FROM MY
MEXICAN KITCHEN
TECHNIQUES AND
INGREDIENTS

DIANA KENNEDY

FROM MY
MEXICAN
KITCHEN
TECHNIQUES
AND
INGREDIENTS

PHOTOGRAPHS BY
Michael Calderwood
and styled by the author

CLARKSON POTTER/PUBLISHERS
NEW YORK

ALSO BY DIANA KENNEDY

The Art of Mexican Cooking
My Mexico
The Essential Cuisines of Mexico
Nothing Fancy

Published by Clarkson Potter/Publishers, New York, New York.
Member of the Crown Publishing Group, a division of Random House, Inc.
www.randomhouse.com

CLARKSON N. POTTER is a trademark and POTTER and colophon are registered trademarks of Random House, Inc.

Printed in China

DESIGN BY JANE TREUHAFT

Library of Congress Cataloging-in-Publication Data
Kennedy, Diana.
    From my Mexican kitchen: techniques and ingredients / Diana Kennedy; photographs by Michael Calderwood.—1st ed.
    Includes index.
    1. Cookery, Mexican.   I. Title.
TX716.M4 K475   2003
641.5972—dc21   2002070405

ISBN 0-609-60700-6

10 9 8 7 6 5 4 3

PAGE 1: FRESH CORN HUSK. PAGE 2: OLLAS AND CAZUELAS. PAGE 3, FROM TOP: TOASTING A CHILE ANCHO; CLEANING A NOPAL; PRESSING OUT A TORTILLA; COVERING A CHILE RELLENO WITH BATTER; TOPPING A SOPE WITH QUESO FRESCO. PAGE 5: CHILES JALAPEÑOS, GREEN BUT MATURE AND RIPE. PAGE 6: NATIVE AVOCADOS. PAGE 7: MOLE VERDE.

Acknowledgments

This is my third book published by Clarkson Potter, under the vigilant eye and guiding hand of my editor, Roy Finamore, to whom I am most grateful (his e-mails keep me laughing through the churning-out process), and, of course, my agent, Susan Lescher, who has championed me through almost three decades. But there are also so many more people, behind the scenes, nameless, faceless, who are responsible for putting one's book together and who never really get thanked. I should like to thank them now and say how much I appreciate their enthusiasm and care at every stage of the book's production: my designer, Jane Treuhaft; production editor, Camille Smith; copy editor, Carole Berglie; production manager, Joan Denman; and publicists, Barbara Marks and Jamie Gass.

Then there are all those Mexican cooks and friends who have generously and patiently contributed to my knowledge. They have certainly not been forgotten; their advice and recipes are there indelibly in all my books.

And don't think I have forgotten photographer and friend Michael Calderwood: how he suffered as the sun went in and out, as the gusts of wind carried off his screens, the awkwardness of ducking his head under the canopy over my kitchen "stove"—far too low for a tall Englishman—not to mention my rushing off at the very crucial shooting moment to scrape once more at my grubby nails, not always successfully (well, doing the food *and* being the hand model is very demanding). Thank you, Michael!

CONTENTS

This book on techniques and ingredients should have been written some years ago, and I really can't think why I didn't do it—except that there were so many exciting recipes to record in my travels when their flavors and textures were still fresh on my palate. Of course, nowadays there is an overwhelming interest in the regional cuisines of Mexico and so many more authentic ingredients are available to enable one to cook the more unusual recipes without tears.

Perhaps I should begin by making it clear that this does not set out to be an—although much needed—encyclopedia/dictionary, or an exhaustive collection of the most abstruse of ingredients known perhaps only in one small area of the country, or for that matter every individual method for making a mole, for instance. But I have tried to distill the information I have gathered through forty-five years of living, or being in touch with, Mexico. This information has come to me from many sources: cooks, botanists, archaeologists, writers, friends, even strangers from many walks of life who have contributed to my knowledge of these varied and complex regional cuisines. I have tried to think and stress (without, I hope, being pedantic) what is important, especially for beginners both outside and in Mexico itself who want to learn to cook authentically. They will be doing so under very different circumstances from their regional counterparts; today's cooks will be using ingredients that do not taste or react in quite the same way, using more up-to-date kitchen equipment and with different nutritional needs, from cooks whom I met, say, when I first went to Mexico in 1957 and in the early intervening years.

Of course, there are many people who still have an indelible concept of that loaded plate of mixed, starchy messes of beans and tasteless corn mush topped with melted waxy cheese. But then again there is a growing number of cooks and eaters who have traveled extensively in Mexico or have learned to appreciate the regional differences by eating in a now-growing number of restaurants that offer traditional regional Mexican food, albeit often with a "nouvelle" presentation. I know that many chefs, and cooks, "doing something different" always think that I won't approve. I wish they (and here I include some of my friends) would stop thinking that they know what I think. Innovations are necessary and amusing, providing they are not passed off as authentic.

To be sure, I would hate to be presented with a full Mexican *comida* (designed to be eaten sometime after 2 o'clock) at a 9 P.M. dinner. More and more people who eat either out or at home want dishes that are lighter; and many of these dishes exist and are totally authentic—this is particularly true of many of the fish, chicken, and vegetable dishes that won't spoil your night's sleep. It is just a matter of spending a little time looking them up in the right books! *But* you have to know what you are doing with the ingredients: how to prepare them and, even more important, how to combine them with other ingredients so that they do not vie with each other for attention. This is particularly true of spices like cinnamon, anise, and clove: their flavors should not stand out in a mole poblano, for instance. Cumin is also generally used with restraint—except in the northeast of Mexico bordering on Texas, and in the odd dish like pollo en ajo-comino, the garlic- and cumin-flavored chicken from San Luis Potosí. You can always come across an exception; for instance, there will be a considerable quantity of aniseeds in the masa of some *antojitos* in the southwestern part of Hidalgo State.

The heavy use of achiote is also to be deplored. Its strong, musky flavor is unpleasant and overpowering when concentrated in a sauce—I shudder when I remember the nouvelle types I have come across—but combined with other spices, as it is in southeast Mexico, it is intriguing and delicious. Aromatics, like hoja santa or avocado leaves, for example, can be used boldly. So if you are going to do the nouvelle thing, you should know and understand both the basic principles of the Mexican regional cuisines and the classical tenets of the French.

When it comes to techniques there are regional differences. They are not enormous, but are sufficient to be able to distinguish more or less what area the dish comes from. Each recipe in my books will give a specific preparation; you will see, for instance, in the case of fresh chiles that jalapeños are usually only roasted and peeled when they are stuffed with cheese, fish, or a picadillo in Veracruz. In Yucatán the light-colored chile xcatik is lightly charred—a process that softens the tough skin and releases the flavor—and, without peeling, put whole into a dish or brothy sauce. The chile poblano is almost always flame-roasted—

CHARRING A CHILE POBLANO.

asado—until lightly charred and peeled, but in the Colima area some cooks put them into hot oil so that the skin blisters and separates from the flesh. In some of the northern areas of Mexico, poblanos or Anaheim-type chiles, are roasted, peeled, and dried for chiles pasados, which is an excellent way of preserving them for the winter months.

Take the general preparation of tomatoes: they can be chopped raw and unpeeled, or they can be char-roasted and then blended for a sauce. For some Michoacán dishes they are cooked whole in the broth with the meat, then blended and strained to remove the skin. In Oaxaca they are often quartered and cooked with a minimum of water until soft, while in Sonora a slice is cut off the top of a large tomato and the flesh is grated from the skin—a method I have seen in a Spanish recipe.

In some areas, depending on the type of mole or sauce, the recipe calls for the dried chiles to be lightly toasted, then soaked and blended. Others require the chiles to be toasted much longer—but not burned—until crisp and then either crumbled to season a soup or blended with other ingredients for a table sauce, or blended with roasted tomatoes for a cooked sauce.

Tortillas are practically synonymous with Mexico, but these too can differ regionally with the type of corn, the methods for preparing the masa, and the type of tortilla made. You cannot compare the large thin *blandas* (soft tortillas) of Oaxaca with those I have seen in the north: thicker and yellow with a pronounced taste of the cal, or lime, with which the corn has been cooked. I remember thicker, more coarsely ground tortillas in the tropical forests of Chiapas; those made of freshly harvested, partially dried corn *(maiz nuevo)* in Tabasco; and those made of masa mixed with wild greens in the Mixteca area of Oaxaca; or masa ground with grains of wheat in the highlands of Michoacán. Of course, the northerners generally prefer flour tortillas; there are the huge thin ones from Sonora, which seem to get smaller as they go east.

Forming tortillas and cooking methods vary, too. Tortillas are still made by hand in many rural communities that respect their traditional foods: some cooks, but very few, still pat the tortillas out by hand and others use a wooden or metal press, while in parts of

PRESSING A BALL OF TORTILLA MASA ONTO A PRESS.

Veracruz and Chiapas you can still see them patted out on a flat surface—usually on a square of plastic substituting for the more traditional banana leaf. But nowadays most Mexicans buy their tortillas freshly made from the *tortillería*—a small tortilla-making business.

Now, take tamales. There are many types of natural wrappers and specific ways to fold them, which often distinguish the tamales from particular regions of the country. Dried corn husks are the most well known and ubiquitous, while fresh green husks are used for fresh corn tamales. The long, narrow leaf of the corn plant is used fresh to wrap the five-pointed corundas in Michoacán and either fresh or dried leaves for bean tamales in the valley of Oaxaca. Fragrant leaves of *Canna indica,* and the fruity cherimole leaf *(Renealmia* sp.) are used in the tropical forest areas of Veracruz and Oaxaca. In Tabasco and part of Veracruz, a large leaf called hoja de to *(Calathea lutea)*—also known as hoja blanca, or white leaf, because of the whitish film on its underside—is used. The unique xocotamales (tamales of soured blue corn masa) in the area of Jalapa, Veracruz, are wrapped in a decorative leaf *(Oreopanax echinops)*. Large avocado leaves provide a fragrant wrapping for very rustic tamales in parts of Morelos and Puebla.

Myths and folklore woven into local religious beliefs still play a part in the preparation of certain foods, particularly in the country areas—making a sign of the cross over the tamale pot, for instance—but these are well documented in anthropological studies of Mexican cultures.

TAMALE WRAPPERS. FROM TOP: FRESH CORN HUSKS; NATIVE AVOCADO LEAF; DRIED CORN HUSK.

Some aspects of Mexican cooking are complicated—the treatment of corn for some types of tamales, for example—and the instructions may seem needlessly fussy until you get the hang of it. But I insist that the cooking of delicious, authentic food is just a question of planning, obtaining the right ingredients (or as near as possible), and careful timing. Many of the more complex sauces can be made ahead of time and in fact intensify in flavor with the wait.

The order of information in this book was a little problematical—like the chicken and the egg. So I have opted for two major sections: a somewhat alphabetical grouping of ingredients, with instructions for the preparation and cooking of specific ingredients as necessary, followed by general techniques for making *antojitos,* sauces, tamales, and the like.

FORMING A TORTA DE HUAUZONTLE.

The availability and variety of traditional ingredients for Mexican foods is continually surprising me: greens like huauzontle and verdolagas, sour tunas called *xoconostles,* the guaje pods, unhulled pumpkin seeds of different sizes, and beautifully dried hoja santa leaves (packed in Florida) are available more sporadically, while a range of fresh and dried chiles, tortillas (most of them miserable), tomatillos, spices, and many of the herbs are available throughout the year. The basic cooking equipment—tortilla presses, molcajetes of sorts, corn grinders—can all be found in many main supermarkets in Latin areas, or small Mexican groceries. (A basic list is given at the back of the book.)

I have throughout the book referred to recipes in my other books. Including those recipes here would simply make the volume too unwieldy, but I cannot resist sending you to these other offspring of mine, where you will find so many wonderful regional recipes.

For ease of reference, I have abbreviated the titles of my books as follows:
The Art, for *The Art of Mexican Cooking* (Bantam Books, 1989)
Essentials, for *The Essential Cuisines of Mexico* (Clarkson Potter, 2000)
My Mexico (Clarkson Potter, 1998) stands without abbreviation.

The task of writing this book is made bearable because I sit in my Mexican home looking at the lush vegetation around me—the result of my year's planting enhanced by a long and generous rainy season. The tall, flaming, red and pink poinsettias that border the steep entranceway to my house are bowing their heads grace-fully; they are natives here. The orange and lime trees are laden with ripe fruit; the strawberries are giving their first small but luscious harvest; and the birds, refugees from the cold north, call to each other scandalously as the sun goes down. The coffee bushes are laden with shiny, green berries, and the grains on the wheat stalks are beginning to swell. The brilliant sun is casting a gloss over the nearby trees and the forested slopes of the surrounding mountains.

I am able to live here in this blessed place thanks to my neighbors' children, who waft between here and the United States passing along their job (with me) to the next one in line. At present there are Carlos and his wife, Consuelo, my *capataz* and housekeeper; and Carlos's brother Manuel, who with Carlos can solve the most complicated of problems be it in the house, in the car, or on the seven acres (he is at the moment trying to convert a normal cheap flashlight into a rechargeable one). Benito completes the trio outside. He is the one who skins and roasts the rabbits that trespass among our crops, picks the wild greens, and smacks his lips at the thought of the edible grubs hiding in leaf-nests in the avocado trees. His feet are firmly planted in the soil. Young Leucardio, or Callito (called "Billy" by his siblings), is tall, handsome, gangling, and sometimes very efficient. He had no idea that the world is round, and in his spells between inside and outside work I make him study the globe on the kitchen table and perhaps learn where his country is in the world. Guadalupe, sister of Benito and Billy, helps run the house, keeps things in order, and sweeps away the fascinating collection of wildlife that presents itself daily inside my adobe walls. Of course, there are two too many—but how can I refuse when they return from their adventures north of the border and want their jobs back? Besides, each one of them has a specific talent or humor that contributes to this very special crew. You may very well ask what all this has to do with this book! Well, without them, it is highly probable that I would never have produced this and my last two books—or at least not for some years ahead. They sustain me by keeping my house functioning and in good repair: painted, watertight, clean, wiring and plumbing in good order, water tanks filled, small diesel generator in working order for emergencies. They keep me supplied with an array of organic vegetables, fruits, avocados, beans, wheat, and corn (in small quantities); and they keep the coffee harvested, processed, and ready to use. I owe them an enormous debt of gratitude!

I sincerely hope this book will achieve its simple objective: to be a beginning guide to the better understanding of what ingredients Mexico has to offer, and how these can best be prepared and cooked to preserve the special flavors and textures that give Mexico its unique place in the world of gastronomy.

Mexico

Mexico is shaped like a cornucopia, its broad top bordering for about 2,000 miles the extreme south of the United States of America. The map shows it has one long, thin arm—the states of Baja California North and South—stretching down its northwestern coast and encompassing the Gulf of California. With the Pacific Ocean to the west and the Gulf of Mexico to the east, and a small fraction of Quintana Roo touching the Caribbean, it has 3,000 miles of coastline. The Tropic of Cancer transverses the country, dividing it almost equally in two. Two huge mountain ranges, the Sierra Madre Occidental and Oriental—running from north to south and seeming to contain the center of the country—end in a central massif, with volcanic plateaus and deep valleys until they fragment into disparate ranges that make up the rugged terrain of Oaxaca and Chiapas.

There still exists a stereotypical belief that Mexico is primarily an arid country with organ cacti galore, and indeed many of the central areas are: Sierra Gorda of Guanajuato, parts of Oaxaca, San Luis Potosí, and a great deal of the northern states. But the higher altitudes around Mexico City, parts of Michoacán, and the states of Mexico and Puebla are thickly forested with fir and deciduous trees (and would be more so without the tree bandits who clear-cut indiscriminately, and far too often go unchecked). The forests of the Sierra Tarahumara in Chihuahua have been almost decimated by American pulp companies, and Durango, another important forested state, is going the same way.

While many parts of the country are riverless, the largest rivers flow down from the eastern mountains into the Gulf of Mexico; Veracruz and Tabasco have the lion's share, with the huge estuaries of the Río Papaloapan in the south of Veracruz and the Usumacinta in Tabasco forming enormous expanses of water that are habitats to fish, crustaceans, and wildfowl. Where the damp air of the Gulf meets the mountain mists—referred to in some areas as *chipi-chipi*—the vegetation is lush and green.

All these geographical and climatic conditions have naturally played their part in making Mexico's animal and plant life one of the more diverse in the world, a diversity threatened (as in so many parts of the world) by uncontrolled urbanization, deforestation, contamination of rivers, lakes, and seas, and unsustainable farming. It is fact that there is no other country in the world that has so many different chiles, for example, or so many varieties of corn, pumpkins, and beans, nor for that matter so many ways of preparing and eating these very basic ingredients.

Cuisines evolve when these natural resources are exploited by man's ingenuity, either through a need to survive or later for pleasure. From codices (pictographs) both pre- and post-Columbian we know quite a bit about how people hunted, fished, and cultivated things to eat—or used them for medicinal purposes—but there is no great culinary history that details how much of this food was prepared. The first manuscripts recording meals and recipes were, not surprisingly, written in the convents, but those were recipes of what could be called the "new cuisine" of the times, combining ingredients of New Spain with cooking methods from Spain. There were other strong outside influences, too—for instance, during the French Intervention. I believe that the use of many more plants, roots, and possibly flowers greatly increased during the Revolution when so many people throughout the country, having lost their stores of food, crops, and animals to marauding soldiers of every side, fled their homes and lived in rough shelters in the forests and caves.

One fascinating aspect of what I call "the true Mexican gastronomy" is that many wild ingredients—ants and flies' eggs, grasshoppers, flying ants, grubs from the maguey, and many exotic plants—have provided free food for the *campesinos* and indigenous peoples living in remote places while at the same time they are considered, like caviar, luxuries and demand high prices in the elegant restaurants of Mexico City.

Mexican food has become one of the most popular and sought-after cuisines in many parts of the world. So far, with notable exceptions in the United States, and perhaps Spain, it is the simplest snack food (except perhaps for mole poblano with its element of chocolate) that has caught the imagination, with *antojitos* based on tortillas, both corn and flour, and tacos, enchiladas, tostadas, quesadillas, and tostadas, with guacamole and tamales not far behind. Tequila—a Mexican drink if there ever was one (pre-Columbian pulque apart)—has become the rage all over the world. It is so much so that the raw material—Agave tequilana—available cannot fill the demand, and prices as a result have soared. And one has to admit that the margarita really is an inspired drink when not messed around with or made overly sweet and slushy. But even the frozen margarita has helped put Mexico on the gastronomic world map!

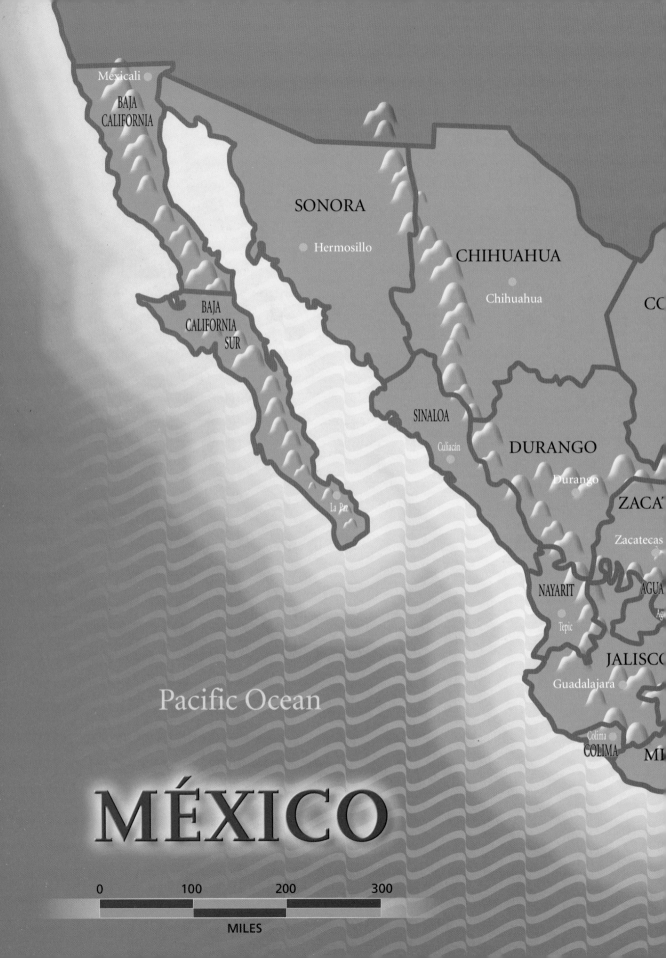

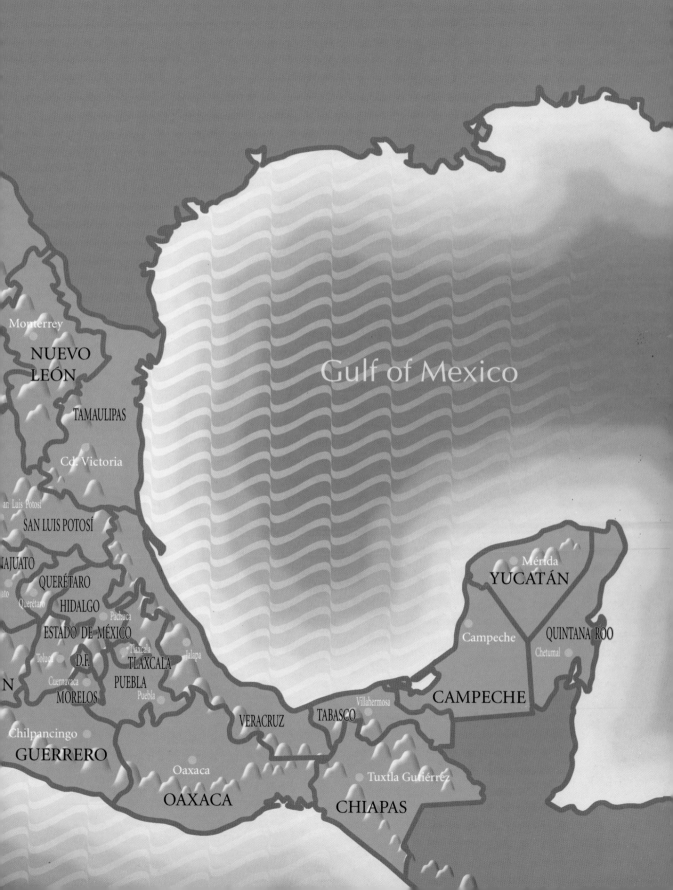

Monterrey

**NUEVO
LEÓN**

TAMAULIPAS

Cd. Victoria

San Luis Potosí

SAN LUIS POTOSÍ

AJUATO

QUERÉTARO

ato

Querétaro

HIDALGO

Pachuca

ESTADO DE MÉXICO

Toluca

Tlaxcala

D.F.

TLAXCALA

Jalapa

N

Cuernavaca

PUEBLA

MORELOS

Puebla

Chilpancingo

GUERRERO

VERACRUZ

Oaxaca

OAXACA

Gulf of Mexico

Mérida

YUCATÁN

Campeche

QUINTANA ROO

Chetumal

Villahermosa

CAMPECHE

TABASCO

Tuxtla Gutiérrez

CHIAPAS

Menus

Mexico has changed so much since I first went there in 1957 and so, to some extent, have family eating patterns. For instance, now many women go out to work, although they almost all have help of some kind at home. They are not in the kitchen all day, preparing complicated sauces. With work and the time spent in traffic between the workplace and home, a leisurely breakfast and afternoon *comida* followed by a siesta are almost things of the past. How easy it is to generalize—and there are so many exceptions—but from observing foods and eating habits in Mexico for so many years, I will attempt it, knowing that these habits can vary widely with so many different cultural and economic layers to Mexican society.

An early morning coffee, with perhaps a pan dulce (sweet yeast roll) and juice, generally starts the day. For affluent businessmen, politicos, or ranking bureaucrats, a business meeting will be arranged over *almuerzo*—equivalent to brunch—when restaurants in Mexico City in particular do a roaring trade. The main meal of the day, *comida,* is eaten anytime during the afternoon. Supper—unless there are guests—tends to be light: leftovers from *comida,* an enchilada, a sandwich, some fruit, or just coffee with a pan dulce, still the starchy mainstay of the day.

Almuerzo is such a great meal: it is so hard to make a decision among eggs cooked a dozen ways, beans, sauces, chilaquiles topped with chicken and cheese, menudo, and so on—all very substantial and enormously satisfying! (The breakfast buffet in the popular chain hotels in Mexico is in my opinion by far the best meal of the day.) A traditional *comida,* the principal meal of the day, eaten in the afternoon from about two o'clock on, is still a family affair in many parts of Mexico, with a rather rigid progression of dishes. To give one example, after a soup comes a *sopa seca*—like the pasta course in Italy—rice, usually, or pasta. This used to be followed (although menus generally have been simplified) by a vegetable dish—even as elaborate as chiles rellenos—before the main course of a stew, mole, or pipián, or guiso with meat and vegetables. Of course, the meal would not be complete without some frijoles de olla (brothy beans), which are often served separately. Dessert is very sweet and sticky.

But as a prelude to this is *la botana*, as the snacks with an apéritif are called, and the array is usually more extensive when there are guests, or on weekends and special occasions. The most popular items are guacamole, chicharrón, chilied peanuts, and pickled vegetables. With these, or on their own, are various masa *antojitos* topped with all sorts of crispy and enticing things. After a second drink, moderation is usually thrown to the wind, addiction sets in, and if you are not careful the snack becomes a *comida* in itself. Of course, then *comida* is postponed and postponed.

When thinking of a menu for Mexican food one has to program oneself anew and forget the luxury of a carefully planned French meal or the clean flavors and simplicity of a great Italian meal. Tacos, guacamole, moles, chiles rellenos—the type of foods for which Mexico is primarily known, and delicious as they can be—are filling and not too digestible at night. But there are many lighter dishes, and it pays to take the time to research and experiment with the lesser known ones in my books and then combine them into a harmonious meal. For instance, if you start with a dish like Camarones en Pipián (Shrimp in a Pepita Sauce, *Essentials*, page 376), you would follow with a dish like Cuñete de Pollo (Chicken in White Wine, *The Art*, page 235) and finish with a tropical fruit ice (*The Art*, pages 417–424) accompanied by Polvorones (Crisp Cookies, *Essentials*, page 439). If you select a main dish of fish, like Huachinango à la Veracruzana (*Essentials*, page 368), then choose perhaps a corn soup with its creamy texture to start. You may also decide not to go totally Mexican, but mix and match with recipes from other cuisines. Always remember that contrasting textures and flavors are most important. Simplicity should rule at the evening meal.

What would I prepare for a very soothing supper? The very simple pipián from Oaxaca—a great favorite of mine (*The Art*, page 102) and some simply prepared fish like Pescado al Vapor (Steamed Fish, *My Mexico*, page 338). A casual supper for great friends would be tamales—oh, there are so many delicious ones—that would probably come out of the freezer, and a salad. With guava or quince *ates*, or fruit pastes (*The Art*, pages 412 and 414), to finish.

Invite a lot of people for brunch or a buffet lunch, and that will be the occasion when you can throw the book at them. Anything goes! Cook up a storm! In fairly recent years a relatively new concept has evolved for feeding a lot of people, especially the young, on a modest budget. It is called *La Taquiza*. Just buy loads of the best corn and wheat flour tortillas (and I don't mean whole wheat, although you could use those, too) you can find and make lots of fillings. Possibilities are chorizo with potatoes, chicharrón in guajillo sauce or green sauce, shredded chicken or meats, a variety of sauces, refried beans. And always remember the vegetarians: Esquites (Fresh Corn Kernels with Epazote, *Essentials,* page 224), Chile Con Queso (*Essentials,* page 221), Poblano Chile Strips with Potatoes (*Essentials,* page 220), nopalitos, and chiles. There are lots of such recipes. But don't get too fancy; remember that a *Taquiza* should be simple; no moles or complicated dishes. Choose fillings that are easy to handle. Small quantities can be stuffed into a taco without making a mess on the floor, or your best shoes.

A must for a special occasion is the great mole poblano meal. Start with a ceviche, or my favorite, Mariscos a la Marinera (*Essentials,* pages 363 and 13) followed by Mexican Rice (*Essentials,* page 160) served alone as a *sopa seca,* then the mole (*Essentials,* page 324) with unfilled or bean tamales (using recipes in *Essentials,* page 112, omitting the filling, or the recipe from Oaxaca, *The Art,* page 75). Although I always opt for fruit, the finale has to be the traditional flan (*Essentials,* page 414).

Buen provecho!

CHEESES
AND
CREAM

CHEESES

Cows were introduced into Mexico very early on in the colonial period, but curiously enough the now "traditional" cheeses have never attained a high measure of sophistication. To be sure there are some very good European-style cheeses made in Mexico, but they are not used in the truly authentic dishes.

Most of the cheeses are made of cow's milk, with the occasional exception of goat's milk—which is not particularly liked for its strong flavor. Not so long ago, however, I did come across small, round, flat goat cheeses that the vendor said he had recently started to make. They were not selling very fast, but they had a pleasant, mild flavor; I was assured by veterinarian companions that there was no Malta fever in the area (where Puebla meets northern Veracruz) so clearly the goat's milk was safe to eat. To my knowledge, sheep's milk cheeses are not made or sold commercially.

Most commercial cheeses are made of milk that has been clabbered with an industrial liquid rennet, but there are still many small, more isolated areas and *rancherías* where the rennet used is an infusion of the dried part of the cow's stomach called *cuajo* (meaning precisely the enzyme, or curds). One fascinating sidelight on this is that in the north of Mexico, especially Chihuahua and Coahuila, a wild berry *(Solanum eleagnifolium)* about ¼ inch (7mm) in diameter is used either fresh or dried to make the local asadero cheese.

I am always fascinated by the cheese section of the market in Huetamo, in the Tierra Caliente of Michoacán. It seems that everyone makes cheese at home, judging from the number of small stands selling pieces of *cuajo* (dried cow's and pig's stomach). They are encrusted with a pinkish local salt that is said to act as a strong disinfectant. To give the cheese its characteristic, strong flavor, the people there do not assiduously scrub the *cuajo!* Set beside each piece of *cuajo* is a small plastic cup with a little clabbered milk in it—supposed proof of its setting qualities.

The quesos secos (dried cheeses) from tropical areas are often formed into large barrel shapes, with a high percentage of salt to preserve them; they develop a strong flavor through the maturing process of the raw milk, *leche bronca.* Most of these cheeses do not melt. They are grated very fine and used mostly to sprinkle over *antojitos,* or in certain types of enchiladas.

There are the soft cheeses like queso fresco, fresh cheese, and panela, a round breadlike form with a mild acidic flavor. The strongest-tasting cheeses are the quesos de Chiapas, usually sold in oblong bars and covered with silver or gold

MEXICAN CHEESES: COTIJA, QUESO FRESCO, AND QUESILLO DE OAXACA.

paper—the latter to indicate "double cream." They tend to be very crumbly, fairly moist (depending on age), and salty. These cheeses melt easily when heated.

Of course, one of the famous cheeses of Mexico is the quesillo from Oaxaca. It is somewhat like mozzarella but with a much more rubbery texture and is more pleasantly acidic and creamy; it melts slowly with low heat.

The remainder of cheeses used most popularly are semisoft, mild, and eponymously named: tipo Manchego, Chester, and, of course, Chihuahua, a commercial version of the real Chihuahua Mennonite cheese.

In the markets of Aguascalientes, Guadalajara, or Zamora—to name only a few places—you will find local cheeses with different names or shapes, sometimes covered with a chile powder to distinguish them, but they will always be the generally accepted, unso-phisticated cheeses. Wherever you get these locally made cheeses you will find requeson (ricotta), sold for *antojitos* of various types.

With very minor exceptions, the Mexican-style cheeses made in the United States are nowhere near as tasty as their Mexican counterparts—although the quality of the latter has been much diluted in the sweep of greater industrialization to keep up with enormous demand.

Queso Asadero

Queso asadero is a very mild, acid cheese with a soft but slightly chewy consistency. The true queso asadero is difficult to find these days in northern Mexico because it is not made on a large scale, even though there are plenty of commercial copies that don't come close to resembling the real thing—certainly those made in the United States do not. The method of making this cheese is the same as that of the Oaxacan quesillo (see page 26): half of the milk is left to sour for two days, then it is mixed with the same amount of fresh milk from the morning's milking. The milk is clabbered with trompillos, the local wild berries, which are crushed in warm water, then the liquid is strained into the cheese. The mixture is then heated gently for about 15 minutes. The person showing me the process took out a small piece of the curd to see if it had coagulated sufficiently to stretch into the traditional flat ovals. Once satisfied, she continued to break off pieces of the curd and stretch them. Correctly speaking, in Chihuahua this is Asadero and another local, crumbly cheese made in a different manner is referred to as Queso.

Asadero is used in Chihuahua for chiles rellenos and chile con queso, and often it is formed into small "tortillas" and served as a *botana*. The closest substitute for asadero would be a good, soft string cheese made of whole milk, or in California, a Teleme would be near enough. And if neither is available, then just use what I always recommend: a domestic Muenster cut from a square block—not the individual ones, since they don't melt as easily. And Muenster is cheaper than the much-touted Monterey Jack.

Queso Chihuahua

One of the most popular cheeses in Mexico is the queso Chihuahua, or tipo Chihuahua, since production of the real thing in the Mennonite communities of Chihuahua is very small. The Mennonites came to Mexico at the beginning of the 1920s, when Alvaro Obregon was president. They worked hard and were successful in making their land productive, and they began to produce a cheese that is high in butterfat and that resembles a young, mild Cheddar. When properly aged it can be quite tangy.

The best cheese was formed into a large wheel with the name of the Mennonite Community stamped on it. Now it is much more difficult to find because some of the communities moved to Central America and others to the southern Mexican states of Tabasco and Campeche. There they often sell their cheeses in the streets, going from door to door, or from car to car last time I saw them. The cheeses are formed into oblong bricks, and the ones I bought did not have the character of those I have tried from Chihuahua. Now there are many companies producing a tipo Chihuahua, but they never quite attain the taste or texture of the real thing.

Queso Chihuahua is used for chiles rellenos, queso fundido (a Mexico fondue), and chile con queso (Chihuahua version, see *Essentials,* page 221), or grated for cheese toppings. The so-called Chihuahua cheese made in the United States is very bland and not worth buying; a good domestic Muenster or medium Cheddar can be substituted.

Queso Fresco

It is always difficult to generalize, but in my experience the most ubiquitous cheese in Mexican food is queso fresco, a fresh cheese as its name indicates. Of course, there are other local names: queso de metate, queso molido, queso ranchero. While there are many inferior commercial brands, and the odd good one, the best are made in small quantities. On small farms, the extra milk left over from breakfast or supper is clabbered, cut, and drained overnight. The dryish curds are then ground on the metate and pressed into small circular molds. The cheeses are then removed and left to drain once more. They are used fresh as a *botana,* crumbled to top many types of *antojitos,* or sliced for stuffing chiles or quesadillas.

Queso fresco has a pleasant acidity and creaminess—if made with whole milk— and it melts well. Occasionally you can see the cheese *oreado,* or air-dried, which gives it a more concentrated taste and deeper color.

There are some passable and downright bad copies of queso fresco in the United States. The quality suffers because they are made of skimmed or semi-skimmed highly pasteurized milk with lots of rennet, which makes for a very tough curd. They have very little acidity and do not melt well. Of course, there are a very few well-made queso frescos, like those of the Mozzarella Company in Texas (see Sources), for instance, and I am sure there are others hidden somewhere. You will have to use what is available. But here is a recipe for true aficionados.

To make queso fresco

Makes just over 1 pound (500g)

4 quarts (4L) raw milk

Liquid rennet (follow instructions on the bottle)

2 rounded teaspoons finely ground sea salt, to taste

Heat the milk to 110°F (50°C) in a pan at least 4 inches (10cm) deep. Stir the rennet in thoroughly, cover the pan, and set aside in a warm place to set for at least 1 hour. The curds should be slightly firm to the touch, and should not adhere to your finger.

Cut the curds into squares of about 1 inch (2.5cm), making sure you cut to the bottom. Leave for about 2 hours for the curds to separate as much as possible from the whey. Transfer the curds with a slotted spoon to a cheesecloth bag and hang up with a bowl underneath to catch the drips. Leave hanging until the curds are well drained and fairly firm—12 to 24 hours, depending on the humidity in your kitchen.

Tip the curds out into the bowl of a food processor, add the salt, and process until you have a fine, crumbly mixture. Scrape into a mold about 2 inches (5cm) deep and press down firmly. Leave to drain for about 3 hours, preferably in a basket or on a bamboo (not on a metal) rack. Turn over once.

As soon as the cheese feels a little firm, carefully press it out of the mold and let it sit in an airy place to dry a little and season. It should acquire a pleasant acidity.

For requeson (ricotta), don't discard the whey, unless, of course, you have a pig in the backyard. Make requeson. Put the pan over low heat and let it simmer until a layer of curds forms on the surface of the liquid. Cook until the texture of the curds is a little firm. Drain in a cheesecloth bag until the curds are moist but not juicy, about 12 hours.

Quesillo de Oaxaca

When you visit markets in the central valley of Oaxaca, you will see the cheese stands prominently displaying balls of a whitish cheese, wound in flat, broad skeins, from about 6 inches (15cm) in diameter to ½ inch (1.25cm). Those are the quesillos for which Oaxaca is renowned.

A well-made cheese is creamy in color and has a pleasant acidity. The curds are a little stringy and have a fairly low melting point. They should be made of a full-fat cream, raw milk, half from the morning's milking, and half slightly soured from the day before. After the milk has been clabbered, the curds are cooked in some of the whey and stirred in a regular clockwise motion until the curds melt and string in solid bands. With dexterous movements the women make the cheese by gathering the skeins and forming them into balls. The cheeses are then drained before being packed for the market.

The smallest of the cheeses are used as *botanas,* to snack on with a drink. The large ones are used in the same way, but often the skeins are shredded very finely to use on top of *antojitos,* tostadas, or tortillas con asiento. Sliced quesillos are also used for chiles rellenos and quesadillas.

Of course, the production of quesillo is not large enough to meet the great demand from all over Mexico, so a "queso tipo Oaxaca" is made industrially. Most of it is an acceptable substitute, although made in bulk it looks and acts right but lacks the authentic flavor and slight stringiness. A good whole-milk string cheese can be substituted, and if that is not available, then there's the usual suggestion: a domestic Muenster.

Queso Panela

Queso panela is the simplest cheese to make, but much depends on the quality of the milk, which of course should be whole and unpasteurized. One summer years ago, when traveling up the Pacific coast of Mexico, and when little settlements like San Patricio were virtually undiscovered, I saw in simple family kitchens the ever-present basket of dripping curds hanging up. The excess milk from the evening's milking—practically each family had a cow sheltered in the backyard—was clabbered for the next day's panela cheese.

For aficionados, follow the steps for clabbering the milk for queso fresco (see page 25), but instead of cutting the curds up, transfer large portions of them with a slotted spoon into a round shallow basket. The curds should be lavishly salted and left to drip overnight. The shape and textured surface will be formed by the basket.

This cheese is best eaten as fresh as possible. It is often served as a *botana,* or sliced on top of a cold dish or salad. There are available many unremarkable so-called panelas of many brands on both sides of the border. You can also substitute a slightly acidy mozzarella-type cheese.

Crema

Crema is used liberally in some regions of Mexico—Michoacán, for instance—but not in others—the cooking of the Yucatán Peninsula, for example. Sometimes it is used thick to enrich a cooked sauce, like the Minguichis of Michoacán (*The Art,* page 330), and the Molito de Camaron Seco (*My Mexico,* page 414), Chicken Breasts in Cream (*Essentials,* page 347), and the like. More often, a thinner cream is used to top off masa snacks like tostadas and tacos, or even some enchiladas.

The real stuff is naturally soured cream from raw milk—in essence the same as crème fraîche of France, with obvious differences in taste owing to the type of cattle and feed or weather. It is now very difficult to come by, since suppliers cannot keep up with the huge demand and there are, predictably, commercial fillers added to give more volume. The commercial so-called Mexican cream (crema mexicana), sold in glass jars at rather a high price in the United States, is not recommended. There is some good commercial crème fraîche on the market; it is quite expensive but worth the price for a good sauce if you cannot be bothered (or think of it too late) to make your own. Julia Child wisely started us all on this.

To make crème fraîche

Makes about 1 cup (250ml)

1 cup (250 ml) heavy cream (not ultra-pasteurized)

3 tablespoons buttermilk or whole yogurt

Mix the cream and buttermilk well in a nonreactive container.

Cover with a piece of thick toweling and set in a warm place—an oven with a pilot light or yogurt maker—until it thickens; this can take up to 8 hours depending on the quality of the ingredients. Then set in the refrigerator overnight, or better still, 36 hours, until the cream thickens even more.

As a less expensive topping for *antojitos,* thin some commercial sour cream with milk to the right consistency. About 1 cup (250 ml) sour cream mixed with ⅓ cup (83ml) whole milk will do it.

POURING CREMA.

Natas

Natas are the rich skimmings that form on top of scalded raw milk. They are exactly the same as the famous clotted cream (for scones and strawberry jam, for afternoon tea—so rich and delicious—in the west of England) except that they have considerably less butterfat. You will often see natas sold in saucers on the market stands offering coffee, chocolate, and sweet rolls in the morning. In fact, natas are often slathered on these yeast rolls, but they are also used in cakes and cookies, to enrich a cooked sauce, or to enhance a vegetable dish.

I mention natas here because you should at least try them—if you haven't already done so—and forget about cholesterol when you are next having breakfast in a Mexican market. Natas would be hard to find in restaurants. Alas, I don't know where you would find them in the United States, unless you have a friend with a cow or can get raw milk. I have very few recipes in my books that include natas, and where they do I suggest a substitute depending on the type of recipe.

CREMA, AND A PLATE OF NATAS.

Mantequilla de Rancho

RANCH BUTTER

I mention this butter, which really resembles a buttery, soured cream, because it is one of the delicious little-known tastes of southern Mexico in the areas around the Isthmus of Tehuantepec, Tabasco, and Chiapas. It is used mostly in the cooking of local breads and tamales, or spread on tortillas.

COOKING
FATS
AND
OILS

M

exican food has the reputation of being greasy. Far too many people still have that impression, or will tell you that most of it is fried. Some of it is, but as in any cuisine, there is a lot of Mexican food that isn't.

We don't really know whether fats of animals or oils extracted from seeds were used in pre-Hispanic food preparation, as some writers have suggested, or were used to any great extent. Presumably not. Nor can we assume that as soon as the Spaniards introduced the "pig culture" and lard—or olive oil, for that matter—everyone wanted or could even afford to use them. Cookbooks compiled in the nineteenth century show that lard had become the most commonly used fat, certainly among urban, well-to-do Mexicans. Oil (the type not specified) was often combined with lard; butter was used quite frequently, as was olive oil—often added at the end of a recipe—and something called raw oil. Nowadays, especially with the cholesterol scare, the majority of cooks in Mexico, like those in the United States, use vegetable oils made from corn, or safflower, or sunflower seeds, and blends with those and other ingredients for everyday cooking. But, thank goodness, pork lard is still used for tamales, and in many cases for frying beans. Lard has a definite affinity for corn masa and beans. And how delicious they are!

Asiento

"Asiento" translates as "a seat" or "sediment," but in central Oaxacan culinary terms it refers to the little crispy bits of fat that fall to the bottom of the frying vats when chicharrón or lard are prepared. The name varies regionally: *zorrapa* in the Isthmus, *migas* in Michoacán, for example. In some areas, it is used to fill gorditas or mix into masa, but in the Isthmus, it is blended before being added to the masa of tamales.

Asiento is sold covered in lard that has acquired a deep caramel color. As a substitute, I suggest you use either the little fatty pieces left over when you make your own lard, or buy some fatty chicharrón from a Mexican market and grind it into textured crumbs.

Lard

In the pork butcher stands in Mexican public markets, rendered, pure pork lard is nearly always on sale. It is not deadly white like the stabilized commercial stuff, but a very pale caramel color and very soft. As one travels farther south in Mexico, one sees a much darker lard used for tamales, straight—sometimes still hot—from the *cazos,* or vats, in which the pork skin—chicharrón—has been fried crisp. The residue of little crispy pieces that sink to the bottom (known as *asiento* in central Oaxaca, *zorrapa* in the Isthmus) is also used to enrich the dough of certain masa snacks, *antojitos,* tamales, and little dumplings, called *chochoyotes* in Oaxaca.

To make one feel a little better about eating some lard I will quote from Paula Wolfert's masterpiece (among her many) *The Cooking of Southwest France.* She writes: "An interesting fact I discovered in a U.S. Department of Agriculture Publication: Handbook 8-4 revised 1979—is that rendered poultry fat (goose duck and chicken) contains 9% cholesterol, and lard contains 10%, compared with butter with 22%. Since one needs less poultry fat, oil or lard than butter to sauté meat or vegetables, one will ingest far less saturated fat . . . one needs less of these because butter breaks down and burns at a high temperature, whereas the others do not."

I make my own lard, and for those who want to, I suggest making it in two heavy skillets, either in a 325°F (165°C) oven or on top of the stove.

To make lard

Makes about 4 cups (1L) or 1¾ pounds (790g)

2 pounds (900g) unsalted fatback or pork fat pieces

Have ready enough stone crocks or heatproof containers and a strainer.

Cut the fat into small cubes, discarding any pieces of tough skin. Using about one-fourth at a time, process the fat in the food processor for a few seconds to chop it finer and divide the quantity evenly between two skillets. Place the skillets on the middle shelf of the oven, or over low heat, and cook until some of the fat renders out. Pour it through the strainer into the crock. Continue cooking, turning the pieces over from time to time until they are crisp and lightly browned. Strain off the remaining liquid fat. Set aside to cool and store in the refrigerator lightly covered. The lard will keep very well for several months. Use the residue of crispy pieces of fat for some gorditas or winter food for the birds.

White Solid Vegetable Fats

Rather like Crisco in the United States, these are used for pan dulce, the semisweet yeast breads eaten by the millions in Mexico daily for breakfast and supper. The everyday white flour tortillas that predominate in the northern states of Mexico are also generally made with this vegetable shortening. Use plain Crisco—please *not* the flavored varieties.

Rendered Beef Fat

This is sometimes used in the dough of certain types of tamales and the *antojitos* known as bocoles in Tamaulipas, and mixed with lard in some tamales typical of the northwestern state of Sonora. Rendered marrow fat is used for the tostadas, or toto-pos de la Mixteca Baja, or pimpo in the Isthmus. The process of rendering both is the same as that for lard.

Olive Oil

Olive oil is not used a great deal in traditional, regional Mexican cooking. Of course, the exceptions are for dishes with strong Spanish roots: cuñete de pollo in Michoa-cán, pollo en ajillo in Veracruz, for example, and fish recipes from the Gulf ports, and Tabasco, Campeche, and Yucatán. But in all cases it is best to use a lighter oil, not an extra-virgin oil, which would overpower the flavors in the recipe. Do not use that tasteless insipid stuff put out as "light" olive oil in the United States. Mexico does produce some olive oil, but the industry has yet to mature and Spanish oils are still preferred.

FRESH
AND
DRIED
CHILES

There is no doubt, nor room for argument, when it comes to chiles: Mexico reigns supreme. Whether they originated in Mexico (some haven't), and whether they were domesticated or cross-pollinated naturally or by human hand, the varieties that exist and are used in Mexico today are uncounted; many are unknown, except in their own small areas of cultivation. The spelling of the word *chile* is the Hispaniolized version of the Nahuatl (Nahuatl was the lingua franca of the inhabitants of the Central Highlands of Mexico when the Spaniards arrived and is still spoken in many modified forms today) word *chili*, which curiously persists in India where chiles were introduced by the Portuguese in the sixteenth century.

While botanists agree that some chiles originated in South America, traces of both domesticated chiles and wild varietals found in the caves of Tehuacan in the state of Puebla and Ocampo in the state of Tamaulipas date back to the seventh century B.C. This suggests that they predate the cultivation of both tomatoes and corn. In my sporadic and uncharted wanderings I am always coming across a new *chile criollo* specific to a small area. It often appears only at a given time of year—irrigated in the winter and the dry months of spring, or at the end of the summer rainy season. The wide variety is often bewildering. Many chiles look alike but taste slightly different, especially when dried. Maddeningly, different chiles may have the same name—for instance, chile manzano is often called jalapeño in Chiapas; chile gordo ("fat chile") refers to the jalapeño in Veracruz, and the poblano in Jalisco; the long green chile of the north is often referred to as chilaca, the name usually applied to the long, thin blackish green chile of Michoacán and the Bajío.

Then there's that controversial subject of heat! The heat is not, as generally supposed, in the seeds but from the capsaicin in the papery placenta that holds the seeds at the top of the chile and the veins running vertically down the sides. By association the inside flesh and seeds will appear hot as well.

Can we really predict how hot a certain chile will be? Long before Scoville, the Aztecs had seven words to describe the gradations of heat of their chiles—and I emphasize *their*. Scovilleites will be shaken to hear me say that nowadays one cannot be sure about the "supposed" measure of heat, particularly with the now wild swings of climate, sporadic unseasonal rains, and changes in soil content with the overuse of chemical fertilizers. And let's face it, the so-called improved varieties of chiles bombarding Mexico from the north, developed for long shelf life or packability, have had an impact. Who are these moguls who decide what they think the public wants? This augurs the downfall of variety and taste!

There is a lot of written misinformation, too! I would invite the author of "a chile with broad shoulders is not as hot" to bite into a manzano grown in the altitudes of Michoacán, or into an habanero or chilhuacle, for that matter—they too have broad shoulders. And to return to the manzano, which another writer proclaimed as mild and fruity (she may have tried one from the Mazateca in the rainy season), let her try the more prevalent ones from the states of Mexico or Michoacán! So beware! In my many years of experience in Mexico buying, cooking, and tasting chiles I have noticed changes: the poblano chile is often fleshier, lighter in color, and no longer has the nuance of flavor of the thinner-skinned, inky-green poblanos of former years. The dried guajillo is often represented by a much broader, fleshier chile more like those from the north and the chilacates of Jalisco. It used to be called the "naughty chile" because of its bite; no longer does it bite! Anchos and pasillas are much hotter than they used to be and, oh dear, where did that insipid pale green banana-like pepper come from? They never seem to know in the markets and it drives me mad! Is it that NAFTA and globalization have had a hand in this? Those delicious little green peppers from Yucatán—chile dulce or botanik—are hard to find except (I hope still) in Campeche, and crops of chilhuacles in the Cañada of northern Oaxaca have been almost driven to extinction through lack of demand, appreciation, and the cost of fighting the new pests that appear in this age of rapid change.

While lamenting what is happening in this era of homogeneity we should also celebrate the chiles that miraculously still exist: the extravaganza of color, shapes, sizes, flavors, and textures that provoke memories of places, occasions, and tastes of years gone by. It is fascinating to watch their colors change through greens to yellows, orange, mulberry, even the color of chocolate, and reds of every shade. Notice surfaces that are shiny, matte, ridged, pleated, or just bumpy, and with flesh translucent or densely opaque. I learned a long time ago that trying to generalize about the uses of certain chiles—either fresh or dried, small or large—is deceptive. No sooner do you think you have established a norm than an exception or two pops up. For example, if I am about to say that only the smaller chiles are pickled, I almost immediately remember the glorious pickled anchos—the recipe from Maria Dolores Torres Yzabal from Sonora (*The Art,* page 355). Say that anchos are not used as a table sauce, then I remember the Aunt Georgina's sauce that I first published in *The Cuisines of Mexico* and more recently in *Essentials,* page 247. Be that as it may, there are certain accepted rules: the large chiles like poblanos, chilacas, and Anaheims are toasted and skinned to remove the rather bitter skin and release the flavor of the flesh. The smaller chiles are used whole—unskinned, unseeded— either raw or *asado* (that word again, which is untranslatable, but see *asar* on page 304), or simmered. They appear in sauces or are added to broth, rice, or beans just as they are, *except* when you are preparing stuffed jalapeños; then they have to be skinned first.

Chiles either fresh, dried, or smoked are used in every phase of the Mexican regional cuisines—less in the northern states than in the central and southern areas. And they are used not just to make food hot, *picante,* but to add flavor as well. The larger ones are to stuff with one of innumerable fillings, cut into strips to use as a vegetable, pickled as a relish, toasted and ground dry as a condiment, or toasted and soaked before grinding with other ingredients for cooked sauces and moles. The variety is infinite. And don't forget to save the seeds: they too can be toasted and ground, to be used as a condiment or added to ground pumpkin or sesame seeds for an intriguing paste for tortillas (see Chiltatis, *My Mexico,* page 267) or to be added to pipianes (*The Art,* page 102). The leaves of some chiles are also used in the green huatape, a regional soup from the northern area of Veracruz. But let me repeat here my favorite anecdote about chiles—it has been recorded twice before in my other books.

A renowned Mexican botanist, the late Dr. Alfredo Barrera, once told me that not all chiles can be combined in a sauce—there is such a thing as *chiles peleados,* "fighting chiles." When his mother saw her husband coming home from the cantina with some of his *cuates,* all a little tipsy, she would hurriedly make a sauce of habaneros and chiles verdes yucatecos, and after a few bites they would excuse themselves and depart. He said the same effect can be produced with pasillas and serranos. I must add that a Yucatecan friend said that Dr. Alfred's mother strenuously denies all knowledge of this.

FRESH CHILES

I commented in the general introduction to chiles about the number of varieties of *Capsicum annuum* that exist. They are as bewildering as they are exasperating. Just when you think you have the varieties in one area listed, then another pops up. While many mature, but are still green, toward the end of the rainy season—about the end of August—others occur in January, yet others are grown under irrigation and ripen in the dry, hot spring. There are locos and zacalapeños in Puebla, toros in the state of Mexico, de huerto in eastern Michoacán, acatleños in Guerrero, tuxtas on the Oaxacan coast, de dos and tres venas (types of mirasol) in Zacatecas, and los criollos of the Isthmus, as well as at least one hundred more criollos, often domesticated from a wild plant, in very small areas, particularly in southern Mexico.

I have described here the most commonly used and obtainable fresh chiles that, unless specifically mentioned, are *Capsicum annuum* var. *annuum*.

Chile de Agua

The chile de agua is very much a local chile grown the year round in the valley of Oaxaca. The production is relatively small and almost exclusively for use in that area. A field of these plants is a very colorful sight when the chiles are ripening from a lightish green to various shades of fiery orange-red. Their shape is that of an elongated triangle tapering to a pointed tip. The surface is smooth, shiny, and slightly undulating; the flesh is thinnish with a sharp and biting flavor and is very, very hot. The sizes vary so much that it is difficult to give a standard size, but let's say 1 inch (2.5cm) to 1¼ inches (about 3cm) across the shoulders and about 4 inches (10cm) long.

Chiles de agua are relatively expensive for local consumers and are sold in groups of say six or twelve—for 10 or 20 pesos, depending on the season—attractively displayed in Oaxacan markets, fanned out in a circle on a small, flat tray generally lined with a large green leaf.

These chiles are used in fresh and cooked sauces, but perhaps most popular is char-roasted *(asado),* peeled, and then stuffed with a picadillo, shredded meat filling, or cheese or cut into strips and used in a relish (*The Art,* page 359). Chiles de agua are also used ripened and dried, but rarely now, since they have been supplanted by guajillos, which are less expensive. As a substitute, use any large, light green, hot chile available—the look may be right if not the flavor.

PREPARATION

A S A D O : Follow the instructions for poblanos (see page 50), but take care not to let the rather thin flesh scorch. The skin can then be peeled very easily from the flesh.

FOR STUFFING: Make a vertical slit down one side and carefully remove the seeds and veins, taking care to leave the top intact.

FOR STRIPS: Open up the chile, remove the seeds, veins, and fleshy top, and cut the flesh into strips about ½ inch (1.25 cm) wide. If you want an even more *picante* relish, leave the seeds and veins intact.

FOR A MOLE VERDE AND OTHER COOKED SAUCES: Some cooks still peel their chiles de agua before blending with the rest of the ingredients. But leave the seeds and veins in.

There is a variation of a sauce in Oaxaca, although not given here because it is very local, referred to as "mortajada." Chiles de agua are *asado* and roughly chopped, sometimes unskinned (depending on the taste of the cook), and roughly crushed, not finely ground, into the tomato base in a *chilmolera* (see page 296).

Rajas de Chile de Agua

OAXACAN CHILE STRIPS IN LIME JUICE

In Oaxaca this healthy "relish" of chile strips in lime juice (full of vitamin C) is used to accompany Enfrijoladas (page 259), a mole Amarillo or Chichilo negro, or as a topping for rice. It is made with the fiery chile de agua, asado, peeled, and cut into strips, then marinated in lime juice with white onion and dried oregano. As a substitute for the chile de agua, which is light to mid-green in color, any thin-fleshed light green or yellow pepper or even Anaheim will do—although it is not very hot.

MAKES ABOUT 1½ CUPS (375ML)

1 cup (250ml) charred, peeled, and
    cleaned chile strips
⅓ cup (83ml) thinly sliced white onion
    (half-moons)

⅓ cup (83ml) fresh lime juice
1 teaspoon dried Oaxacan oregano,
    or ½ teaspoon Mexican oregano
Sea salt to taste

Mix all the ingredients in a glass or nonreactive bowl and set aside to marinate for several hours. This will keep for several days in the refrigerator, but it is not suitable for freezing; the chile flesh tends to disintegrate.

Chilaca

Chilacas are long, narrow chiles, sometimes curling at the end; this has earned them the Michoacán name of cuernillos, or "big horns," or chiles para deshebrar, since they are torn, not cut into strips. They are prevalent in the cooking of central-western Mexico, especially Michoacán, and Mexico City. They are a deep, almost blackish, green and they ripen to a dark chocolaty brown. When ripe, they are dried and become pasillas or negros (see page 74). The surface is very shiny with vertical ridges—which makes them easy to shred—but the flesh is thin, therefore skinning them is rather labor-intensive. Because of their diverse sizes, choosing an average is purely arbitrary, but let's go by those I have in front of me: 7 inches (18cm) long and ¾ to 1 inch (2–2.5cm) wide.

The chilaca—one of my great favorite chiles—has a complex fruity flavor and while not usually among the hottest chiles, they can sometimes surprise you. While chilacas are sometimes stuffed, they are mainly used skinned and shredded and added to other vegetables like potatoes or corn, or to mushrooms and cream, or as a colorful topping for sauces or in a filling for tamales.

Although I saw chilacas many, many years ago in a Los Angeles market, they never caught on. Only now are they making a comeback, and are appearing in some supermarkets catering to a large Mexican population. But if they are not available, substitute poblanos, as recipes will tell you to do.

PREPARATION

ASADO: Follow the instructions for poblanos (see page 50), but take care because the flesh is very thin and can easily burn. Leave them to steam in the bag longer than you would for poblanos, about 15 minutes.

FOR STRIPS: After charring and skinning, cut the tops off the chiles, make vertical slits, and remove the seeds and veins. Tear the flesh into narrow strips.

FOR STUFFING: Make a vertical slit in the chiles and carefully remove the seeds and long veins, leaving the tops intact. They are not usually covered with batter, which would seal them by covering the slits, so always be prepared with toothpicks.

Chiles Güeros

Any chile in Mexico that is a light yellowish or very pale green is called *güero,* and it seems that a new tasteless varietal is introduced (mainly I suspect from the gene-shufflers in the United States) every year. This makes writing about the güeros very difficult. I shall therefore confine myself to those that have stood the test of time and have some flavor. These chiles are fleshy and are generally, with minor exceptions, not dried.

Chile Cera

These small triangular chiles with a smooth, light yellow waxy surface are fairly regular in size, unlike many other types of chiles, about $2\frac{1}{2}$ inches (6.5cm) long and about 1 inch (2.5cm) across the shoulders. Depending on the area they are also known as (erroneously) caribes, hungaro, and in the United States, as wax or Fresno chiles, which are always available. They can vary from mild to fairly hot.

I have come across these chiles in markets in Zacatecas, where many are grown. They are used mainly in northern Mexico, often pickled whole with fruits and vegetables or added to soups and stews. It is unusual to see them charred and peeled, but then there is always the exception to the rule, as in the case of the dish Carne en Chile Güero from the Restaurant Bar El Paraiso (*My Mexico,* page 146).

Chile Xcatik

The name means "blond" in the Mayan language. The xcatik is very much a local Yucatecan chile that can vary from mild to fairly hot. An average one measures $4\frac{1}{2}$ to 5 inches (12–13cm) long and $\frac{3}{4}$ inch (2cm) wide. It has a smooth, shiny, slightly undulating surface. It is most generally used whole, charred but not peeled, in escabeches, sauces, or broths. Substitute an Italian or banana pepper.

Chile Largo o Carrecillo

When I first went to Mexico in the late '50s, these slender, pale yellow chiles would be sold fresh in the markets during the rainy season. Now I think the entire crop, which is not on a grand scale, is bought up by the canning industry. Unskinned, they are canned in a light pickle with onions and carrots and used in tomato sauces a la Veracruzana or in dishes like Cuñete de Pollo (*The Art*, page 235). They have a light distinctive flavor and are mildly hot. An average chile largo, as its name suggests, is about 3 inches (7.5cm) long, ending in a curled, sharp tip and is less than ½ inch (about 1.3cm) wide. The surface is shiny, but undulating, with a thin, almost transparent skin. You can always find them canned in Mexican markets.

Chile para Rellenar Amarillento, o Cristalino

This chile grown exclusively around Dolores Hidalgo in the state of Guanajuato is shaped like an elongated poblano about 5 inches (13cm) long and 2 inches (5cm) across the top. It has a light green, shiny skin with a slightly undulating surface and much thinner, almost transparent flesh than a poblano, and a fresh, fruity flavor. It is usually charred, skinned, and left whole for stuffing; it can vary from mild to quite hot.

Chile Habanero

A chile habanero plant in full production is a decorative masterpiece about 3 feet (1m) high with dark green glossy leaves interspersed with what seem like green and orange lanterns. The chiles ripen from light green, through yellow, and finally a deep orange. There is one rare type that ripens to red (found only on a small island off the coast) and another from a darker green to an aubergine color, which they call cubano; in Campeche, I have also used a habanero that is a pale apricot color with a

pushed-up tip, which they call rosado.

The chile habanero has a smooth, shiny skin and undulating surface. It is an average size of 1¾ inches (4.5cm) long and 1¼ inches (3cm) at its widest part. It is not only among the hottest of chiles but also has a distinctive and appetizing aroma and flavor that are released more potently when the chile is *asado.* While this chile is mainly grown in the Yucatán Peninsula, where it is consumed in local dishes, it is now much more widely available in supermarkets in the main cities of Mexico, as well as in specific areas of the southwestern United States.

The chile is not used dried in Mexico. I don't recommend the dried ones that are to be found in some areas of the United States, since the juiciness, flavor, and character of the fresh are lacking. Substitute Scotch bonnets, which are found in Caribbean and West Indian stores. Chile habanero is used whole as a flavoring in sauces, pickled, or made into a strong relishlike sauce. The seeds are not removed, and the chiles are never skinned.

PREPARATION

WHOLE, RAW: When preparing frijoles colados—with black beans—or a Yucatán tomato sauce, either a whole raw or charred chile habanero is added for flavor.

WHOLE, ASADO: Place the whole chile on an ungreased griddle or grill over medium heat and turn it from time to time until the flesh is slightly wilted and the skin is very slightly charred.

FOR CEBOLLAS EN ESCABECHE: The chiles are chopped raw, with seeds.

FOR A HOT SAUCE: The chiles are *asado,* as for poblanos (see page 50), and mashed with lime juice and salt. A unique expression is used in Yucatán when a chile habanero, either raw or *asado,* is slashed several times at the tip and dipped a few times into the sauce, for both flavor and a light piquancy: "The chile takes a walk through the sauce."

Chile Jalapeño

This chile hardly needs an introduction since it is perhaps the best known outside of Mexico, possibly because so much of the crop goes to the canning industry, not only for home consumption but also for export. The name derives from Jalapa, the capital of the state of Veracruz.

Among the fresh chiles, the shape of the jalapeño is unmistakable. Some are more cylindrical than triangular, tapering slightly to a blunt tip with an average size 2½ inches (6.5cm) long and just under 1 inch (2.5cm) wide at the top. The skin is a shiny to dark green, some with blackish-purple patches and others with vertical light brown stripes known as corking, which makes for a somewhat abrasive, as opposed to an otherwise smooth, surface. They vary from hot to very hot. When ripened on the plant and deep red in color, they are smoke-dried as chipotles and moras (see pages 67, 71). There are many local names for the jalapeño, among them chile gordo in parts of Veracruz, chilchota in la Sierra Norte de Puebla, cuaresmeño in central Mexico, and tornachile in the early cookbooks.

Jalapeño chiles are available fresh the year round and have a wide distribution. They are available in many supermarkets, as well as specialty stores, in many parts of the United States. But do not fall for the hybrid dark red ones that do not have the same crispness or flavor.

Jalapeños are used in many different ways: pickled with vegetables (either whole or in strips), blended into cooked or raw sauces, or charred and peeled to be stuffed with cheese, meat, or fish.

Always rinse and dry the chiles first. For some cooked or uncooked table sauces, chop the raw chiles roughly *with their seeds,* and grind them together with the rest of the sauce ingredients.

Chiles Jalapeños en Escabeche

PICKLED CHILES JALAPEÑOS

These chiles are an indispensable part of any Mexican meal, except for the southern areas of the country, which have their own regional condiments. Most people would buy industrially canned jalapeños en escabeche, *but as always the homemade ones are fresher, healthier, and tastier.*

Providing these pickled chiles are refrigerated they will last several months, but make sure they are cooked thoroughly and pickled with enough salt and vinegar. Insufficiently cooked fresh chiles (as opposed to dried) allow the growth of bacteria; at the least hint of fermentation, throw them out. It is best to let the chiles mature in flavor for a couple of days before using.

MAKES JUST UNDER 4 CUPS (1L)

1 pound (450g) jalapeños
About ⅓ cup (83ml) vegetable oil
2 medium white onions, thickly sliced
2 medium carrots, trimmed, scraped, and
    thinly sliced
1 small head garlic, cut across
    horizontally, left unpeeled
About 3½ cups (875ml) mild vinegar

2 tablespoons sea salt
2 bay leaves, Mexican if possible
½ teaspoon dried oregano, Mexican if
    possible
4 sprigs fresh thyme, or ¼ teaspoon dried
4 sprigs fresh marjoram, or ¼ teaspoon
    dried
1 tablespoon sugar

Have ready sterilized jars and lids. Rinse and dry the chiles. Leaving the stems intact, cut each chile lengthwise into six strips; for appearance' sake, and a little less heat, you may remove seeds and veins but it is not really necessary.

Heat the oil in a deep skillet and add the chiles, onions, carrots, and garlic and fry over medium heat for about 10 minutes, stirring from time to time to ensure even cooking—the chiles will become a dull green color. Add the vinegar, salt, herbs, and sugar and bring to a boil. Lower the heat and cook for about 10 minutes. Test for seasoning. The liquid should just cover the chiles.

Pack the mixture into hot, sterilized jars and set aside to cool. Store in the refrigerator.

PREPARATION

ASADO: Place the whole chiles on an ungreased griddle over medium heat and turn them from time to time until the flesh is fairly soft; there will be brownish blistered patches on the skin and the color will have changed to a dull green. Chop roughly unskinned, with seeds, and blend with the other ingredients.

FOR STUFFING: Follow the instructions for peeling poblanos (see page 50), and while still hot, place in a paper or plastic bag for about 10 minutes to steam. The skin will be loosened from the flesh, making them easy to peel. Make a vertical slit down the length of the chiles and carefully remove the seeds and veins.

TO MAKE STRIPS FOR PICKLING: Cut each raw chile into about four strips and remove the seeds for appearance' sake.

Chile Manzano

This bulbous, fleshy chile is also known as perón in Michoacán, canario in Oaxaca, and, annoyingly, jalapeño in parts of Chiapas. It is a native of South America (known there as rocoto) but has adapted well to the cool, highland areas of Mexico. I have even seen it growing in the shade of pine trees in Michoacán. The chile is produced by a rangy plant that can become a tall bush *(C. pubescens)* and differs from other chiles in that it has purple flowers, as opposed to the usual white. Curiously there are two separate plants of chile manzano: one bears chiles that ripen from green to yellow or orange, while the other bears chiles that ripen from green to a deep red.

Chile manzano has a smooth, highly polished skin, black seeds, and thick flesh that is not suitable for drying. It is, with very minor exceptions, terribly hot. An average size might be about 2 inches (5cm) from the top to its blunt, rounded base and almost as wide. The chile is a particular favorite in the higher altitudes of the state of Mexico, where it is chopped raw with peaches for a pico de gallo (see *Essentials,* page 250). In Michoacán it is sometimes charred and skinned and prepared like chiles rellenos. But mostly it is prepared unskinned, with lime juice and onions for a relish or added whole to stews of pig's blood *(relleno)*. In Veracruz, I have also seen the unskinned chile with the top cut off to serve as a lid, then seeded, stuffed with ricotta and epazote, and *asado* on the comal to make a fiery snack. I have seen these chiles in supermarkets catering to Latin American populations in Texas and growing in window boxes in the Mission area of San Francisco.

Preparation

RAW FOR SAUCES OR PICKLES: The very hard, black seeds are always removed before chopping.

FOR STUFFING: *Asado,* following the instructions for poblanos on page 50, and then soak or simmer in salted water for about 20 minutes to remove some of the fiery piquancy.

Chile Píquin

There is as yet an uncounted number of minute chiles, domesticated from wild plants, found throughout Mexico. They can be round, like some in the northern areas, triangular, oval, or tubular. All have a shiny, smooth skin, mid- to blackish green in color ripening to a brilliant red. They pack a lot of concentrated heat and their flavor varies slightly with soil and climatic conditions. Some plants produce fruits the year round while others are seasonal, and these chiles are used both fresh and dried.

There is, for instance, a very tiny chile de monte that grows wild in the damper valleys of Nuevo León. I am told by a chile expert there that it is reproduced only through the digestive tract of birds—obviously Mexican birds can tolerate the heat! And I am also told that there is a noticeable difference in flavor in the chile, small and hot as it is, depending on the area where it is found.

In Yucatán, it is the chile max (pronounced *mash*), amashito in Tabasco, and chilpaya in Veracruz, while chiltepin and chilito are the names used in other areas. But most commonly it is referred to as píquin. When used fresh, it is often pickled in

vinegar or crushed with onion and salt, or lime juice as a *picante* condiment. When dried, it is toasted and ground to a powder as a condiment for beans or pozole (in Sonora), among other uses.

You can always find small packages of these little chiles in Mexican markets and large supermarkets with a Mexican section.

Chile Xigole

I have seen two little chiles by this name. One is small like any píquin in a market in Oaxaca City; the other is a small and triangular chile from the Sierra Sur above Puerto Escondido. They are mostly used for uncooked table sauces. This is not a commercial chile.

Chile Poblano

The chile poblano is, in my opinion, one of the most delicious foods in the world. It is cultivated in many parts of Mexico and now exported to the United States. It is also known as *chile para rellenar,* or "chile for stuffing," as *gordo* in Jalisco, and as *jaral* in the state of Mexico, among others. In the United States it is often marked "pasilla," which indicates something dried and wrinkled, or the oxymoronic name, "fresh pasilla." When ripened on the plant, then dried, the poblano becomes the chile ancho. Poblanos are also used for chiles pasados (see page 74).

The poblanos I remember from more than thirty years ago (which you can still sometimes get from Puebla in the summer rainy season) were a deep, blackish-green color. They were thinner fleshed than those of today, with a marked deep depression around the base of the stalk. These poblanos were pleasantly hot and had a complex, inky-fruity flavor. Nowadays they are often lighter in color, thicker fleshed, and much more *picante*. The chile poblano is a large, triangular chile, an average one being about 4½ inches (about 11.5cm) long and 2½ inches (6.5cm) across its broad shoulders. It has a smooth, lustrous skin and a slightly undulating surface.

This is the most versatile of chiles: *asado* and skinned poblanos can be stuffed, cut into strips to be cooked with other vegetables or as a topping for soups, or blended, sometimes without skinning, for cooked sauces, green moles, and so on.

Poblanos are being grown on a commercial scale in Washington and Oregon states, but they are exceedingly hot and do not have the pleasant characteristic flavor of the Mexican originals.

These chiles are now easy to find in the United States in larger supermarkets or Mexican groceries, but often marked incorrectly.

PREPARATION

ASADO: Place the whole chiles over the open flame of a gas stove or on a charcoal grill, turning them from time to time until the skin is blistered and lightly charred. If you do not have a gas stove, then wipe the surface of the chiles lightly with oil and put them up

 under a hot electric grill, about 2 inches (5cm) from the element and turn them from time to time until blistered all over. Place them immediately inside a paper or plastic bag and set aside to steam for about 10 minutes; this process will loosen the skin. Then remove the skin by just running your hands down the chile. Wipe off any pieces of reluctant skin with a damp cloth. Do not rinse as some cooks and writers suggest; you will lose all the concentrated juices and impair the flavor.

Do not put into a hot oven; the skins may blister, but the flesh will be cooked too much.

FOR STUFFING: Make a vertical slit on one side of the charred and peeled chile and carefully cut out the placenta at the top, which holds most of the seeds; take care to keep the top intact. Try to remove some of the veins without shredding the flesh of the chile.

FOR RAJAS (STRIPS): Cut the top with the stalk base off the charred and peeled chile, open down one side, and remove the seeds and veins. Cut into vertical strips about ⅜ inch (about .75cm) wide.

FOR BLENDING RAW: If you are not going to skin the poblanos, but just blend them with other ingredients, you still need to remove the placenta with the seeds at the top.

FOR PASADOS: See page 74.

REMOVE THE SKIN BY RUNNING YOUR
HANDS DOWN THE CHILE.

CAREFULLY CUT OUT
THE PLACENTA.

REMOVE SOME OF
THE VEINS.

Chiles Rellenos

STUFFED CHILES

Chiles rellenos is one of the dishes that is practically synonymous with Mexican food. It provides one example of the gastronomic vagaries of foods. The pepper from Mexico was adopted in Europe and the Mediterranean area (and later other parts of the world), but the practice of stuffing it came back from Europe and the Mediterranean.

While more often than not chiles poblanos are used for this dish, other chiles, mostly fresh but occasionally dried, will be stuffed. Some examples are the fresh chile de agua and dried pasilla in Oaxaca, anchos and pasillas (dried) in central Mexico, jalapeños (fresh) in Veracruz, and pasados (dried) in Chihuahua. In many—but not all—cases, the prepared, stuffed, and lightly floured chiles are covered with a coating of beaten egg and fried; they are called "rebozados" (as if covered with a rebozo, a Mexican type of shawl). Some are served in a tomato and meat broth, or a mild, dried chile sauce, others with the sauce or even cream on the side.

There are many other ways of stuffing and serving chiles that can be found in my books: poblanos lightly pickled and stuffed with guacamole (Nuevo León) or with seasoned beans (Colima), stuffed with squash and served as a salad, or with cheese and sautéed, and so on. There are so many such enticing recipes that never see the light of day on the normal restaurant bill of fare.

Poblano chiles may be filled with a number of stuffings, the most popular being shredded and chopped meat—called picadillo—or cheese. Recipes for a pork and a cheese filling follow (see pages 54 and 55). Other options are fresh corn and cheese (Essentials, page 214); potatoes and cheese, although the recipe calls for pasilla chiles (My Mexico, page 114); and a seasoned shrimp filling (My Mexico, pages 74 and 350). Or invent your own!

FOR 6 POBLANOS

6 stuffed poblanos (see above)	**Salt to taste**
Vegetable oil, for frying (not canola)	**⅓ cup all-purpose flour**
3 large eggs, separated	

Have the stuffed chiles ready. Stack paper toweling or opened paper bags nearby, ready to drain excess oil. Heat oil to a depth of 1 inch (2.5cm) in a skillet. I have never taken the temperature, but the oil when tested with a dry wooden spoon should sizzle around it. Another test is that the batter should sizzle and froth up as it enters the oil. But do not let the oil overheat and smoke or the batter will brown—and in fact burn—and the chiles will not be cooked on the inside, nor will the stuffed chile be heated through, or any cheese stuffing melted. Do not attempt to fry chiles in a deep-fat fryer. The batter will stick to the wire basket and the batter will absorb the strong residual flavors in the oil.

Meantime, beat the egg whites until they form soft peaks, but not too stiff and dry. Tip the bowl just to make sure they do not slide around, which indicates there is still

some unbeaten egg white at the bottom; or turn the bowl upside down. They should not fall out. Gradually beat in the salt and yolks. When they are well incorporated, lightly dust one of the chiles with the flour. With a perforated spoon, or two forks, dip the chile into the beaten eggs and turn it around until it is well covered—not too thin a coating and not too thick—and carefully lower into the hot oil.

It is useful to have two clean spatulas or two forks to turn the chile around. When the batter is well set and a deep golden color, carefully turn the chile over as if folding it into the batter, and fry again until golden all the way round (see Note)—this should take about 6 minutes in all. However, if there are some uncooked patches of batter around the stem, carefully upend it and fry until evenly colored. This will take a few moments more. Drain on paper towels or brown paper bags and repeat with the remaining chiles.

If you are going to serve the chiles immediately, heat them in the sauce—if called for in the recipe—to absorb the flavors for about 10 minutes. Of course, the batter will become a little sodden.

N O T E : *Until you have done your first hundred I don't suggest you do what adept young cooks do: grab the chile by its stalk and twirl it around in the batter and then the oil! Very showy and effective . . . but!*

Of course, this frying procedure is nerve-wracking if carried out while your guests wait at the table. You can fry the chiles several hours ahead, and reheat by placing the chiles on a double layer of absorbent paper on a cookie sheet. Place in a 350°F (180°C) oven for about 15 minutes to heat through. This method has the added advantage of reducing excess oil.

FROM TOP: BEAT IN THE SALT AND YOLKS; LIGHTLY DUST CHILES WITH THE FLOUR; COVER THE CHILE WITH THE BEATEN EGGS; LOWER INTO HOT OIL; TURN THE CHILE OVER.

Relleno de Puerco para Chiles Poblanos

PORK FILLING FOR POBLANO CHILES

There are countless fillings for rellenos, for poblano chiles, and this is my favorite, probably because it was the first I learned back in 1957. Some cooks prefer to mix pork with beef or other meats—a popular filling is now made with chicken. But whatever meats you want to use, you will have better results if you poach and shred the meat—ground meat just doesn't give the same flavor and texture, and besides you don't have the delicious broth for the tomato sauce. Fry the meat in lard if you can bear it. You will need about ½ cup (125ml) filling for each poblano chile.

MAKES ABOUT 3 CUPS (750ML)

COOKING THE MEAT

2 pounds (900g) boneless pork with some fat, cut into 1-inch (2.5-cm) cubes

½ white onion, roughly chopped

4 garlic cloves, unpeeled

Salt to taste

SEASONING THE MEAT

4 to 5 tablespoons lard or vegetable oil

⅔ cup (163ml) finely chopped white onion

3 garlic cloves, peeled and finely chopped

8 peppercorns, lightly crushed

½-inch (1.25-cm) cinnamon stick, broken into small pieces

1¼ pounds (562g) tomatoes, roughly chopped, about 2¾ cups (690ml)

3 heaped tablespoons raisins

2 tablespoons blanched and slivered almonds

2 heaped tablespoons acitron or candied pineapple cut into small cubes

Salt to taste

Put the meat into a large saucepan with the onion, garlic, and salt. Barely cover with water, cover the pan, and cook over medium heat until tender but not soft, 35 to 40 minutes. If you have time, leave the meat to cool in the broth for better flavor. If not, strain and reserve the broth; set the broth and meat aside to cool.

When cool enough to handle, shred the meat roughly, discarding any large pieces of fat and cartilage. Then chop the meat to a medium consistency. You should have about 3 cups (750ml). Skim the broth and set aside.

Melt the lard in a large skillet and cook the onion and garlic over medium heat until translucent, about 2 minutes. Add the meat, sprinkle with the spices, and cook over medium heat, stirring from time to time and scraping the bottom of the pan to avoid sticking until it begins to brown very lightly, about 8 minutes.

Blend the tomatoes to a textured puree, add to the pan, and cook over fairly high heat until the juice has been absorbed, about 10 minutes. Just before the end of the cooking time, stir in the raisins, almonds, and acitron. The mixture should be moist but not juicy. Stir in salt to taste.

Relleno de Queso

CHEESE FILLING FOR CHILES RELLENOS

An equally delicious filling—and a very simple one—is that of just cheese. In Mexico, queso Chihuahua or quesillo de Oaxaca is used, but since their counterparts in the United States do not come up to scratch, I suggest you use a domestic Muenster or mild Cheddar with a low melting point.

You will need about 2 ounces (60g) of cheese for each chile, cut into strips about 3 inches (7.5cm) long and ¹⁄₂ inch (1.25cm) square. Be sure to use them at room temperature and not cold from the refrigerator so that they will melt as the batter-coated chiles are fried.

Chile Serrano

Chiles serranos, together with jalapeños, are the most ubiquitous. They are what I call the everyday chile, particularly in central and parts of northern Mexico. A general name is chile verde (not to be confused with the chile verde de Yucatán, which is completely different).

The chile serrano is small, on average about 2 inches (5cm) long and about ¹⁄₂ inch (1.5cm) wide. There are now some longer ones from, presumably, "improved" seeds, but their characteristic flavor has been somewhat lost. The chile is narrow in shape, tapering to a slightly pointed or rounded tip. The smooth, shiny surface ranges from mid- to darkish green in color with occasional dark patches. The flesh is thickish, crisp, and juicy with a sharp green flavor that enhances many fresh regional sauces. Like other types of chiles, the serrano can vary between hot and very hot depending on its ancestors and growing conditions.

Despite being such a popular chile in its fresh

state, quite a large proportion of the crop goes to the canning industry, where it is packed in vinegar with onion, carrot, and herbs for Serranos en Escabeche (*The Art,* page 356; *Essentials,* page 237), a favorite relish that is sometimes added to cooked sauces.

For fresh or cooked sauces, the serrano is used either raw or *asado,* chopped, or ground with other ingredients. *The seeds are not removed.* Occasionally serranos are added whole, either raw or *asado*—to some recipes for beans or rice, for instance—but each recipe will give specific instructions. If *asado,* until slightly charred and softened, they are passed separately as *chiles toreados*—in essence, a condiment for those who prefer their food with more fire. When serranos are to be pickled, they are left whole, but two slits are made in the tip so that the flavor is released and the vinegar can penetrate.

There is a wide distribution of these chiles now in the United States, and they are available the year round in supermarkets and specialty stores, but steer clear of the deep red hybrids, which do not have the flavor or texture of the real thing.

Preparation

Rinse and dry the chiles.

RAW: For some raw or cooked sauces, just chop the chiles with their seeds, and grind with the rest of the sauce ingredients.

ASADO: Place the whole chiles on an ungreased griddle over medium heat and turn them from time to time until the flesh is fairly soft; there will be brownish patches on the skin and the color will have faded somewhat. Then, if they are to be ground with other ingredients, chop roughly before blending. Note well: they are to be neither peeled nor seeded.

Chile Verde del Norte

The chile verde grown in the northwest of Mexico is probably the same as, or a close varietal of, the California Anaheim chile. It is always hard to say exactly because the same chile changes in taste and even texture when grown in different soil under different climatic conditions. Confusingly, it is also known as chilaca (totally different from that described on page 40) in Chihuahua and chile Magdalena, named for the town in Sonora near which many of these chiles are produced. If this chile has been overfertilized and/or refrigerated for some time it is quite innocuous tasting, but freshly picked and produced under normal conditions, or evenly under slightly stressed conditions, it has a more interesting character.

An average-size chile verde del norte measures about 5½ inches (14cm) long and 1¼ inches (3cm) wide with very little tapering at the base. It has a smooth, light-green skin and very slightly ridged surface and is usually mild. It ripens to a brilliant red. This chile verde has rather a tough skin so for most uses it is first *asado* and cleaned of veins and seeds, then either stuffed, cut into strips for sauces and stews, or dried whole for pasados (see page 74).

In Mexico, the northern chile verde is found only in the northern states; it is not appreciated farther south, where the chiles are hotter and have more defined flavors. It is of course widely available throughout the United States, where it is sold as an Anaheim.

PREPARATION

ASADO: Place the whole chile over the open flame of a gas stove or grill over medium heat and turn it from time to time until the skin is blistered and slightly browned. Immediately put it into a paper or plastic bag to steam. The rather tough skin will loosen in about 5 minutes. Run your hands down the chile to easily remove the skin. Wipe with a damp cloth to remove any stray bits of skin, but do not put into water—that will wash away the flavor that has been released by the grilling.

FOR STUFFING: Make a vertical slit down one side of the chile and carefully remove the seeds and veins.

FOR STRIPS: Cut the tops off the chile, make a vertical slit down one side, and remove the seeds and veins. Cut into strips as specified in the recipe.

FOR PASADOS: See page 74.

Chiles for drying are left to ripen on the plant and then either dried in the sun or slightly fermented under sacking and then dried in ovens. I recommend that you get to know the extraordinary flavors of chiles that have been ripened and smoke-dried, like the chilpocle (popularly known as chipotle), mora, morita, and the incomparable pasilla de Oaxaca. All dried chiles provide a rich source of vitamin A.

There is one method of drying the poblano or Anaheim (Magdaleno or chile verde del norte) done in northern Mexico that is little known in the rest of the country. These chiles are picked when mature but still green, then charred and peeled but left whole and dried in the sun; as such, they are known as chiles pasados (see page 74).

While in this section I give the preparation of each chile in turn, there are two general rules to remember. First, when soaking chiles to be prepared for sauces like moles and adobos, do not leave them for too long in the soaking water or they will lose their flavor. One famous Zapotec cook I know says that the soaking water should be cold so that the color does not leach out. She should know because she is a weaver and dyes her own wool. However, I am a dyed-in-the-wool adherent to my first cooking experiences and teachers, and I soak chiles in hot water. Second, never attempt to peel the chiles after soaking.

CHOOSING AND STORING DRIED CHILES

When purchasing dried chiles, avoid if possible those that are already packaged. For one thing, they are grossly overpriced and often wrongly labeled. Besides, you can't see what you are getting. Until you are completely familiar with your chiles, take the book with you. Even when sold loose, chiles are often misnamed.

If your supplier or supermarket buys first-quality chiles, they should be flexible, but not damp (sometimes crafty chile sellers dampen them so that they weigh more) and should not have transparent patches where the flesh has been eaten away by a type of fruit fly, which hatch out in damp, hot weather from tiny, but discernible, dark eggs deposited by small moths.

If your chiles have been around for some time and are dried out and even brittle, a slow warming on a medium hot pan for a few minutes will bring them back to life, but they will probably need a little longer soaking to rehydrate. In damp weather, try to keep your chiles in a dry place or even in the freezer. I talk from experience because every rainy season in Mexico my dried chiles develop a mold on the inside and on the lower part of the stem.

How does one describe chiles adequately and as accurately as possible? Yes, one has to generalize and, taking a whole bunch, try to decide on which might be considered the most representative, knowing full well that from one plant, or a late picking, the size and even the shape of chiles can vary considerably. And the more experience I have at looking at the many very similar varieties, the more I realize how difficult it must be for beginning cooks to recognize a particular chile of a certain general group when separated from its companions.

Then there is the dilemma of how to describe the color, particularly of dried chiles, since practically everyone has his or her own concept for naming colors. So I have set out before me a range of ten dried chiles of the main color group to show how to differentiate. Very much depends on how old the chiles are, how they have been dried, and how thick their flesh was when the chile was mature but still green. I have myself erroneously described chiles as reddish-brown—they aren't! Matching them to an official color chart in *Webster's International Dictionary*, I come closest with the description "raisin" (although I have never actually seen a raisin of that color). The chiles with a thinner skin are slightly lighter in tone, while others are the color of very ripe mulberries. But as I have said before, a lot depends on how long they have been around.

During the last five years, the greater availability of dried Mexican chiles has been astounding, and in the most unlikely places you can come across a supply of lesser known (in the United States) chiles like costeños or pasillas de Oaxaca. It is a matter of keeping your eyes open and making inquiries in authentic local Mexican restaurants. I will, however, mention substitutes where and if necessary. I have not referred to the Scoville chart for heat.

TOASTING DRIED CHILES

Although each recipe calling for dried chiles will give instructions on how to prepare them, there are some important points to observe. Very generally speaking—but I can always come up with the odd exception—the large fleshy chiles are used for cooked sauces while the small thinner-fleshed ones are used for table sauces.

When following instructions for toasting chiles, be aware that those with shiny, smooth, and tougher skins, like guajillos, cascabels, and puyas, will burn more quickly than the anchos, mulattos, and pasillas. The former will therefore require less toasting time. Dried chiles are toasted on an ungreased comal or griddle set over medium-low heat.

1. For most cooked sauces like moles, pipianes, and adobos, dried chiles should be slit open vertically, seeds and veins removed, and flattened out or cut into two parts to make toasting easier. They should be toasted slowly, flattening them down with a spatula, on both sides until the inside flesh changes to a tobacco brown. This should take about 25 seconds with a reasonably flexible chile. If your chiles are so dry that they are brittle, place them whole on a warm griddle and, pressing down lightly, heat them through on both sides until miraculously they come to life and are completely flexible; you can then slit them open and remove seeds and veins. The chiles will be soaked to rehydrate before blending with liquid and/or other ingredients.

2. Some recipes for cooked sauces may call for the same type of chiles to be toasted for a longer time—for 50 seconds to 1 minute—so that when they cool they become slightly brittle and can easily be crumbled into a blender jar and then, without soaking, blended with liquid and/or other ingredients. For this method, wipe the chiles first with a damp cloth to clean off any dirt or dust.

3. The smaller dried chiles are usually toasted whole, unseeded. It is useful to leave the stems, if any, intact so as to be able to turn them more easily. Again, these should be toasted over low heat, turning them from time to time so they toast evenly and do not burn. This process should take no longer than about 50 seconds; when they cool, they should be brittle. But do take care not to let them burn or the resulting sauce will be bitter.

Chile Ancho

The chile ancho (or wide chile, as it is more commonly known in Mexico) is the poblano ripened and dried. Confusingly, in parts of Michoacán and Colima it is called pasilla, or sometimes pasilla roja, and since a great number of Michoacános have migrated to the United States, the name for these chiles has gone with them. I have even seen bags of identical chiles, side by side, some marked ancho and some pasilla. So beware!

A first-quality ancho chile is flexible, neither damp nor dried out. It is triangular with broad shoulders tapering to a blunt tip. It is a deep red, with a wrinkled, shiny skin and an average size of 4½ inches (11.5cm) long and 3 inches (7.5cm) across the top.

Anchos have a fruity, slightly acid flavor. Although they have the reputation of being mild, they can surprise you and be very hot, depending on where they were grown, the soil, and the heat and if irrigated or grown in the rainy season.

Some anchos are darker in color than others, and as they dry out they become increasingly difficult to distinguish from chiles mulatos (see page 73). If you are unsure, open one up and hold it up to the light. The ancho will have a reddish hue and the mulato a chocolate brown and, generally, a smoother skin.

PREPARATION

Very generally speaking, ancho chiles are not used in fresh table sauces—often referred to in Mexico as *salsas de molcajete*—with one notable exception: Salsa de Tía Georgina (*Essentials*, page 247). However, that is really more of a relish than a sauce. Depending on the recipe, where it will always be stated, there are slightly different ways of preparing anchos.

FOR STUFFING: Leaving the top and any stalk intact, make a careful vertical slit down one side and again very carefully—so as not to tear it in an unsightly fashion—remove the seeds and veins. If the chile is very dry and brittle, soften it for a few moments on a medium-hot ungreased griddle or comal as mentioned on page 60. Cover the chile with hot water and leave to soak until rehydrated—in other words, until pliable and fleshy. This should take 10 to 15 minutes—no longer.

FOR COOKED SAUCES: Remove the stem, if any. Make a vertical slit down one side of the chile and remove the seeds and veins. Flatten the chile out as much as possible, and then follow one of these three options: (1) Cover with hot water and leave to soak until fleshy and soft—about 10 minutes. Drain, discarding the water. (2) Put cleaned chiles into a pan, cover with water, bring to a simmer, and cook over low heat for about 5 minutes. Set aside to soak for a further 5 minutes or until fleshy and soft. (3) Heat an ungreased comal or skillet over medium heat—it should not be too hot or the chiles will burn and affect the flavor of the sauce. Press the opened chile

TOASTING A CHILE ANCHO.

down lightly onto the hot surface and leave for a few seconds; turn and repeat on the second side for a few seconds more. The inside flesh should turn a golden brown and there will be a pleasant aroma from the chile. Put the chile into a bowl, cover with hot water, and soak for 10 to 15 minutes or until fleshy and soft.

For some recipes, especially moles, the instructions are to fry the chiles before soaking. Remove the seeds and veins, flatten the chiles, and fry lightly on both sides in just enough oil to cover the surface of the skillet. Again, the inner flesh will turn a tobacco brown—this will take about 5 seconds on each side. Remove and drain the chile before covering it with hot water to soak for about 10 minutes.

FOR POWDERED CHILE: Remove the seeds and veins, open the chiles, and flatten as much as possible. Place on an ungreased comal over medium heat and toast slowly on both sides until well cooked, 3 to 5 minutes per side. When cold the chiles will be quite crisp and crumble easily to a powder.

Chile de Árbol

The chile de árbol is not from a tree as its name implies but from a rangy plant that can grow about 3 feet (1m) high. It ripens from a mid-green to bright red, a color it retains when dried.

It is a smooth-skinned, slender chile with a slightly undulating surface. It tapers to a sharp point. An average-size sample measures 3 inches (7.5cm) long and ⅜ inch (about .75cm) in width. It is thin fleshed and very, very hot, with a sharp flavor that develops, and is more discernible, when it is lightly toasted.

The chile de árbol is mostly used for hot table sauces, for frying whole—with black beans, for instance, in Veracruz—or toasted until crisp, ground to a powder, and used as a condiment on sliced fruit, cucumbers, or jicama.

Very rarely will you see this chile sold in its fresh, green state, for growers can realize a better price when it is dried, either in the sun or in commercial ovens. The chile is readily available in the United States, usually packaged in small quantities and sold in the spice section of some supermarkets and Mexican groceries.

Nobody in Mexico would attempt to remove the seeds and veins from the chile de árbol; they want the heat.

FOR TABLE SAUCES: Heat a small quantity of oil in small skillet and fry, turning it from time to time until it changes to a slightly darker color and sends off a sharp, appetizing aroma.

FOR POWDERED CHILE: Place the whole chile, with stalk if it has one, on an ungreased griddle or comal over low heat. Turn the chile occasionally so that it is evenly toasted all around—about 1 minute. Allow the chile to cool. When it is quite crisp, remove the stem and crumble it, with the seeds, into a blender or an electric grinder. Grind to a very lightly textured powder. If stored in an airtight jar in a dry place, the powder can be kept for several months.

Chile Cascabel

The true cascabel (as opposed to the guajillo, which in some parts is also called cascabel) is a deep reddish sphere with a tough, smooth, polished surface. And it does indeed rattle as you shake it, as its name implies. Although it can be found in most Mexican markets, it is more prevalently used in the dishes of the central-western and northern parts of the country.

An average-size chile cascabel measures about 1¼ inches (just over 3cm) wide and 1 inch (2.5cm) from the base of the stalk to the rounded base, and it is quite fleshy when rehydrated. It is pleasantly hot.

The chile cascabel is used mainly, but not exclusively, for table sauces in which its character can be appreciated (rather than being combined with other chiles in a more complex cooked sauce). One of my favorite table sauces, in fact, is where the skin and the seeds are both toasted to give the sauce an extraordinary nutty flavor (see *Essentials*, page 246). This chile can be found in the United States, but beware when buying: the guajillo is also marked "cascabel."

PREPARATION

Some recipes call for the cascabel chile to be soaked or simmered in water—omitting the toasting, of course—and then blended with the other ingredients, usually tomatoes or Mexican green tomatoes and garlic. In this case, it should be cleaned first of the seeds and veins.

TOASTING: Providing the surface of the chile is not irregular, wipe the whole chile clean with a damp cloth and place it on a warm ungreased griddle over medium heat. Toast, turning it from time to time, until it is crisp to the touch and sends off a delicious (for chile lovers) aroma. It can then be slit open and the seeds and veins removed.

If the surface of the chile is uneven, wipe it clean, but then cut it open and remove the seeds and veins before toasting the pieces over medium heat. Take care to turn them over from time to time because the surface can burn very quickly and ruin the flavor of the sauce.

Chile Chilacate

In the Jalisco-Colima area of western Mexico the chile chilacate is used often with anchos instead of guajillos, although it is often packaged and sold as "guajillo" in both Mexico and the United States. It is one of those innocuous chiles of which there are many strains in northern Mexico, California, and New Mexico. In form it is an elongated triangle, full at the top and tapering to a point, with an average size of about 5 inches (13cm) long and 2 inches (5cm) across its shoulders. It has a smooth, shiny, almost transparent skin the color of a ripe mulberry, with an irregular surface. It is generally mild as chiles go, with a pleasant fruity flavor, but it is not very fleshy when rehydrated.

In the Jalisco-Colima area chilacates are used in cooked sauces for enchiladas and meat dishes like *birria*, and other cooked sauces often combined with anchos.

PREPARATION

FOR COOKED SAUCES: Slit the chiles open vertically and remove the seeds and veins (or leave the veins intact). Cover the chiles with hot water and leave to soak for about 15 minutes—no longer or the flavor will be diminished. Drain and blend according to the instructions in the recipe. The skin is not as tough as that of the guajillo and there is generally no need to strain the sauce.

Chile Chilcosle

The name derives from the Nahuatl words *chil* for "chile" and *costli* meaning "yellow." It is another native chile of Cuicatlán in Oaxaca. It is reddish, not yellow, as its name would imply, and is probably a cousin of the chilhuacle rojo. The typical chilcosle is long and narrow, often curling dramatically at the end, with an average size of about 5 inches (13cm) long and a little less than 1 inch (2.5cm) at the shoulders. The surface is slightly undulating and matte. It is used for mole amarillo, and other cooked sauces, but not for table sauces.

PREPARATION

Prepare the chilcosle as you would the chile chilhuacle (see page 67).

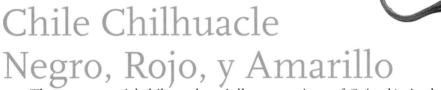

Chile Chilhuacle
Negro, Rojo, y Amarillo

These very special chiles—the criollos, or natives, of Cuicatlán in the far northeast corner of the state of Oaxaca—are the most expensive of all the dried chiles. Unfortunately production is very small and dwindling. They are unique in appearance, the most representative being full bodied and squat, almost square at the base and about 2 inches (5cm) wide and 2 inches (5cm) long. Others are more like elongated triangles tapering and slightly pointed, about 3½ inches (9cm) long and 1½ inches (4cm) across the shoulders. They have a matte skin, very slightly abrasive to the touch, a deep depression around the base of the stem, and are generally very hot.

There is certainly no doubt about distinguishing the blacks, or the reds, for that matter, with their translucent, rusty-red color. Some of the yellows, really amber colored, also have a translucent quality while others are quite dark and need to be opened up to be identified exactly.

Unfortunately because of their high price many cooks are turning to the ubiquitous and relatively cheap guajillos—a pity because the sharp piquancy of the chilhaucles is missing in sauces made with guajillos.

Dried chilhuacles are not used in table sauces, but are used in the typical moles and stews of that region and the central valley of Oaxaca. One of the prominent growers told me that some years ago large quantities of black chilhuacles went to Puebla for the preparation of mole poblano.

I have seen chilhuacles on sale only once in the Market Place in Austin, but I hope they will be more widely available in the future. The recipes calling for them will give an appropriate substitution wherever possible.

FOR A MOLE: Slit open and remove the seeds (the veins are usually left in) and tear into halves. Toast on an ungreased griddle over low heat, pressing them down slightly and turning them so that they are evenly toasted. The inside flesh will turn golden brown, about 50 seconds. Take care as they burn easily. Rinse the chiles in cold water and then soak them for about 15 minutes in hot water or until fleshy. The skin will never soften, but it does blend well. Drain and blend as indicated in the recipe; there is no need to strain the sauce.

Some cooks prefer to grind their toasted and rinsed chiles dry, omitting the soaking step, while others fry them in lard, omitting both the rinsing and soaking. In all cases save the seeds, which are included in many recipes for Oaxacan moles.

Chile Chipotle

The chile chipotle—as it is generally referred to, or more correctly, chilpocle—is the jalapeño ripened to a deep red on the plant and smoke-dried. The name derives from the Nahuatl words *chil*, "chile," and *pectli*, "smoke." The large tobacco-brown chipotle is known as meco (it is actually red but with wrinkled highlights that give it that color); the smaller is called chipotle mora and is mulberry colored.

An average-size chipotle is 2½ inches (6.5cm) long and 1 inch (2.5cm) at its widest part. It is fleshy when rehydrated and very *picante.*

Chipotles are used whole to flavor soups, and for pickling in vinegar and piloncillo, and even for stuffing with cheese, picadillo, or shredded fish. They are also blended in sauces for albóndigas, shrimp or meat dishes, or in some mole poblano recipes. These large chipotles are not used as much as they were twenty-five years ago since the smaller mora are used much more in the canning industry, being a more convenient size for the small cans.

Dried or canned chipotles are readily available in the United States, and, owing to their popularity it seems with chefs the world over, they are now distributed widely.

Preparation

FOR SOUPS OR FOR PICKLED: Rinse the whole chiles in warm water to remove any dust, then pierce them with a sharp fork to release flavors before following the recipe further.

FOR COOKED SAUCES: Soak the whole chiles in hot water for about 10 minutes, then drain, tear into pieces, and blend with the rest of the ingredients. You don't have to bother to remove the seeds and veins; it will not reduce the heat since the capsaicin will, in the smoke-drying process, have penetrated the flesh.

FOR STUFFING: Soak the chile in hot water for about 10 minutes. Make a vertical slit down one side and carefully remove the seeds and any bits of veins that you can scrape out easily. Pat dry and follow the recipe for stuffing.

Occasionally a recipe will require the chile to be lightly toasted before the next step of soaking, or whatever. Always use an ungreased comal or griddle over low heat and toast briefly on both sides.

Chile Costeño Rojo y Amarillo

The chile costeño is grown, as its name implies, in northern Oaxaca and Guerrero coastal areas, as well as the Mixteca Baja. It is used almost exclusively there, and in the central and western part of the state. Although a small portion of the crop is sold during the late summer and fall when ripe but still green, the majority is dried.

The costeño is among the smaller-size chiles, although this past year's crop seems to have grown extra long—an average would be about 3½ inches (9cm) long and about ½ inch (1.25cm) wide tapering to a pointed tip. It is a beautiful bronzy-red color with a thin, almost transparent, shiny skin and slightly undulating surface. It can be very hot, although there is a milder strain.

The bronzy-yellow chile from the same area is not used quite as much as the red variety, but is equally delicious in a rustic table sauce made the same way. It tends not to grow quite as long as the red, with an average length of 2½ inches (6.5cm) and ½ inch (1.25cm) in width tapering at the tip. The skin is not quite as transparent, but it is smooth and shiny with a slightly undulating surface. It is very hot.

The chile costeño is most popularly used toasted and ground with garlic salt and water for a rustic table sauce, sometimes with tomatoes added. It is used in the local moles and in sauces for flavoring tamales. I have also seen it used in a brothy mole amarillo, and in chilates in the Mixteca Norte area around Tlaxiaco.

Since so many Oaxacans have emigrated north of the border and brought with them their traditional foodstuffs and seasonings, you can often find costeños in Mexican markets, particularly in Los Angeles and parts of Texas and New York. The yellow chile is rarely found in the United States.

Preparation

Costeños can be toasted whole, as mentioned above, and ground with their seeds. Or they can be cleaned of their seeds and veins, toasted, and ground with other ingredients and very occasionally soaked after the toasting process. For local moles and cooked sauces, preparation varies from cook to cook, some removing and others leaving the seeds for more piquancy. For recipes see *My Mexico,* pages 423–434, and Salsa de Chile Costeño, page 206.

Chile Guajillo

The chile guajillo (literally meaning "a big pod"), as well as the ancho, is the chile most commonly used in Mexico, probably because it is the cheapest and is very easy to come by. It is reddish in color, with a tough, shiny, smooth skin that is opaque. Its shape is that of an elongated triangle with narrow shoulders tapering to a pointed tip. An average-size chile measures about 1¼ inches (just over 3cm) across the top and about 5 inches (13cm) long.

In recent
years often
what is sold as
guajillo does not have
the typical shape—it is
fuller at the top—nor is it
as pungent in flavor. Normally
the guajillo has a crisp, sharp flavor
and can vary from fairly hot to hot. When rehydrated it
is fairly fleshy but the skin remains tough, therefore blended guajillo sauces should
be strained.

This chile is sometimes referred to, in its green or dried state, as mirasol (literally "look at the sun"), which is misleading because, with a few exceptions, it does not normally point upward on the plant. It is very confusing also that the regional name in parts of central and northern Mexico is cascabel, and this has carried over into parts of the United States. Beware!

Guajillos are used in some areas for table sauces, enchiladas, adobos (seasoning pastes), and stews. They are readily available in the United States.

PREPARATION

FOR COOKED SAUCES: Remove the stems if any, slit open vertically, and remove the seeds and veins, then follow methods 1, 2, or 3 for anchos (see page 61), but note that for cooked sauces, the blended guajillos should always be strained because some of the tough skin never seems to disappear completely.

FOR BLACK MOLE: The guajillo chile is often used in Oaxacan black mole instead of the very expensive chilhuacle negro (see page 66). In this case the whole chiles are toasted until black and crisp, rinsed, and then soaked briefly until partially rehydrated.

Chile Mora

The chile mora is a smaller jalapeño—probably a second picking—that is smoke-dried until it is thoroughly wrinkled and a mulberry color *(mora)*, from which it gets its name. It is also known in different locations as chipotle mora, chile seco, and when devoid of its seeds, chile capón. It is sometimes called, erroneously, morita.

The mora is a narrow, blunt-ended chile, with an average size of about 2½ inches (6.5cm) long and 1 inch (2.5cm) wide. It is fleshy when rehydrated and extremely hot.

These chiles are readily available in the United States, particularly when canned as chipotles en adobo (see page 72), now an all-time favorite seasoning with cooks everywhere. They are used in exactly the same sauces and pickles as the larger chipotle, although too small to be stuffed.

PREPARATION

Moras are prepared in the same way as chipotles (see page 68).

Chile Morita

The chile morita—literally "little mulberry"—is the last picking of either serranos or jalapeños, ripened on the plant and smoke-dried. This accounts for their diverse shapes—small elongated triangles or longish and narrow—which makes it difficult to give an average size. The triangular ones are about 1 inch (2.5cm) long and ¾ inch (2cm) wide at the top. They all have a skin that is

Chipotles en Adobo

Chipotles en Adobo really are the flavor of the decade; their gutsy, acidy, smoky heat lends itself to many types of seasonings whether traditional or nouvelle: in tomato sauces either raw or cooked, in mayonnaise (in Veracruz), with potatoes, in soups—the list is a long one.

I was inspired to make up this recipe, first published in My Mexico, *after a visit to Ciudad Camargo, Chihuahua, one fall when the crops of small, ripe jalapeños chiles were being smoke-dried for chipotle moras (not "moritas" as so many people, even some Mexican cooks, call them). They were so cheap I bought a sack full of them to give away to friends and the rest I decided to can. Why buy commercially canned chiles when you can do it yourself, and without preservatives? Besides, many commercially canned chipotles are now packed in a tomato-based sauce rather than a true adobo made primarily of anchos.*

MAKES ABOUT 3 CUPS (750ML)

4 ounces (115g) chipotle mora chiles
3 ancho chiles, seeds and veins removed
About 1½ cups (375ml) water
4 garlic cloves, roughly chopped
3 sprigs fresh marjoram, or scant
    ¼ teaspoon dried
3 sprigs fresh thyme, or scant ¼ teaspoon
    dried
Pinch of cumin seeds, crushed

1 bay leaf, Mexican if possible, torn into pieces
2 tablespoons olive oil (not extra-virgin)
¾ cup (190ml) mild vinegar
¾ cup (190ml) strong vinegar
2 ounces (60g) dark brown sugar,
    about ⅓ cup (83ml) firmly packed
1 tablespoon sea salt

Rinse the whole mora chiles and drain. Pierce each one through with a sharp skewer. Put into a pan with a tightly fitting lid, cover well with water, and cook over medium-low heat until tender but not mushy, 30 to 40 minutes. (If you have a pressure cooker, this will take about 15 minutes.) Drain; discard the cooking water. Remove any stems and stray seeds.

Meanwhile, put the anchos in a small pan, cover with hot water, and simmer for 5 minutes. Drain and transfer to the blender with 1 cup (250ml) of the water. Add the garlic, marjoram, thyme, cumin, and bay leaf plus four of the cooked moras. Blend to a textured sauce.

Heat the oil in a shallow pan or deep skillet, add the blended ingredients, and fry for about 3 minutes over medium heat, scraping the bottom of the pan to avoid sticking. Add the remaining ½ cup (125ml) water, the vinegars, the brown sugar, and the salt and cook for about 5 minutes more. Then add the rest of the moras and cook over low heat, scraping the bottom of the pan to avoid sticking until the sauce has thickened, about 15 minutes.

Cool and store in the refrigerator. Allow the chiles to mature in flavor for about two weeks.

NOTE: *If you prefer to have a less* picante *version of the recipe, cook the chipotles first for about 5 minutes, drain and discard the water, slit them open, and remove the seeds and veins if visible. Cover with fresh water and start at the beginning of the recipe, reducing the cooking time by about 5 minutes. If you would like a lighter sauce, add 6 ounces (180g) tomatoes to the adobo.*

smoother than other chipotles' and of a lighter tone of red. They are extremely hot. Moritas are sometimes available in the United States.

PREPARATION

FOR TABLE SAUCES: Wipe clean, then lightly toast whole on an ungreased griddle for a few seconds on both sides. Grind with the other sauce ingredients.

FOR COOKED SAUCES: Rehydrate in hot water and then blend without removing seeds.

Chile Mulato

The chile mulato (the name refers to its brown color) plant is essentially the same as the poblano, with slightly different genes that affect the color and taste of the fruit. When mature the chiles are a very dark green that turns to a rich brown as they ripen. Like poblanos, mulato chiles are left to ripen on the plant and dried in the same way. Since the growers can get a higher price for the dried chiles you will very rarely come across them fresh in the markets.

A first-quality mulato is flexible, neither damp nor dried out. It is triangular with broad shoulders tapering to a blunt or slightly pointed tip. It has a shiny chocolaty-brown skin that is not as wrinkled as the ancho's. An average size is 5 inches (13cm) long and 3¼ inches (8.75cm) wide.

Mulato chiles range from mild to fairly hot and have a mild, sweetish taste that, with their color, makes them so suitable for mole poblano. When rehydrated they are fleshy and have a mild, faintly chocolate taste. They are readily available in the United States.

PREPARATION

The preparation of mulato chiles is the same as that for anchos, although frankly I have never seen them stuffed or ground to a powder. While chiefly used for cooked sauces like moles, you will occasionally find them used in a salsa borracha—a table sauce often accompanying barbecued meats.

Chile Pasado

This method of drying chiles is typical of some areas in northern Mexico, particularly Chihuahua and Zacatecas, where they are known as chiles orejones, or "big ear" (a word usually applied to vegetables and fruits that are sliced and dried in the sun to preserve them for the winter months), but they are all but unknown in the rest of Mexico. Either poblanos or the large green chiles of the north are charred, peeled, and dried whole. They look most unappetizing all shriveled and black, but when rehydrated, cleaned of seeds, and cooked they have a delicious, concentrated flavor. They are used in recipes that normally call for fresh chiles when available: cut into strips for Chile con Queso (*Essentials,* page 221), for example, and even stuffed for Chiles Rellenos (*My Mexico,* pages 179 and 180).

To make chiles pasados

2 pounds (900g) poblano or Anaheim chiles, about 16 medium

Char the chiles whole, preferably directly over the flame of a gas stove or right up under a gas or electric broiler—do not put them into a hot oven, which will cook the flesh—and turn them from time to time until they are slightly charred and blistered. Without letting them cool off, put them into a thick paper or plastic bag and set aside for about 10 minutes to steam—or sweat, as the Mexicans put it. This will loosen the skin and make the peeling easy. Do not put into water or rinse under a running tap, which will impair their flavor; simply wipe the skin off with a damp cloth. A few pieces of stubborn skin can stay; they can't hurt.

Put the chiles, still intact, on a rack, or hang them up if they still have their stalks intact, and set them out to dry, preferably in the sun or a very airy, dry place, taking them in at night if outside. This drying process can take up to a week depending on heat and humidity. The thick top part, with the placenta that holds the seeds, will take the longest and must be completely dried out; if not, the chiles will become moldy. If they are stored in a dry place, they will last at least a year.

Chile Pasilla

The chile pasilla (*pasilla* means "large") is the dried chile chilaca (see page 40). In some areas it is known as chile negro. It is a long narrow chile, blunt or slightly pointed at the end. It has a shiny black skin and a surface puckered with vertical ridges. An average-size chile pasilla is about 6 inches (15cm) long and 1 inch (2.5cm) wide and can range from fairly hot to hot; when rehydrated it has a sharp but rich flavor.

This is a versatile chile: it can be stuffed (*My Mexico*, pages 114 and 115), used for table sauces, in moles, fried whole, or in strips for a garnish. The toasted veins are also used for a condiment. It is readily available in the United States.

PREPARATION

For preparation of these chiles, see anchos (page 61). The pasilla is not usually ground to a powder for classical Mexican recipes.

AS A TOPPING AND CONDIMENT FOR SOUP: If the chile has a stem, leave it intact. Wipe the surface thoroughly with a damp cloth. Heat oil in a small skillet to the depth of about ¼ inch (.75cm). When hot but not smoking—or the skin will burn—add the chile and fry over low heat, turning it from time to time until the whole surface is shiny and crisp. If it is not torn or punctured the chile will inflate impressively. Not only does it look nice to put whole on the top of a soup, but leaving it whole will ensure that the chile is thoroughly crisp. It can also be crumbled easily—together with seeds and veins—to use as a condiment.

FOR RUSTIC TABLE SAUCES: Wipe the surface of the chile with a damp cloth. Heat an ungreased comal over medium heat—if it is too hot the chile will burn and the sauce will be bitter—and toast the whole chile, turning it from time to time, for about 5 minutes, until thoroughly crisp. Crumble the chile, seeds and veins included, into a molcajete or blender and blend briefly with the other sauce ingredients to a textured consistency (see *Essentials,* page 246).

THE VEINS AS A CONDIMENT: When a recipe calls for the seeds and veins to be removed from pasilla chiles, do not throw them out. Save them because they may be useful for other recipes. The veins, for instance, can be toasted on an ungreased griddle for a minute or so or until a rich, golden brown color. They can then be crumbled and used as a condiment (see *Essentials,* page 128).

Chile Pasilla de Oaxaca

This unique and delicious chile is used almost exclusively in Oaxaca and in a limited part of neighboring Puebla. It is also known as the chile mije because it is grown exclusively in the Sierra Mije, which rise above the valley of Oaxaca to the east. It is grown in relatively small quantities in very isolated valleys in this extremely rugged terrain. The chile is ripened on the plant and then smoked under very rustic conditions. When the chile is mature but still green it has very little flavor, but the ripening and smoking do wonders and produce a very fruity, smoky flavor. With occasional exceptions, the chiles are extremely hot.

The chile pasilla has a very wrinkled but shiny skin, and is fleshy when rehydrated. The indigenous Mijes bring their smoked chiles to the markets in large, high baskets separated and priced according to size. But the price will be given for 100 chiles, as opposed to weight.

Small chiles, about $1\frac{1}{2}$ inches (4cm) long, are usually used for table and cooked sauces, or cooked with beans. Medium chiles, about $2\frac{1}{2}$ inches (6.5cm) long, often are used for pickling in vinegar. Large chiles are about $3\frac{1}{2}$ inches (9cm) long, between $\frac{3}{4}$ and $1\frac{1}{4}$ inches (2cm and 3cm) wide, and taper to a pointed, or slightly rounded, tip. They are usually stuffed.

Because of the small production, the chile pasilla de Oaxaca will probably never be imported on a large scale—like anchos, for instance. Since they are popular among the Oaxacans themselves, immigrant families will no doubt see that there is a future supply, however small, and a few restaurateurs do import them privately. I suggest you bring some back when you visit Oaxaca; you are allowed to.

PREPARATION

FOR TABLE SAUCES: Wipe the chiles clean and heat through, toasting them whole for about 30 seconds on each side on an ungreased griddle over low heat. They will soften slightly at first and then begin to dry out and toast. Take care not to let them burn. Do not attempt to deseed, but tear them into small pieces and blend or grind them with the rest of the sauce ingredients.

FOR PICKLING IN VINEGAR WITH VEGETABLES AND HERBS: Wipe the chiles clean, then heat them whole on an ungreased skillet over low heat until they become flexible, then follow the recipe for pickling.

FOR STUFFING: Heat the chiles on an ungreased comal over low heat until they become flexible. Carefully flatten them as much as possible and make a vertical slit down one side. Carefully remove the seeds, then cover with hot water and leave to soak just until they are fleshy, about 10 minutes. Drain well, and follow the recipe for stuffed chiles.

FOR COOKED SAUCES: Toast lightly, tear into pieces with the seeds, and blend.

There is one unusual way of very lightly toasting dried chiles for table sauces that I have seen only in country areas of central Oaxaca: whole pasillas de Oaxaca are buried in hot, but not glowing, ashes of a cooking fire and left for about 50 seconds. They send off a delicious aroma and if not punctured they will inflate. Excess ash is just shaken off, not wiped thoroughly. This counteracts the acidity of the green tomatoes.

Chile Puya

The chile puya (the word literally means "a goad" or "steel point") or guajillo delgado ("thin"), as it is sometimes known, has the same color and characteristics as the larger guajillo, but is narrower—an average ¾ inch (2cm) wide—and about 4 inches (10cm) long, terminating in a sharp point.

The chile puya is considerably hotter than the guajillo, and they are often used together for a more *picante* sauce.

These chiles are not so readily available but can always be found in larger supermarkets catering to Mexican customers. The methods of preparation are the same as those for guajillos (see page 70).

Chile Seco de Yucatán

The chile seco as it is known in Yucatán is *the* dried, local chile verde (small, lightish green in color with a unique taste). It ripens on the plant and dries to a golden-orangy color. It has a thin, shiny, translucent skin and a rather wrinkled surface, and it is very hot. An average size is 1½ inches (4cm) long and just over ½ inch (1.25cm) wide.

These dried chiles are usually ground to a powder and used as a condiment, but they have another rather extraordinary use: the whole chiles are actually charred by dousing them with alcohol and setting them aflame. The blackened chiles are then ground with other spices to make the chilmole, or black seasoning paste, recado negro, used for the very special dish of Yucatán, *pavo relleno negro* (turkey seasoned and filled with blackened stuffing). These chiles are available only in Mexican groceries that carry some Yucatecan ingredients.

FRESH
AND
DRIED
HERBS

${\large A}$romatic herbs—many indigenous and highly regional, with a few others introduced from other parts of the world—add a fascinating complexity to the dishes of Mexico.

Cilantro, mint, and parsley are generally known and used in most of the country; others like hoja santa *(Piper auritum),* chepil or chipilin *(Crotolaria* spp.*),* and avocado leaves are found and used in only specific areas.

The bay laurel is not used in the traditional cooking of Mexico, but an aromatic leaf *(Litsea glaucescens)* of a tree of the laurel family that grows wild mostly, but not exclusively, in the cool highland forests of oak and pine is called "laurel" and is one of the triumvirate of Mexican *hierbas de olor,* or potherbs. Small sprigs of the half or completely dried leaves are tied together in small bunches with thyme and marjoram and sold in local markets pretty well throughout Mexico. The one exception that I know of is in Tuxtepec, in the low area of Oaxaca that borders on the southern part of Veracruz. There, the *hierbas de olor* for soups, broths, and stews consist of the broad-leafed, fleshy oreganon *(Plectranthus aboinicus),* a flat-leaved chive *(Allium schoenoprasum),* and the sharply pointed and long serrated leaf of culantro *(Eryngium foetidum).* They are all used fresh.

Now we come to the complex question of oregano. There are many plants referred to as oregano in different regions of Mexico—I have nine of them in my kitchen at the moment—some of which defy classification. (To quote a botanist friend, who would certainly wish to remain anonymous: "There is certain taxonomic confusion on the subject.") How frustrating it is never to see the plant when it is flowering, which would certainly help matters along! But in any case, look at page 88. Oregano is generally used dried, though there is the occasional exception.

In parts of Hidalgo, Michoacán, and Guerrero, a very fragrant wild anise *(Tagetes micrantha)* is used in the cooking water with fresh corn; in Patzcuaro, it is used for a fragrant atole made of fresh corn. Leaves of the allspice tree *(Pimenta dioica)* and those of a tree called arrayan *(Psidium sartorianum)* are added, depending on the area, to caldos or stews, or escabeches. Then there is the very fragrant leaf of a wild avocado aguacatillo (as yet unclassified), in Veracruz, used to flavor beans, tamales, and barbecued meats. In the area of the Papaloapan River in Veracruz, the moste leaf *(Clerodendrum ligustrinum)* is toasted until it burns; the powder is then used to season local dishes of turtle like Galápago en moste. There are many others, but moreso in the damp tropical areas of southern Mexico. I shall also describe some of them in the following pages.

TOXIC CULINARY HERBS

In a paper published (undated but probably around 1992) by the Department of Agriculture and Natural Resources, Delaware State University, Arthur O. Tucker and Michael J. Maciarello wrote that hoja santa and epazote, among others, have toxic properties.

✳ Epazote, *Teloxys* (formerly *Chenopodium*) *ambrosioides:* "Taking the (concentrated) oil has proven to have many serious consequences to health and the leaves reported to be carcinogenic to rats."

✳ Hoja santa, *Piper auritum:* "Leaves contain about 70 percent safrole and caphoradione A &B, two aporphine-type alkaloids of unknown physiological activity."

I include these aromatic herbs in my recipes because they are, and have been for centuries, used in the indigenous and everyday foods of Mexico. However, with the exception of a recipe for tortas de epazote given to me in the state of Morelos, these plants are not consumed in concentrated form. Nonetheless, I must make you aware of this warning; people who are highly allergic should take particular heed and caution.

See also the note on avocado leaves (page 87).

Mexican Bay Leaf, or Laurel

The Mexican bay leaf, or laurel, as it is called in Mexico, is not the *Laurus nobilis* used for cooking in Europe and the United States. It is the fragrant leaf of another species of laurel *(Litsea glaucescens)*. I have seen it growing in tropical mountain pine and oak forests in Oaxaca and Michoacán but also in subtropical areas of Veracruz.

The leaf when fresh is more delicate than the better known and more ubiquitous bay laurel. It is narrow, tapering to a sharp point. When dried, it turns an olive green and the edges become slightly fluted. This laurel is most commonly sold along with

marjoram (mejorana) and thyme (tomillo), half or completely dried, in small bunches as *hierbas de olor,* (potherbs). Large sprays of the laurel with intricately woven strips of palm are sold in the streets of Michoacán (and maybe elsewhere) on Sabado de la Gloria, the day before Palm Sunday, when it is also customary to throw buckets of water at passersby.

I have come across only one other type of laurel with a smaller, round leaf that is used in the cooking of the central state of San Luis Potosí and the northeastern state of Nuevo León.

The Mexican bay leaf is now being imported and sold packaged in some Mexican markets and supermarkets catering to a Mexican clientele. However, if you cannot find it, substitute the more common bay laurel, using just half the quantity stipulated.

Chepiche

Chepiche *(Porophyllum tagetoides* and *P. coloratum),* as it is known in Oaxaca, is a native Mexican aromatic herb with a pungent flavor similar to that of papaloquelite (see page 89). In other parts of southern Mexico it is known variously as *pipitza, pipicha, tepicha,* or *papalo delgado,* while in the Chilapa area of Guerrero it is called *escobeta* and has a slightly wider leaf. It is a stringy herb with very narrow, slightly notched leaves that are grayish green in color; when mature, it has small purple flowers.

Chepiche, like papaloquelite, is usually eaten raw either

accompanying or inside a taco or torta, but in the central valley of Oaxaca it is cooked in a sopa de guias, a soup made with squash vines and other herbs (see *My Mexico*, page 401).

Although I have not yet seen it in Mexican markets, keep a sharp lookout, especially where Mexican residents are from Oaxaca and Guerrero. There is no substitute, but you should at least try it when you visit southern Mexico.

Chepil or Chipilín

There are various species of this plant (*Crotolaria* spp.) that are used in the cooking of southern Mexico. *Chepil*, as it is called in the central valley of Oaxaca, has a smaller leaf and flower than that used either on the Pacific coast or in Chiapas, where it is called *chipilín*. While chepil usually grows like a weed and is collected

during the rainy season, it is also cultivated with irrigation in the dry months because of its importance in many local dishes—soups, tamales, and rice, in particular.

The leaves and flowers are used preferably before the little bulbous pods mature, and when the plant is abundant, it is dried for the scarcer months. Chepil has a distinctive but delicate taste that is released when cooked. I have never come across an instance when it is eaten raw.

There is no substitute for chepil (see Sopa de Guias, *My Mexico*, page 401), but it is a taste that any lover of southern Mexican food should try when visiting.

Cilantro

CORIANDER

Coriander *(Coriandrum sativum)*, always referred to as *cilantro,* the Spanish word, in the United States, is one of the most important aromatics in Mexican food. It is a native of the Old World that was introduced by the Spaniards in the colonial period.

Cilantro is used fresh and coarsely chopped in many raw salsas and salads, and is sprinkled lavishly over the top of many *antojitos.* It is also used to flavor cooked dishes. Cilantro is often blended with other ingredients for green moles. Popular new dishes include a cilantro soup and small beignets of the chopped leaves.

When using this herb, discard only the thicker stems and chop the leaves and smaller stems coarsely—if you chop too finely much of the juice and flavor will be left behind on the board.

Try always to purchase cilantro with the roots intact. To keep for a few days, store upright in a jar with water to come halfway up the stalks, and cover the tops with a plastic bag. In Dominican and other Caribbean markets, cilantro is often labeled "cilantrillo."

Culantro

This spiky-leafed herb *(Eryngium foetidum)* grows wild mainly in the tropical coastal areas of southern Mexico. Its rather tough leaf is dark green in color with long, narrow leaves ending flat with a point in the middle. The sides of the leaf are

slightly serrated with a minuscule hairlike thorn on each serration. Confusingly, in Tabasco (where it is used frequently), it is called *perejil* (parsley). Among its many other names are *cilantro extranjero* and *cilantro habanero.*

Since the culantro leaf is too tough to be used raw, it is added to broths and stews and to dishes like a (traditional) arroz a la tumbada en Veracruz (see *Essentials,* page 373), but it tends to lose flavor if cooked too long.

Culantro can be found in the United States in Dominican and other Caribbean stores; it will usually be marked "cilantro" (while the cilantro is called cilantrillo). I have also found it in Vietnamese markets, marked "ngo gai" (pronounced *go' guy*).

Epazote

Mexican Tea or Wormseed

Like other aromatic herbs with hard-hitting flavors, epazote (*Teloxys*, formerly *Chenopodium, ambrosioides*) takes some getting used to. But once you have acquired the taste, no black beans or tortilla soup will be acceptable without it.

The name of this herb—which is used for cooking but not usually eaten raw—comes from the Nahuatl word *epatzotl* (*epatl* meaning "skunk" and *tzotl* meaning "dirty"), which is descriptive of its wild taste. I always liken it to creosote, and indeed it likes to grow in many an American tarred parking lot. While generally it is called *epazote,* in some areas the word has evolved into *apasote.*

Epazote is a native of Mexico and seeds itself rapidly, taking over any spare land. The mid-green leaves are long, narrow, and serrated, and the little round green seeds cluster on elongated spikes. Traditional recipes call for either the whole stem with leaves or whole or chopped leaves alone. In traditional herbal medicine epazote is recommended for dispelling gastrointestinal worms or in a tisane for flatulence. Crushed and thrown down on the floor, or wherever, epazote will make ants scurry away fast.

I first identified this herb in New York's Central Park when I started my cooking classes in 1969, when hardly anyone knew what it was. Epazote is now available fresh practically all the year round in many markets catering to Mexican cooks and aficionados. I do not recommend it dried since it will have lost the essential oils that make it so pungent. Seedlings are also available in many nurseries selling culinary herbs. Alas, there is no substitute.

Hierbabuena

MINT

Fresh mint (*Mentha* spp.) is omnipresent in Mexican markets, and although it is not one of the most used of aromatic herbs in Mexican dishes, it nevertheless is essential in some dishes in some areas. For instance, in Jalisco mint is called for in some meatball and mushroom recipes; in Yucatán for black beans, or frijoles huachas; and in the blood sausages of the state of Mexico. In various areas of Oaxaca it is used with cuitlacoche and is a must in a broth with chicken, in some beef stews, and in moles verdes.

Fresh mint is often used in other regions for brothy beef stews. You will also find it used more often in dishes (adapted, not traditionally Mexican) in Lebanese communities—for example, in Zitacuaro, Michoacán—cooked with eggs and chile serrano and eaten as a snack.

These are only a few examples of its culinary use, while an infusion of mint is recommended as a stomach comforter.

Hierba de Conejo

This aromatic herb (*Tridax coronopiifolia*) grows wild in the valley of Oaxaca; I have not seen it used in cooking elsewhere. There are actually two types of "rabbit herb" (*hierba de conejo*) used principally to flavor beans. They both have long, spiky, rather tough leaves that are slightly abrasive. When mature, one plant has a darker green leaf and has a yellow flower, while the other has a hairier leaf and a white flower. The slightly waxy but pleasant flavor is released with cooking. There is no substitute.

Hoja Santa

Hoja santa *(Piper auritum)*, to call it by its most popular name—literally, "holy leaf"—is one of the great Mexican native aromatics. It is used principally in many regional dishes of southern Mexico and the eastern lowlands bordering the Gulf of Mexico. It has many regional names: *yerba santa* in Oaxaca, *hierba santa* or *momo* in Chiapas, *tlanepa* in Veracuz, *acuyo* or *acoyo* in Tabasco.

Piper auritum is a rangy shrub native to the Mexican tropics; there are many varieties—one in particular has deep purple-red stems and veins that I have seen only in semitropical Veracruz. The leaf is heart-shaped but tapers to a point with a pronounced central vein; it has a strong anise flavor. I am told that a variety of hoja santa grows wild along riverbanks in Texas, and in one area in the U.S. South it is called "the root-beer plant."

Hoja santa leaves are used extensively in Veracruz, Oaxaca, Tabasco, and Chiapas to wrap and/or season tamales, meats, fish, mushrooms, and even rice. Blended with other ingredients, they lend a unique flavor to green moles or seafood sauces; torn

into rough pieces, they add the final touch of flavor to some yellow moles of Oaxaca. While the leaves are usually used fresh, I have also seen them toasted for sauces in the Zapotec cooking of Oaxaca's Central Valley.

Several cooks I know grow the plant in California and Texas (and probably elsewhere), but it is shy of frost and will almost always die down in the winter. However, some enterprising spice company is now packaging whole dried leaves and I have seen some in very good condition in small groceries catering to Mexicans. There is no substitute for hoja santa, but an alternative is suggested in recipes that call for it.

Hojas de Aguacate

Avocado Leaves

One of the most intriguing flavors of the dishes of the central part of southern Mexico (areas of Morelos, Puebla, Veracruz, and Oaxaca) is that of leaves from a native avocado tree: *Persea drymifolia*. The mature leaves, which have more flavor, are usually toasted first and ground and added to preparations of black beans. In fact, outside the main market in Jalapa, Veracruz, you can buy them already prepared in powdered form—but they always look too suspiciously green.

Fresh avocado leaves are used for covering the meats for barbacoa in Oaxaca, and for flavoring or covering tamales, particularly in certain areas of Morelos and Puebla—they add a delicious anise flavor to the masa. Toasted leaves are added whole to the seasoned meats cooked in mixiotes (the membranous skin of the maguey leaves) in Hidalgo, Tlaxcala, and Puebla. The dried leaves from Mexico are now packaged and distributed on a wide scale to markets carrying a large range of Mexican cooking products. In a pinch for certain recipes, avocado leaves can act as a substitute for hoja santa when the latter is not available.

According to well-known editor Fran McCullough, in answer to queries I had received on the use of leaves,

Because there has been some concern about toxicity of avocado leaves, among some Californian aficionados, I think it is time to set the record straight. The toxicity reports relate back to a study done in 1984 at the University of California at Davis, which showed that dairy goats suffered some toxic effects from ingesting very large amounts of avocado leaves (the toxic agent remains unknown). The crucial point, according to Dr. Arthur L. Craigmill, toxicology specialist at Davis and one of the authors of the study, is that the toxic effects were traced to the Guatemalan avocado (Persea americana). When the goats were fed Mexican avocado leaves (Persea drymifolia), a different variety, there were no problems.

The Hass avocado, the best-tasting one grown in America, is a hybrid of indeterminate origin though its DNA tests positive for a Guatemalan ancestor—hence the suspicions. No one has ever tested the Hass leaves for toxicity, but it seems unlikely that the small amounts used in cooking would cause any problems in any case. When in doubt, choose based on taste, and that leads you to the aromatic Mexican leaves which are now available in the U.S.

Mexican "Oregano"

You see that I have put *oregano* in quotes; I have done so because the so-called oregano used in Mexico is not the same as the true oregano from the Mediterranean *(Origanum vulgare)*. The most commonly found Mexican oregano *(Lippia berlandieri)* is always used dried and is distributed widely in Mexico. It is also available either loose or packaged, sold in Mexican groceries and supermarkets that carry a variety of Mexican ingredients.

But there are also many regional plants referred to, and used as, oregano in local dishes. One of the most distinctive is that used in the Yucatán peninsula—*Lippia graveolens,* with a much larger leaf. Curiously, it is always dried and then toasted to a dark brown color. Another distinctive oregano is that used in the north of Mexico, especially Nuevo León, with thin, pointed, dark green leaves and very small purple flowers, which is probably a *Satureja.*

I have at the moment about nine different varieties of "oregano" that I have collected in recent years in the mountains of Jalisco, the Mixteca of Oaxaca, in Guerrero, and including the light, minty-flavored oregano used in the central valley of Oaxaca, which is nearer to a marjoram. In his large volume, *Plantas Mexicanas, Catalogo de Nombres Vulgares y Cientificos,* originally published in 1927, Maximino Martínez listed eighteen plants from different regions of Mexico known as oregano. Little wonder there exists today, to quote a botanist friend of mine, some "taxonomic confusion." So whenever you visit a rural market in Mexico make sure you look for the local "oregano."

Oreganón

It is difficult to know what to call this aromatic leaf of a plant *(Plectranthus aboinicus),* a native of Africa, that has taken root mainly in the regional cooking of the tropical lowlands of the southern Gulf coast of Mexico (and in Asia). It has many regional names: *entre otros, oregano grueso, orégano grande, orejuda o extranjero,* among others. Of course, it isn't an oregano as such, but it is used in much the same way as a seasoning for caldos, fish dishes, rice, and meat stews. In the Tuxtepec area of Oaxaca that borders on Veracruz, it is used as a potherb.

The crisp, fleshy, spade-shaped leaf has a mid-green surface, slightly fuzzy to the touch, while the underside is a lighter green with a pronounced, highly intricate vein structure. The leaf has a light minty aroma that is released dramatically when broken. Obviously this leaf is used fresh—it cannot be dried because it discolors and rots—but for optimal flavor, in a shrimp rice for instance, it should be added toward the end of the cooking time.

I mention this herb because many visitors to markets in Veracruz or Campeche have asked me about it or have identified its flavor in local dishes there. There is no real substitute, but if it is called for in a recipe, I always give an alternative. Although I have not seen it personally, you may find it in Asian markets, since it is used in Vietnamese and Thai food.

Papaloquelite

The leaves and tender stems of papalo (*Porophyllum ruderale* or *macrocephalum),* as this indigenous plant is called in the markets of central Mexico, are eaten raw, either chopped on top of a table sauce or stuffed inside a taco of guacamole or carnitas. Papaloquelite also lends its indispensable flavor to a semita (a crunchy bread roll topped with sesame seeds) stuffed with meat, avocado, tomato, or chipotles—a specialty of Puebla. Either you hate or you love its strong pungent flavor that, like that of guajes (page 131), lingers in the mouth.

The leaves are almost round in form and slightly notched. They are light green in color and feel almost velvety to the touch. Although it grows wild, the plant is also cultivated to provide a year-round supply because it cannot be dried. A more delicate plant with smaller leaves is found in the Chilapa, Guerrero, market called copanquelite (see *My Mexico,* pages 372–378). I have occasionally seen papalo in Mexican markets in the United States, but be sure to look for it in areas where there is an immigrant population from the state of Puebla or even Mexico City.

I am afraid there is no substitute, but it is another Mexican aromatic par excellence that you should at least try whenever you go to central Mexico.

Perejil

PARSLEY

Italian parsley *(Petroselinum neapolitanum)*, with the flat leaf, is used in Mexican cooking. It is used whole, but sparingly, for some dishes like meatballs, rice, soups, and stews. In Oaxaca, very tender leaves are used to decorate dishes like enfrijoladas or entomatadas. Small quantities of parsley, ground with other ingredients, are sometimes called for in regional recipes for green moles.

The curly parsley, called *perejil chino,* is used mainly for European and American recipes.

Piojito

This is another one of the essential wild greens for sopa de guias, also exclusive to the valley of Oaxaca. The soft, triangular leaves and tender stems of piojito *(Galinsoga parviflora)* are used in the soup. At a recent reunion to demonstrate different ways of using indigenous herbs and greens, a cook flavored rice with piojito; I tried it and it was delicious. There is no substitute. But be sure you make a point of trying these herbs when you next visit Mexico.

Tequelite

This is a very unusual aromatic plant *(Piper pseudo-alpino)* that I first came across in the market of Huejutla, in the northeastern part of the state of Hidalgo, which borders Veracruz. It is used, mostly, to season beans in that tropical cloud forest belt that slopes down toward the Gulf through parts of Puebla, Hidalgo, Veracruz, and Oaxaca.

This is a creeping vine with fleshy stems and leaves that are shaped like large teardrops. The face of the leaves is dark green in color with lighter veins and a matte, very slightly abrasive surface. The underside is a very light lime green outlined with a slightly darker edge and central vein. It is like touching—as I am now—a very cool (in temperature) piece of suede. If you double the leaf over it will break crisply and release a cilantro-like flavor. Tequelite cannot be dried. One of its names is in fact *cilantro silvestre,* or *de monte* in the Sierra Juárez, *causasa* in the Sierra Norte de Puebla, *oreja de burro, nascaullo, nacastequelite,* and other variations depending on the area.

I have only seen tequelite added in bundles to be cooked with black beans or used to season Tamales de Vigilia (*My Mexico,* page 254). Of course, this rarity is not available in the United States, but its obvious substitute is cilantro. It is mentioned here because I have had several inquiries about it from travelers to those parts of Mexico.

VEGETABLES, BEANS, AND FRUITS

Aguacate

Avocado

Avocados, or *aguacate,* must now surely be one of the most popular of foods worldwide—with obvious exceptions, of course. These fruits of a tree (*Persea americana* and var.) native to Mexico and Central America are almost synonymous with Mexican food. Rich in nonsaturated oils and vitamins A, B, and E, their qualities and flavor were appreciated and cultivated as early as 8000 B.C.

According to a Mexican botanist writing from the very early part of the 1900s (and for fifty years thereafter), there are twelve varieties of avocado in Mexico. However, many of these are no longer appreciated, owing to the introduction and wide distribution of the grafted Hass and Fuerte varieties from the large avocado-growing areas, principally Michoacán.

The typical *aguacates criollos,* or indigenous avocados, grown in semitropical areas vary slightly in characteristics; generally they have a thin, shiny, edible skin and a large pit surrounded by a thin layer of flesh. The flavor is incomparable: aniselike, nutty, and altogether delicious. The variety with a skin that turns black when ripe is preferred over that with the green skin—referred to in Michoacán as *blancos.* The flesh, too, varies in texture: that of the former is more compact and oily while the latter is quite moist. Of course, there are always exceptions, but it would be unlikely

Guacamole

Guacamole is one of those popular Mexican foods that is easy to make and very nutritious. There are many versions in Mexico itself, like a delicious one with tomatillos and avocado leaf, as well as many distortions that find their way back to Mexico (like the version in My Mexico *from Zacatecas with of all things sour cream!). Guacamole is often served alone or as part of a* botana *with totopos, to accompany tacos, or as part of that extravaganza of a dish, Carne Asada a la Tampiqueña (*The Art, *page 287).*

There is a lot of advice about how to keep guacamole from turning brown if it is not eaten when freshly made: by adding lime juice (which is not always appropriate), leaving the pits immersed in the mashed flesh, keeping it in an airtight container, and the latest foolproof one of pressing plastic wrap over the surface. (I shudder to think of the action of the fat of the avocados on the plastic!) My advice is don't make it in advance. Have everything already chopped, crush the base ahead of time, and mash the avocados at the last minute in front of guests. Why not? But be sure you have a nice-size molcajete (see page 298) to do your show in style. Of course, the perfect guacamole has to be made in a molcajete so the flavors are intensified by the crushing of the ingredients—cutting them just isn't the same. But if you don't have one, you can blend the base of onion, chile, cilantro, and salt and then mash in the avocados to a rough texture; don't blend to a smooth consistency—texture means flavor!

*The recipe that follows is one that I first came across when I went to Mexico in 1957, and it seems to me to be a classic. One of the simpler northern versions with little wild chiles, onion, and lime juice is delicious, as well as the guacamole with the surprising combination of fruit, chiles, and avocado from Guanajuato (*My Mexico, *page 106). See the advice about buying avocados in advance on page 95, and no sweet onions, please!*

MAKES ABOUT 2½ CUPS (625ML)

2 heaped tablespoons finely chopped white
    onion
4 serrano chiles, finely chopped (yes, seeds
    and all), or to taste
3 heaped tablespoons roughly chopped
    cilantro
Sea salt to taste
3 avocados, (about 1 pound/450g)
About ½ cup (125ml) finely chopped,
    unskinned tomatoes

THE TOPPINGS
¼ cup (63ml) finely chopped tomatoes
1 heaped tablespoon finely chopped white
    onion
2 heaped tablespoons finely (but not too
    finely, just prettily) chopped cilantro

Put the onion, chiles, cilantro, and salt into a molcajete (see note above) and crush to a paste. Cut the avocados in half and, without peeling, remove the pit and squeeze out the flesh. Mash the avocado roughly into the base and mix well. Stir in the tomatoes and sprinkle the surface of the guacamole with the toppings. Serve immediately.

to find these avocados in markets outside Mexico because once ripe they spoil very quickly. But make sure you try them when you go there!

In the hotter lowlands of southeast Mexico you will find *chinnin,* large, elongated, pear-shaped avocados with reddish dark-brown skin; in other areas there is also a roundish avocado with a shell-like skin called *pagua.* Both of these have a more compact flesh that is not as rich, which makes them more suitable for slicing rather than making guacamole.

When using avocados for either guacamole, a soup (see *Essentials,* page 127), or other sauces, it is best to buy avocados well ahead as it is rare to find perfectly ripe ones in supermarkets; from my experience they are as hard as rocks and need several days to ripen at room temperature. There are two things to avoid when buying: if the skin has separated from the flesh and if the pit rattles when the fruit is shaken.

Always buy more than you think you need; sometimes there are brown patches on the inside flesh, which will make your sauce bitter.

You need not peel a ripe avocado: just cut it in two, pry out the pit, and squeeze the flesh from the cut halves. For slicing into segments: make a vertical cut from the top to the stalk end through both the skin and the flesh, and loosen the segments with a small paring knife.

FROM TOP: CRUSHING THE BASE IN THE MOL-CAJETE; SQUEEZING OUT THE AVOCADO; ADDING THE TOMATO; GUACAMOLE READY TO SERVE.

BEANS

Frijoles Mexicanos

Apart from being delicious, even addictive, and nutritious, beans play an indispensable role in the Mexican diet, especially for people with low incomes, since they form a complete protein when cooked and eaten together with properly treated dried corn.

There are many regional varieties of beans. Some have ordinary names that denote their color: *negros* (black), *blancos* (white), *bayos* (beige); others have descriptive names: *cacahuate* (peanut), *ojo de liebre* (hare's eye), *flor de mayo* or *junio* (may or june flower), *montañero* (mountain climber), *garrapata* (tick). There is also the misnamed delicious yellow *peruano,* which in fact is the mayocoba bean from Sinaloa. Then there are the whitish combas from the hot country of Michoacán and Guerrero and the xpelon (limas) from the Yucatán Peninsula, among many others. Regional bean varieties come in all colors: red, yellow, mauve, fawn, all shades of brown, white and black, and russet, mottled or plain—although I admit I have never seen blue ones!

Bean sizes generally do not vary that much; the smallest I have seen is a light orangy-brown bean no more than ¼ inch (about 6mm) long from southern Veracruz. There are the diminutive black chimas from the Chimalapas in Oaxaca, and the very small whites and blacks from the Central Valley. The largest are the multicolored ayocotes from the central Mexican states, and the silvery-gray variety from the Oaxaca valley (the red flowers of both are used for fritters, and in stews).

Beans are prepared in many ways, the principal being the brothy frijoles de olla and refritos, fried to a paste. They are made into soups, fritters (see *My Mexico,* page 170), sauces (see Enfrijoladas, page 259), or toasted, ground, sieved to a powder, and reconstituted for another type of soup. Cooked and whole they are used as a filling or mixed with corn masa for *antojitos* or tamales. In Hidalgo and Michoacán there are recipes for beans roughly ground when still dry, and the loose skins are skimmed off the surface of the cooking water. And all are seasoned to regional dictates.

Frijoles de olla—soupy beans in the first stage of their cooking—are often served in their broth just after the main course. Frijoles refritos are generally served with breakfast eggs, grilled meats, and enchiladas, although there are no hard-and-fast rules. See frijoles rancheros or Frijoles Borrachos in *Essentials,* page 158.

Frijoles de Olla

MAKES 7 TO 8 CUPS, WITHOUT THE BROTH

1 pound (450g) dried beans (*bayos, flor de mayo,* or pinto)	1 tablespoon lard (optional)
	Hot water
½ medium white onion, roughly sliced	Salt to taste

Pick over the beans carefully to get rid of any little stones or bits of chaff. Cover them in a bowl with cold water and skim off any flotsam, shriveled beans, or anything else you might have missed while picking them over.

Drain the beans and put them into a heavy pot with the onion and lard, if using. Cover well with hot water; it should come about 4 inches above the level of the beans. Cover the pot and set over high heat until it comes to a boil. Lower heat to medium and continue cooking until the skins become tender. Add the salt and continue cooking until the beans are soft but not falling apart. This will take anywhere from 2 to 3 hours, depending on the age and quality of the beans.

Keep some hot water on hand to top off the water if it is getting low—never add cold water.

FRIJOLES NEGROS DE OLLA

MAKES A SCANT 7 CUPS, WITHOUT THE BROTH

Follow the method for Frijoles de Olla, using 1 pound (450g) black beans and adding a sprig of epazote when you add the salt. Allow for a longer cooking time.

There are regional differences in what is added to beans cooked this way, but each recipe will guide you—or should.

FRIJOLES DE OLLA OAXAQUEÑOS

Follow the Frijoles de Olla recipe, adding ½ small head of garlic, cut horizontally, and a large sprig of epazote from the beginning.

Above are some of the basic guidelines for the preparation of frijoles (dried beans) in Mexico. Unless you or your neighbors grow and dry your own beans, you will not really know how old they are and therefore how long they will take to cook. Always cook beans well ahead, even the day before. (How one's tastes change! I used to like frijoles de olla, or plainly cooked beans, when they were soupy the day after cooking. Now I can't resist eating them the minute they are cooked in their broth.) The aroma

Frijoles Refritos

REFRIED BEANS

You can always cook more than you need and keep some frozen for yens or emergencies. The fried paste will last about three months.

MAKES ABOUT 3 CUPS (750ML)

About ⅓ cup (83ml) lard, melted

1 heaped tablespoon finely chopped white onion

3½ cups (875ml) cooked beans in their broth

Heat the lard in a heavy 10-inch (25-cm) skillet, add the onion, and fry over medium heat without browning until translucent, about 30 seconds. Gradually add the beans and their broth and continue cooking over fairly high heat, mashing them down to a textured paste, about 10 minutes.

FROM TOP: ADDING FRIJOLES DE OLLA TO SAUTEED ONION; REFRITOS, FRIED TO A PASTE.

of the beans when they are almost finished, and their very special taste when they are just tender, is intrinsically Mexican. Nor do they need any elaborate seasonings: salt, a little white onion, and perhaps an aromatic herb depending on the region.

What is the best pot to use for cooking beans? Traditional Mexican cooks use an earthenware olla or bean pot (see page 300) and cook them very slowly. They say the beans develop the best flavor cooked in this way.

For cooks living at low altitude, I suggest using a slow-cooker with a ceramic lining; this way you will never scorch your beans. For cooks in a hurry, use the pressure cooker despite the fact that this is frowned upon by some. Although it may not produce the most fragrant of beans, it certainly saves enormously on time and energy, particularly if you are living at an altitude of over 4,000 feet.

Well, having got your beans into the kitchen, pick through them carefully, removing any little stones or bits of chaff. Cover them with cold water and remove any flotsam, shriveled beans, or anything else you may have missed in sorting through them.

I do not agree with soaking the beans overnight—whether you discard the soaking water or not. To my taste, the skins always develop an unpleasant flavor. Drain and put into the bean pot and cover with water—hot if you like—which should come at least 3 inches (7.5cm) above the surface of the beans. At this stage some cooks add nothing at all; others add some onion slices and a tablespoonful of lard, others some onion and a head of garlic. Most, but not all, Mexican cooks say that adding salt to the beans too soon will toughen the skin. I follow their advice despite this not having been proven scientifically.

Bring to a boil, lower the heat, cover, and cook over low heat until just tender. Add the salt and continue cooking until tender. This can take from $2\frac{1}{2}$ to 4 hours depending on the age of the beans. If the bean water is getting low, have some hot water on hand to add to the pot—never add cold water. Generally speaking smaller black beans take longer to cook than larger, lighter-colored beans; the larger beans absorb more water, so be watchful. The beans can be used in other ways. Never serve the beans al dente; they will be gassy and indigestible.

Frijoles Colados Yucatecos

YUCATECAN SIEVED BEANS

When I first went to learn with the Mayan cooks in Yucatán in 1969 they were actually using hair sieves for these beans; now the blender does the work (not the food processor). This purée of black beans is ever present in a Yucatecan meal. The habanero chile is used more for flavor than for giving a hot touch to the beans. These beans can be prepared well ahead and will keep in the refrigerator for about three days, after which they tend to sour. But the paste freezes very well and can be kept in the freezer for about three months.

MAKES $2\frac{1}{2}$ TO 3 CUPS (625–750ML) DEPENDING ON THE QUALITY OF THE BEANS

2 to 3 tablespoons pork lard or vegetable oil
$\frac{1}{4}$ cup (63ml) roughly sliced white onion
$3\frac{1}{2}$ cups (875ml) cooked small black beans with their broth

1 habanero chile, *asado* and left whole
2 large sprigs epazote
Sea salt

Heat the lard in a large skillet, add the onion, and fry over high heat for a few seconds, until translucent. Meanwhile, blend the beans with their broth in a blender and add to the pan with the chile and epazote. Cook over fairly high heat to reduce, stirring and scraping the bottom of the pan from time to time to avoid sticking, until the beans form a loose shiny paste that plops easily off a spoon, about 15 minutes. Add salt as necessary, although remember that the beans have been seasoned before.

CACTI

Nopales

EDIBLE CACTUS PADDLES

The fleshy new leaves, or paddles, of various species of the nopal cactus are cooked and eaten in many parts of Mexico, particularly in the semi-arid highland areas that favor their cultivation. There are many wild varieties that produce tender paddles in the spring, but because of the popularity of nopales in central Mexico, there are plantations of hybrids producing paddles most of the year. Nopales generally have a pronounced acidic flavor and crisp texture; when cut, a viscous juice exudes.

People in the country gather the wild ones when they abound, starting in late March or April, just in time for the vegetarian Lenten dishes that are mandatory at that time of year. These wild nopales tend to have larger and more prominent green sheaths dotted over the surface that envelop hairlike, almost invisible, and very sharp thorns (aguates). The hybrids also have aggressive thorns that are more apparent, but shaving them off is still a chore unless you have lots of practice.

The most delicate nopales are those called lenguitas, or "little tongues," named for their elongated oval shapes and cooked in the central valley of Oaxaca. They are light green in color and only about ⅛ inch (.5cm) thick. There are also larger, round ones known as nopales "de castilla"—as though they came from Spain—also used in local regional dishes; but the rarity is the large, nonacidic nopal grueso. It is indeed thick, about 2 inches (5cm). It is cut into large pieces and cooked until soft and roughly mashed in its broth at the time of serving with a pasilla de Oaxaca sauce in typical Zapotec style. (There is a charming belief in the villages that if you cut these nopales on a cloudy morning or are feeling jealous the nopales will be acidic.) In the markets of Zacatecas there are some delicious local varieties quite unlike others I have seen around the country.

Nopales are now available in many supermarkets, especially in the southwest, and in Mexican markets generally. Often sold whole and with thorns intact, they also can be found already prepared and cut up, although carelessly. However, unless recently packaged, they are often discolored and a lot of their juice has exuded.

When purchasing them whole, if you have a choice, select those that are fairly rigid, denoting freshness, and are not too thick—a little more than ¼ inch (.75cm) is ideal. When they are flaccid they are past their best but still edible.

Preparation

Holding the base of the nopal, preferably with tongs, and using a very sharp knife, shave off the spines but try not to remove too much of the green skin. There will still be some spines left around the periphery of the paddle, so trim those off by cutting a thin strip all the way round. Try not to let the hairlike thorns get into your skin, but if they do, pass some very clear adhesive tape over the area (rubber gloves won't help much). Then cut the nopal into the size required.

FOR NOPALES COCIDOS: Most recipes call for nopales to be added cooked. The main reason is to get rid of the viscous juice that they exude; they are only very occasionally used or added raw. Mexican cooks generally boil the nopales in water and then rinse them thoroughly, a method I don't recommend because many of the nutrients are lost. However, if you want to, cover the prepared nopales with boiling water and salt to taste. Add a small bunch of green scallion tops and cook over high heat until the nopales are just tender, about 10 minutes. Rinse thoroughly in cold water until the nopales are free of the slimy liquid, drain well, and then follow the recipe.

ALTERNATIVE COOKING METHODS (FOR GOOD OR FOR BAD): (1) Cook with a teaspoon of baking soda (terrible thought, but commonly used); (2) cook in an unlined copper utensil; (3) add a copper coin to the cooking water.

FROM TOP: SHAVING SPINES FROM NOPALES; BEFORE AND AFTER TRIMMING.

Nopales al Vapor

"STEAMED" NOPALES

Many years ago I learned this method from a bus driver/cook (see Essentials, *page 208), which helps to preserve certain nutrients and a crisper texture.*

MAKES JUST UNDER 2 CUPS (500ML)

1 tablespoon vegetable oil
1 tablespoon finely chopped white onion
3½ cups (875ml) diced cactus paddles,
    about 1 pound (450g)
Salt to taste

Heat the oil in a skillet over medium heat, add the onion, and fry for a few seconds, then add the cactus pieces and salt. Cover the pan and cook over medium heat, shaking the pan to avoid sticking and stirring from time to time to ensure even cooking, for about 8 minutes. You will see that the viscous juice will exude and the nopales will start turning from a bright to a yellowish green.

Remove the lid and continue cooking until the juice has been absorbed and the nopales look shiny and still slightly crisp, about 8 minutes more.

FROM TOP: STIRRING UNCOOKED NOPALES; AFTER COOKING, THE NOPALES EXUDE A VISCOUS JUICE.

Nopales Asados

GRILLED NOPALES

Heat a grill or comal over medium heat. Shave the spines off the surface of the nopales and around the periphery. Make four or five vertical slits (depending on the size of the nopal) from about 2 inches (5cm) from the base down to the rounded tip—like a hand. Grill the nopales on a lightly greased surface (if using a comal) over medium heat until the flesh changes color to a yellowish green and has a few brown patches, about 4 minutes. Turn and cook the second side for a further 4 minutes.

Nopales con Chiles Poblanos

This is a delicious and lesser known preparation of nopales that serves either as a separate course or as a vegetable with broiled meats or fish, or as a filling for tacos. While you could add the nopales to the sautéed chiles, I find that the flavor and texture are better if cooked separately.

MAKES ABOUT 6 CUPS (1.5L)

3 tablespoons vegetable oil
½ cup (125ml) thinly sliced white onion
1½ cups (375ml) loosely packed strips of
    poblano chiles (rajas de chile poblano;
    see page 50)
Salt to taste

1½ pounds (675g) nopal cactus pads,
    cleaned and cut into small squares,
    about ¼ inch (7.5cm); makes about
    5¼ cups (1.315L)
2 tablespoons roughly chopped epazote or
    cilantro (optional)

Heat 2 tablespoons oil in a skillet over medium heat, add the onion, and cook for a few minutes until translucent. Add the chile strips, salt to taste, and cook over medium heat, stirring from time to time, until tender but not soft, about 5 minutes. Set aside.

Heat the remaining 1 tablespoon oil in a heavy, deep skillet, add the cactus pieces with a little salt, cover, and cook over medium heat until they are almost swimming in the viscous juice, about 5 minutes. Remove the cover and continue cooking over medium heat, stirring from time to time to avoid sticking until the juice has been absorbed, about 5 minutes more. Stir in the chile strips and epazote, adjust the seasoning, and serve either hot or at room temperature.

This dish can be prepared several hours ahead and then reheated, but it is always better to let it sit and season for about 30 minutes before serving. I do not recommend freezing.

Nopales Rellenos

"STUFFED" NOPALES

This is really a nopal sandwich. Choose two cleaned nopales—the smallest you can find. Place some slices of cheese on one and cover with the second nopal. Secure the two together with toothpicks and grill on a comal or outside grill for about 4 minutes each side, until yellowish green and browned in spots. Serve with corn tortillas and a red or green table sauce.

Nopales Rellenos y Rebozados

"STUFFED" NOPALES IN BATTER

Follow the previous recipe but first dip the nopales into an egg batter and fry as you would for Chiles Rellenos (page 52).

Xoconostles

Many types of cactus of the genus *Opuntia* give edible fruits, known as *tunas* (the Spanish invaders called them "figs of the Indies"), most of them sweet and with very hard seeds dotted throughout the flesh. The *tuna agria,* known as *xoconostle* (the fruit of the cactus *Opuntia*), is acidic and the seeds are encased together in the center of the flesh, which is about $1/2$ inch (1.25cm) thick.

An average xoconostle is squat—about $1 1/2$ inches (4cm) wide and 2 inches (5cm) in length—and weighs about $1 1/2$ ounces (45g). It has a thin skin that varies in color from pale green to pale pink.

I have included xoconostles here because I think that it is an extraordinary fruit in its various preparations and, to my surprise, it is now exported to the United States, although not in enormous quantities.

Xoconostles are skinned and cleaned of seeds for adding raw to a mole de olla in Michoacán (see *Essentials*, page 146); *asados*, skin removed and cleaned of seeds for a table sauce from Hidalgo (see *My Mexico*, page 197); for an *ensalada*, or salad, which is more like a relish, from San Luis Potosí; in broths and moles in Querétaro; and for a dessert, also from Hidalgo. I am sure there are many others, but these are the most representative recipes.

Xoconostles en Almíbar

SOUR TUNAS IN SYRUP

These tunas make a great agridulce—*sweet and sour—dessert, to eat either by itself or better still with crème fraîche, ice cream, or cream cheese. It is attractive to look at, too; the flesh and syrup turn a lovely orange-pink as they cook. Since the flavor is very intense it should be served in small quantities.*

I like to cook the xoconostles in one layer in a nonreactive pan.

6 SMALL SERVINGS

12 xoconostles
About 1¼ cups (313ml) water
1 cup (250ml) sugar

1 vanilla bean or a 2-inch (5-cm)
  cinnamon stick

Prepare the xoconostles by removing the thin skin, cutting them open horizontally, and removing the seeds concentrated in the center. Cut each into strips about ½ inch (1.25cm) wide.

Put the water, sugar, and vanilla bean into a nonreactive pan and stir over medium heat until the sugar has dissolved. Continue cooking the syrup until it starts to thicken, about 8 minutes. Add the fruit and stew, still over medium heat, until the flesh is cooked through, about 15 minutes. It will always remain crisp-tender. Set aside to cool and serve at room temperature.

Xoconostles prepared in syrup will keep very well for about one week and in fact improve in flavor.

Ensalada de Xoconostles

SALAD OF SOUR TUNAS

I came across this recipe many years ago in a family cookbook in San Luis Potosí. This way of preparing these very acidic tunas as a salad—in fact, it is more like a relish—may not be wildly popular, but it makes an interesting accompaniment to serve with broiled meats, enchiladas, or beans.

MAKES ABOUT 1½ CUPS (375ML)

6 xoconostles
⅓ cup (83ml) finely chopped white onion
2 serrano chiles, finely chopped, or to taste

2 tablespoons vegetable or olive oil
Salt to taste
¼ cup (63ml) finely chopped cilantro

Prepare the xoconostles by removing the thin skin, cutting them in halves lengthwise, and removing the seeds concentrated in the center. Cut the flesh into thin strips and put into a nonreactive bowl. Add the onion, chiles, oil, and salt and set aside to season for about half an hour.

Stir in the cilantro and allow to season for about 15 minutes before serving at room temperature. This relish will keep for about two days. I do not recommend freezing.

Acitrón

The large, round biznaga cactus *Echinocactus grandis* is candied and sold as acitrón. It should not be confused with citron, which is a large citrus fruit. Acitrón is sold in traditional candy stores in Mexico in the form of square bars. Cut into small cubes it is used in several types of desserts, in sweet tamales, and in some types of picadillos.

Acitrón can usually be found in the United States in Mexican bakeries and groceries. It has a crisp texture but no pronounced flavor. When not available I have often substituted candied or dried pineapple.

Camotes

SWEET POTATOES

One of the most important staples of the Mexican diet are sweet potatoes, or camotes *(Ipomoea batatas),* from the Nahuatl *camotli* (although the name is also used when referring to other bulbous roots). The sweet potato is native to Mexico, cultivated from early pre-Columbian times. It has the advantage of flourishing in poor soil with little water, and is more nutritious than the white potato, with a higher percentage of vitamins and minerals. There are many varieties of sweet potato, even one with deep purple flesh, but the most popular commercially grown ones have either orange or white flesh.

Sweet potatoes are cooked in soups and stews, baked in hot ashes (the *camoteros* can still be heard as they push their little cart-ovens through the streets in the evenings, alerting people with a steam whistle that the camotes are for sale). They are also baked, bathed in syrup, for eating just like that, skin and all, for breakfast or supper; or boiled and mashed with other ingredients—pineapple, for instance—and reduced with sugar to a paste for dessert. To get the best flavor from your camotes, when they have been dug up leave them, without cleaning off the soil, in the sun for three to five days. This serves to intensify the natural sugars (see *The Art,* page 163).

Cebollas

ONIONS

Onions are used a great deal in Mexican cooking, either blended raw with other ingredients for cooked or fresh sauces, or finely chopped to add to or use as a topping for table sauces and to scatter over *antojitos.* They are often *asado*—cooked and slightly charred on a comal—particularly for sauces in Yucatán and Oaxaca.

The most commonly used onion is a medium-size, sharp white onion. It is not at all sweet, unlike most of its counterparts in the United States. Red, or rather purple, onions are used particularly in Yucatán, Campeche, and Guerrero, and sometimes in the fresh sauces of Jalisco and Colima.

The "peasant" onion preferred for cooking in broths, stews, beans, and the like is called *cebolla de rabo*, or "onion with a tail," because it is sold with its green tops of furled leaves attached. It is a large bulbous scallion occasionally sold in markets in the United States as knob onions or Texas scallions. It is also the onion grilled with the meat for *tacos del carbon* (tacos of charcoal-grilled meat).

The small bulbous scallion, called *cebolla de cambrai*, is used mostly in pickled vegetables and also chopped with some of its leaves for fresh sauces in the western states of Colima, Jalisco, and Sinaloa.

PREPARATION

PICADA: Finely chopped but slightly larger than the French chop, and please no grating! Used for fresh sauces and garnishing *antojitos*.

REBANADA DELGADA: Thinly sliced, usually in rings or half-moons. Sometimes seasoned with lime juice and salt as a crisp topping for simple meats in adobo or dried chile sauces.

BLANCHED: Submerged very briefly in boiling water, and drained immediately before adding the vinegar and seasonings. This method is particularly used for preparing Yucatecan *cebollas en escabeche*.

ACITRONADA: Fried gently in oil until translucent.

FRITA: Fried in oil to a deep golden color; a method used particularly in parts of Oaxaca.

ENTERRADA: Literally meaning "buried," this is a term used particularly in the Yucatán Peninsula when ingredients, particularly chiles, garlic, and onions, are cooked on the hot stones of the pit-barbecue called a *pib*. The outer layer becomes lightly charred; inside, the flesh really steams. These are then added whole to broths, escabeches, and so on, without peeling.

ASADA: The most difficult word to translate because it has several culinary meanings. Here it refers to lightly cooking an ingredient on an ungreased surface. In Mexico the surface would be a comal. Usually an onion is thickly sliced and cooked until it becomes translucent and slightly charred. Unpeeled, it is used in sauces, giving an incomparable flavor.

Chayote

The chayote *(Sechium edule)*—of which there are, according to Mexican botanist Rafael Lira, many wild varieties—is a Mexican native and has been cultivated since early pre-Columbian times. Many regional varieties are eaten today, from the very small, pale yellow one to the large, dark green variety with sharp prickles. The joy of the chayote vine is that not only is it decorative but also the tender vines can be cooked and eaten as a green, in soup, or with eggs. An added bonus is the swollen, bulbous root—chinchayote or chayotestle—that is also prepared in different ways. When cooked the flesh is almost transparent with a slightly crisp, starchy consistency and a delicate potato flavor. It is either eaten alone or made into tortas: cooked, sliced, and sandwiched with cheese, covered with beaten egg, and served in a tomato sauce.

The chayote itself is used in soups and stews, stuffed with cheese, breaded and fried, or made into fritters; it is even cooked as a dessert with sugar and dried fruits. Unless the chayote you buy is very tender and completely smooth, it should be peeled before cooking. The skin can be very tough after any amount of cooking and it will cause intestinal pains. Try to get the crisp, almondlike seed before anyone else—it is the most delicious part. In my part of Michoacán the large prickly chayotes that grow wild in the orchards are usually cooked or baked whole and eaten straight out of the skin with no adornments.

Commercially grown chayotes tend to be watery and don't have a lot of flavor, so they have to be seasoned judiciously.

CITRUS

Bitter Orange

The bitter orange tree, *naranja agria,* is particularly adaptable to different climates and soils and is thus found and used in many parts of Mexico. A native of southeast China and northern Burma, it is well traveled and came to Mexico with the Spaniards, where it arrived in the tenth century (well before the sweet orange).

The tree, with its abundant blossoms and brilliant orange fruits, is often used just for decorative purposes. I remember seeing avenues of it in the northern cities of Mexico and around the Capitol Gardens of Sacramento, California, and along the principal avenues of Marrakech. I came to know the fruit in my youth in England, when February was devoted to the making of marmalade with Seville oranges from Spain, so imagine my delight to find many trees already planted on my land in Michoacán.

One cannot think of the food of the Yucatán Peninsula, or Tabasco, without the bitter orange *(Citrus aurantium).* There, however, the oranges have a green peel even when ripe, which is removed before juicing to avoid bitterness from the pungent oil it contains. The *recados,* the typical seasoning pastes of Yucatán, are usually diluted with the juice; onions are lightly pickled in it; meats and fish are seasoned with it; and tripe scrubbed with it to remove any germs or odors. In parts of Guerrero and Puebla, as well as Mexico City, the juice is used in adobo to season pork. In Zitacuaro, Michoacán, the hollowed peels of these oranges are one of the fruits cooked to a dark stickiness for the traditional *frutas en tacha* sold in the local markets.

Bitter Orange Substitute

MAKES ABOUT ½ CUP (125ML)

1 teaspoon grated Meyer lemon rind
2 tablespoons Meyer lemon juice

2 tablespoons fresh orange juice
4 tablespoons fresh lime juice

Mix together and use as indicated in the recipes. It will keep three or four days.

They are eaten for dessert or during Lent, stuffed into a bread roll for breakfast.

These Seville-type oranges are usually available the year round in Caribbean, especially Dominican, groceries, and at the Fiesta Market in Austin, Texas. The best season for them is in February, when many specialty stores will carry them. When you find them, buy more than you need and freeze the juice with a little of the grated rind for future use. I do not recommend the bottled stuff; it is preferable to make the fairly acceptable substitute opposite.

The best oranges are of medium size, slightly flattened in shape, with a rough, thick rind, and very juicy. They have lots of flattish seeds and should therefore always be squeezed into a strainer. When the oranges are large, with an even rougher, thicker skin, and spongy to the touch, they are generally dry inside and cannot be used. See page 162 for the *recados*.

Lima

Among the hybrid varieties of the *lima (Citrus limetta)* that I have come across in my travels around Mexico, many of which defy classification, one of the most interesting is the *lima agria,* and the sweet variety called *lima* or *lima chichona* (big nipple). In fact, both types have very pronounced, pushed-up nipples. The fruits are squat, about 2 inches (5cm) in length and width (if they have not been fertilized and overwatered), and a shiny, rough rind, light green in color, maturing to yellow. Scratch the rind and you get a strong, delicious citric aroma.

The sweet variety is actually insipid, but it is very much in demand for filling the piñatas during Christmas festivities (children eat them whole). The juice is also drunk; but one of the most refreshing tisanes is made by infusing the whole fruit in boiling water with a couple of the leaves. Local lore has it that it is good for high blood pressure. I have only once come across the *lima* cooked; in Morelia it was stewed in rellena (pig's blood) and rue.

The *lima agria,* which is extremely acidic, is perhaps better known by those who are familiar with the famous soup of the Yucatán, *sopa de lima.* Although a little of the juice is squeezed into the soup, it is the fragrant rind that gives it its special flavor. One extraordinary use of the *lima agria* is found in Chilapa, Guerrero, where a typical accompaniment to a mole would be a curl of red onion seasoned with a squeeze of the juice, or a relish made of hoja santa, seasoned with chiles, and moistened with the juice. And in Mascota, Jalisco, a strong relish is made of the segments of *lima agria* combined with cucumber, onion, and chiles.

There is no substitute, but I look for it in Mexican markets.

Limones

LIMES

Extensive areas of Mexico are suitable for growing citrus fruits, so it is not surprising that it is the world's biggest producer and exporter of limes. It is little wonder also that Mexicans eat limes in one form or another in enormous quantities and with practically everything: as limeade, with beer, in relishes with chile and onion, and candied and stuffed with coconut at the end of a meal—to mention just a few of their uses.

The most popular by far are the fragrant little Mexican or Key limes *(Citrus aurantifolia).* Those grown in tropical areas bear fruit the year round, but at higher altitudes in semitropical areas they have one late summer crop.

Confusingly for strangers to Mexico, they are called *limones.* On rare occasions only will you come across the real yellow lemon. Limes are picked and used when mature but still green. Once fully ripened to yellow, they are considered beyond the pale. The flesh is at first greenish, developing to a greenish yellow. They are slightly elongated, with a small nipple and no neck.

Persian limes *(Citrus latifolia)* have been introduced on a fairly small scale. They are larger, with a full oval shape and a small round nipple at the tip. They are seedless, with rather coarse-grained flesh and a thicker skin. These limes tend to have an off taste once they pass a certain point of maturity. They are picked when mature but still green.

Mexican and Key limes are not always available in the United States, and the Persians have to be used as a substitute. However, since they are not as juicy, you will need to buy more than you think.

Cuitlacoche

CORN FUNGUS

Cuitlacoche *(Ustilago maydis),* or corn fungus, also known in Mexico as *hongo de maiz (cuervos,* in Michoacán, is one of its local names), has been eaten since pre-Columbian times. The name derives from the Nahuatl words *cuitlatl,* "excrement," and *cochtli,* "asleep"—not very flattering for such an exotic and delicious foodstuff. Cuitlacoche appears like a misshapen ear of corn, bulging out of its husks in a most unseemly manner. Each kernel is encased in a silvery-gray skin while the inside fibrous flesh is black.

Drearily, many new corn varieties are supposed to be resistant to the fungus, but happily, so far, it occurs naturally in many varieties in Mexico during the rainy season and can also be induced in irrigated corn. Studies of cuitlacoche (initiated by a food writer on Mexican subjects and an enthusiastic consumer of the fungus) carried out in a Swiss laboratory proved that it had properties likened to those of rye grain, and although it might cause an allergic reaction—like any fungus—it did not contain toxins.

Cuitlacoche is now available in several areas of the United States. Farmers in the Middle West used to burn it in disgust; now, if it does occur, I do not know whether they would bother to market a commodity that was so sporadic unless they had several neighbors who were avid fans with big appetites! But there are some very acceptable canned Mexican products that are distributed in the United States—I can recommend the San Marcos label.

Recipes for cuitlacoche used in soup, crepas, tacos, quesadillas, budines, and cooked with other ingredients appear in both *The Art* and *Essentials*. Cuitlacoche left to dry in the cornfield is also used in a unique mole in Tlaxcala (see *My Mexico,* page 456).

If you have a choice, always buy fresh cuitlacoche still attached to the cob; sometimes it is sold in Mexico already shaved off, and that is rather mushy. If you find it in prime condition, and your source is not constant, buy extra and cook and freeze it. It freezes well and will last at least six months.

Again, if you have the luxury of a choice, choose ears that have the gray kernels intact and not broken open—the latter will tend to be dryish and starchy. Unfurl the green husks around the ear of corn and discard. Pull off the fine strands of corn silk. (You can dry them and keep them for a Mexican home remedy: an infusion that is said to be beneficial to the kidneys.) Cut off the fungus, and any remaining normal kernels, as near to the cob as possible. Chop roughly just to break them up so they will cook evenly. Weigh at this stage.

To prepare cuitlacoche

Makes about 5 cups (1.25L)
3 tablespoons vegetable oil
3 tablespoons finely chopped white onion
2 small garlic cloves, finely chopped
1½ pounds (675g) cuitlacoche (see above)
Sea salt to taste

Heat the oil in a large skillet over low heat. Add the onion and garlic and cook until translucent, about 2 minutes. Add the cuitlacoche and salt, cover the pan, and cook over medium heat for about 10 minutes, stirring from time to time so that it cooks evenly. If the cuitlacoche is rather dry, add a little water at the beginning. If the mixture is too juicy, then remove the cover and reduce over high heat for a few minutes more. When correctly cooked the cuitlacoche should be tender, not mushy, and moist. And don't be afraid of the salt—it needs more than one would suspect.

The recipe given here is absolutely basic: the appropriate chiles, herbs, etc., should be added according to the recipe you are following. Cuitlacoche is always served hot. If you have a large supply that you cannot use, or have leftovers, then cook it all and freeze it. I have kept it frozen for several months. To reheat, put a tablespoon or two of vegetable oil into a wide skillet (size depending naturally on the amount), add the frozen cuitlacoche, and heat through over low heat until thawed, then cook over medium heat to reduce the juiciness.

Garbanzos

CHICKPEAS

Chickpeas *(Cicer arietinum)* were also introduced into Mexico from the Old World, and while they don't form an important part of the foodstuffs, dried they are indispensable for certain dishes and add protein to an otherwise poor diet.

When the chickpeas are very young and tender during the rainy season in Michoacán and Guanajuato—where they are an important crop at that time of year—they are sold as a snack, still in their husks, by wandering streetsellers, always with a bottle of very *picante* sauce to accompany them.

Dried and powdered chickpeas are made into a soup and into small fritters that are put into a sugar syrup, particularly in Oaxaca. Chickpeas are added to a *caldo de res,* a hearty beef and vegetable stew in Zacatecas, and even made into a sauce for a version of *capirotada,* a type of bread pudding—to mention a few.

Of course, you can use canned chickpeas, but they tend to be mushy, with most of their flavor leached into the canning liquid.

If you want to prepare them yourself, start by soaking them the day before.

To prepare chickpeas

Makes 2 cups (500ml) cooked

1 level cup (about 6 ounces/180g) dried chickpeas

2 cups (500ml) water

Sea salt to taste

Rinse the chickpeas, cover with hot water, and leave to soak overnight. The following day, transfer them with their soaking water to a medium saucepan. Add the water and salt and bring to a boil. Lower the heat and cook over medium heat, partially covered (so that they do not boil over), until tender but not falling apart. This can take up to 1½ hours depending on how old and dry they were. By this time the skins should be loosened and can be removed from the water. If not, then rub them gently to release the skins and discard. Always reserve the cooking water for the stew or soup, however the chickpeas are going to be used.

An alternate cooking method is to put the soaked chickpeas with 3 to 4 cups (750m–1L) water, but no salt, into the pressure cooker and cook at medium pressure for 35 to 40 minutes.

Guayaba

GUAVA

The guava *(Psidium guajava)* is a very popular and abundant fruit in Mexico. The tree on which it grows is native to tropical America—possibly Mexico and Colombia. While there are wild trees that produce small green, rather bitter fruit, there are now many cultivated varieties available the year round.

The most commonly found guavas, *los criollos,* or natives, are round and when ripe have a thin yellow skin. The flesh is firm and about ⅛ inch (.5cm) thick, encasing many small hard seeds set in an opaque, mucilaginous substance. The fruit is very high in vitamin C and highly per-fumed. Many of the "improved" varieties are larger and pear-shaped and while often slightly sweeter, they do not have the same intensity of flavor.

Be careful when choosing guavas. Do not buy the darkish green, puckered, round fruits that probably come from Central America or even Asia (I have seen them in Burma)—they do not have the same flavor or texture. Another fruit often marked as guava is the feijoa—this so-called pineapple guava is a native of South America.

In Mexico, cooked guavas are used in different types of desserts but most popu-larly for making Ate, a fruit paste (see *The Art,* page 412), or for canning. There are many brands of canned pink guavas imported into the United States, and these will do in a pinch for stuffing, although they tend to be overly sweet. Guava shells can be stuffed with coconut as a dessert (see *Essentials,* page 431).

To prepare guava shells for stuffing

8 medium yellow Mexican guavas, ripe but still firm (about 1 pound/450g)
2 cups (500ml) water
½ cup (125ml) grated piloncillo or dark brown sugar

Rinse the fruit well. Dry but do not peel. Remove the small circular base holding the shriveled flower and cut the fruit into halves horizontally. You can remove the inner gelatinous flesh containing the seeds either now or after poaching, which is easier.

Put the water and sugar into a wide, shallow pan into which the guavas will fit in one layer and bring to a boil. Lower the heat and simmer the syrup until it thickens slightly, about 10 minutes.

Place the guavas, cut side down, into the syrup and simmer, uncovered, for about 5 minutes. Turn them over and cook for 5 minutes more. They should be just tender but not too soft (of course, there will be a few soft ones that were riper in the first place). Carefully scoop out the inner flesh and seeds if you have not already done so, taking care to keep the "shell" intact.

Habas

Fava Beans

Fava beans *(Vicia faba)* were introduced into Mexico by the Spaniards and are grown extensively, especially in the highlands of central Mexico, where with irrigation there are two crops a year. They are eaten both fresh and dried. They have a high protein content.

The beans are added to many Lenten dishes, served with fritters of dried shrimp; seasoned with other ingredients and lightly cooked, they are eaten as a *botana* with drinks (see *My Mexico,* page 20).

Once removed from their pods, fresh fava beans have a thick skin, which is sometimes removed either before or after cooking, depending on the recipe.

When fava beans are dried, they turn yellow while the outer skin turns a dark brown and adheres stubbornly, so buy them if possible already peeled. The dried fava beans are most commonly used in a soup prepared particularly during Lent, and for a filling for Tlacoyos (page 184), a popular *antojito* of corn masa prepared in the states of Mexico, Hidalgo, and part of Puebla.

Jicama

The name jicama *(Pachyrhizus erosus),* derives from the Nahuatl *xicamatl.* This creeping plant is native to Mexico and Central America, and has been cultivated in Mexico since pre-Columbian times. While it is the bulbous root that is generally eaten, apparently the tender pods are also edible. The crisp, watery flesh (it is 90 percent water) is eaten raw and is at its best when young; as it matures the flesh becomes more starchy. Peeled and sliced jicama is eaten as a snack, put into salads or pickles, and sometimes added to cooked dishes like Manchamanteles, the chicken and pork stew served on Corpus Christi (see *Essentials,* page 331). The best season for jicama is in the late fall.

Lentils

The small greenish and brown dried lentils *(Lens esculenta microesperma)* are the ones most used in Mexican cooking—they are about 3/16 inch (3–4mm) in diameter and have much more flavor than the larger orange lentil. They are very nutritious, containing proteins, the vitamin B complex, and minerals. Lentils are stewed and seasoned with other ingredients (often a fried mixture of tomatoes, onion, garlic, and green chiles with cilantro and/or cumin). You will find that they are cooked with the addition of pineapple and plantain as well, which no doubt harks back to Moorish Spain. A family I know in San Luis Potosí serves them with slices of raw banana on top. The greatest use of lentils can be seen in the recipes of the many Lebanese communities in Mexico.

Olives

Small green—not black—olives are generally used in more sophisticated Mexican recipes or those that have a Spanish heritage. Whole olives, pits intact, used to be more frequently added to cooked dishes, but now the pitted ones—which are naturally much easier to handle—are widely available. I even suggest using the pimiento-stuffed ones in dishes like Huachinango a la Veracruzana (see *Essentials,* page 368).

Plátano Macho

PLANTAIN

Plantains *(Musa paradisiaca),* or vegetable bananas, as I call them, feature strongly in the cooking of the tropical regions of Mexico, particularly along the coastal areas. They are distinguished from the more common bananas by their shape: plantains are larger, triangular in form, and pointed at the tip.

There are various types of plantains, the most delicious being the smaller dominicos from Tabasco, the plátanos de castilla from Oaxaca, and the even smaller and narrower plátano hembra grown in the plantations of northeastern Puebla and Veracruz. All have thick skins that ripen from green to yellow to black.

With rare exceptions, plantains are peeled before cooking; the way they are prepared and eaten varies according to the region. The most common way of cooking them when they are ripe and almost soft is to peel, slice them lengthwise, and fry them; in this way they accompany white rice or black beans.

Curiously enough plantains are used much more in their ripe but still green and firm state. The *tostones de plátano* in Tabasco and the southern part of Veracruz can become addictive; small lengths of the underripe plantain are fried, then squashed down to a thin disk and fried a second time until crisp (see *My Mexico,* page 335); they are eaten as a snack or to accompany a meal. Boiled and mashed to a paste with a little flour to make the dough for empanadas filled with cheese or a meat picadillo, plantains become a favorite evening snack especially in Alvarado and Tlacotalpan. The same dough formed into a banana shape with the same fillings—*plátanos rellenos*—makes a substantial meal with rice and beans in that part of Veracruz. The dough without flour is used for the molotes de plátano of the Isthmus of Tehuantepec.

Plantains can be found in supermarkets catering to Latin American populations or small Mexican and Caribbean markets in many urban areas throughout the United States. They are usually picked when they are green, and while these may serve for some recipes, you will have to wait for them to ripen well for others.

SQUASH

Calabacitas

LITTLE SQUASH

For convenience' sake, one is tempted to use the word *zucchini* (the long, dark green squash sold in the United States is not known in Mexico). But it really does not apply to calabacita, this most Mexican of vegetables, which plays such a prominent role in everyday regional dishes.

There are three main types of calabacitas, not counting the small, dark green fluted squash (like a slightly compressed acorn squash) with orange-colored flesh so appreciated in the Yucatán Peninsula. The most common are the blimp-shaped pale green squash that are picked before they become too swollen, the round ones (sometimes a darker green), and the pear-shaped ones with prominent vertical ridges.

Calabacitas are used the year round in soups and with other vegetables in meat stews. Seasoned with a tomato sauce or enriched with poblano chiles and cheese, they are often served as a separate dish, either as a first or an economical main course. Another popular way of serving calabacitas is to stuff them with meat, cheese, rice, or corn, and even with their flowers, to serve either as a vegetable or a main course. The outer colored skin of all the calabacitas is so thin and tender that the vegetables do not require peeling. The flowers of calabacitas, despite their name, *flor de calabaza,* are also used (see page 120).

Commercially grown calabacitas are picked from a bunchy, more compact bush plant while those described last as pear-shaped come from a vine that spreads and wanders at will. The tender vines and leaves cut about 15 inches (37.5cm) from the end are used as a vegetable, and most famously as the main ingredient for that extraordinary Sopa or Caldo de Guias, typical of the central valley of Oaxaca (*My Mexico,* page 401). The vine should break crisply at the end (like an asparagus); the pieces are stripped of their tough outer fibers and cut into small pieces ready to boil in water seasoned with onion, garlic, and salt. They are delicious with a delicate flavor.

The Yucatecan squash, commercially known as *chigua,* is the tender fruit of pumpkin that is allowed to mature specifically for the small and delicious dried seeds *(chinchillas)* that are such an important element in the foods—especially the typically Mayan—of the southeastern region of Mexico. The dark green skin of this squash remains a little crisp when cooked and should never be peeled. The flesh is more compact than that of other squash and is slightly sweet. It is cooked in stews, soups, etc., but my favorite way of preparing it is cooked with tomato and chile dulce as an appetizer (see *Essentials,* page 9). Acorn squash should be used for any Yucatecan squash recipes.

In some areas of the north and in more remote villages it is still customary to slice calabacitas when fresh and dry them in the sun; most fruits and vegetables treated in this way are called *orejones,* or "big ears."

Although for most recipes zucchini can be used, the Mexican elongated squash is often available in large supermarkets catering to a Mexican public. I have also seen it sold, of all places, in a Palestinian supermarket in Sunset Park, Brooklyn, where it is called "Arabic squash."

A delicious small, round green squash suitable for stuffing is often used in Mexico, but rarely have I found it in U.S. markets. I have seen it in catalogs as *rond de Nice* and one can sometimes find packets of Italian seeds.

Flor de Calabaza

Squash Flowers

Squash and squash flowers are used in the cooking of many areas of Mexico. References to *flor de calabaza* are a little misleading, since the plants grown for pumpkins do not have as full a flower as those for squash. Strictly speaking it should be *flor de calabacita* or the "flower of little squash."

In many areas, the smaller flower of the squash, calabacita de matón, which is grown throughout Mexico on a large commercial scale, is used. The largest and most

fragrant flower, however, is from the *calabacita India* or *de guia,* which flourishes in Michoacán in the rainy summer months and into the fall; in the valley of Oaxaca, it is available the year round, although production drops off in the winter months.

I have not tried using all types of squash flowers, but I was once given some from a Japanese squash that had such a pungent scent and they were not usable. If you are picking the flowers yourself, make sure you choose the male flower—unmistakable with its long stamen—leaving one in every twenty-five to pollinate the female flowers. Remember that the best flowers are seasonal, so if you come across a great crop, cook and freeze them for other occasions.

Squash flowers can be used raw (as the Italians and French do), but to appreciate their very special flavor it is best to cook them. Some Mexican cooks tell you to remove the stamen and bulbous calyx, saying that it is bitter. No, no, no. To the contrary, they add sweetness and crunch. But do remove the stringy green sepals around the base of each flower. If the flowers are very large, then leave about ½ inch (1.25cm) of the stalk on; again, this adds flavor. Once cooked, they can be used for quesadillas, soups, budines, tacos, crepes, and so on.

To prepare flor de calabaza

Makes about 1½ cups (375ml)

1¼ pounds (562g) squash flowers, cleaned and roughly chopped

2 tablespoons vegetable oil or unsalted butter

3 tablespoons finely chopped white onion

1 garlic clove, finely chopped

Sea salt to taste

2 poblano chiles, charred, peeled, and cut into strips (see page 50; optional)

1 tablespoon roughly chopped epazote (optional)

Rinse briefly and shake excess water off the flowers. Roughly chop the flowers, calyx and stamen included. Heat the oil in a large skillet over medium heat, add the onion, garlic, and a little of the salt, and fry gently without browning until translucent, about 1 minute. Add the chile strips and cook, stirring from time to time, for another 2 minutes. Add the flowers and salt to taste, cover the pan, and cook over low heat until the round calyx is tender, not soft, about 10 minutes. Add the optional epazote after 5 minutes. The mixture should be moist not juicy.

This is enough for twelve to fifteen 4-inch (10-cm) quesadillas, twelve crepes, or soup for six servings. They will freeze well for about two months.

Note that if the flowers are not that fresh they tend to be rather dry. It is best to add a little water to moisten in the beginning.

Calabazas

PUMPKINS

Calabazas, one of the very earliest foods to be domesticated in pre-Columbian Mexico, are grown commercially on a very large scale, not only for their flesh but also for the seeds that play a very important part in regional Mexican dishes like pipián, moles, and many Yucatecan dishes (in fact, Yucatán in 1991 produced 73 percent of all commercial pumpkin seeds).

The calabazas grown in Mexico are mainly four types: *Cucurbita moschata, C. pepo, C. mixta,* and *C. maxima,* although they are known by many different names in different regions. Among these common names are *pipiana, India, chompa, huichi, pipitoria, tamalayota;* those grown extensively in the southeast are called *chigua.* (Calabazas are never allowed to reach the absurd size of those grown for Halloween in the United States and then discarded to rot.)

The flesh of the mature pumpkin is used in many areas for soups and stews, while in northern Veracruz and the Sierra Sur of Oaxaca there is a tamale made with it. One of the very favorite candied sweets in Mexico, mainly as a dessert or breakfast food, is Calabaza en Tacha (*Essentials,* page 438).

The seed encases a delicious dark green pepita; they are sometimes sold, but not marked, alongside those of pumpkin seeds. The flat pumpkin seeds with cream-colored husks are used toasted and salted as a snack; generally—with minor exceptions—other seeds are used whole with husks intact, well toasted and ground to a slightly textured powder for pipián (see *Essentials,* page 209, and *My Mexico,* page 380), mole verde, and dishes of Mayan origin like Dzotobichay (*The Art,* page 78), Sikil P'ak (*Essentials,* page 4), and Brazo de la India.

Hulled green pepitas have always been available in markets and health food stores in the United States, and now you can also buy unhulled seeds, pepitas enteras, or semillas de calabaza enteras in many Mexican groceries or supermarkets catering to a Mexican public. Their availability very much depends on the region from which the local Mexican immigrants come from, or the owner of the store, for that matter. Use whatever you find for the recipes calling for unhulled seeds.

Chilacayote

The chilacayote (*Cucurbita ficifolia*) is the fruit of a climbing plant of the Cucurbitaceae family. A native plant of Mexico, with brilliant yellow flowers similar to those of most squashes and pumpkins, the chilacayote grows wild in central Mexico, not so much creeping along the ground but climbing and spreading over trees and bushes. When the fruit is small and tender—up to about 7 inches (18cm) in length—it is a pale green color flecked with cream and is prepared as a vegetable. It is most commonly cooked unpeeled in a pipián, with or without meat, or mole de olla, or more rarely alone (see *My Mexico*, pages 449 and 451). The flesh is tasteless but crisp textured. Chilacayotes can grow up to 10 or 12 inches (25–30cm) long and about 9 inches (22.5cm) wide. As they mature the skin hardens to a rind and the color deepens to a dark green flecked with lighter tones. The flesh is only about 1 inch (2.5cm) thick, encasing spaghetti-like strands dotted with hard black seeds. At this stage the flesh, and the spaghetti-like strands inside holding the seeds, are candied. Although it is all used for cooking in sugar—*en tacha*—the strands are often cooked by themselves in a syrup for cabellos de angel, "angel hair," a crisp, textured dessert sometimes including the flat, round seeds. At either stage of ripeness chilacayotes do not have much flavor. The seeds, which have a very dark green husk, are also dried and toasted with salt as a *botana*.

Tomatoes

The everyday tomato that is indigenous to Mexico is called *jitomate* in Central Mexico. This is from the Nahuatl words *xitli* meaning "umbilicus" and *tomatl*, because the native tomato in Mexico had an indentation like a belly button at its base. These tomatoes, called *criollos*, are found in the Isthmus and some southern regional markets. They are formed like small, thin-fleshed beefsteak tomatoes and are very juicy and delicious—alas, they do not last long and therefore are not commercially viable in this age of mass production. The common round tomato is referred to as *jitomate de bola* and the plum tomato, which has taken over the markets in Mexico, *jitomate guaje*. In the north and south, however, the name is *tomate*, or *tomate rojo*. There are also miniature tomatoes—about one-third the size of a cherry tomato—in the damp tropical parts of Veracruz and the Sierra Norte de Puebla; they are called, variously, *Zitlali, ojo de venado, tomate de monte*, and *cuatomate*.

Tomatoes are used mainly, but not exclusively, for table sauces. In Tuxpan, Veracruz, the green unripe tomatoes are mixed with the red so that the sauce will not be too sweet. Sliced raw, they are used as a topping for tostadas and salads; chopped, they are for a salsa mexicana or to add to a seafood cocktail or scrambled eggs. But more generally tomatoes are used either raw, cooked in water, or *asado* (see opposite), and skinned or unskinned and blended or ground in the molcajete, for both table and cooked sauces.

TOMATOES *ASADOS*.

PREPARATION

COOKED IN WATER: As a general rule whole tomatoes are covered with water and simmered until soft, about 10 minutes. They are then skinned and blended, or blended unskinned and the sauce strained. There are, of course, exceptions; for instance, in parts of Oaxaca the tomatoes are chopped and stewed in a minimum of water before blending. For some recipes in parts of Michoacán the tomatoes are simmered with the meat and taken out as soon as they are soft.

ASADO: The whole tomatoes are cooked on an ungreased comal or griddle until they are slightly charred and mushy to guarantee a specially delicious table or cooked sauce. About half the cooks I know then skin the tomatoes, while others—including me—blend them unskinned. While the appearance of the sauce may not be as attractive, the flavor and texture are incomparable. This method of cooking tomatoes is particularly recommended for freezing and storing for the months when tomatoes are not at their best (not a problem in Mexico).

You may want to broil them in a more practical way. Choose a shallow pan into which the tomatoes will just fit in one layer—not too large or the juice that exudes will dry up. (I used to line the pan with foil, but no longer. It is high time that we gradually ease foil out of the kitchen or use it very, very sparingly. The mining of bauxite for the production of aluminum has destroyed far too many tropical forests on this planet.) Place the pan about 2 inches below a heated broiler and broil until the top halves of the tomatoes are soft and the skin is blistered and slightly browned. Turn the tomatoes over and repeat on the other side. The exuded juice will be sweet and syrupy so save it to blend with the tomatoes.

ENTERRADO: *Enterrado* means literally buried, and it is an expression from Yucatán

VEGETABLES, BEANS, AND FRUITS 125

where cooking in the villages is still done in a barbecue pit or *pib*. When the stones lining the base of the pit have been heated with wood, the ashes are brushed aside and ingredients like tomatoes, onions, garlic, and chiles are cooked—or perhaps "char-cooked" would be a better word. This method could, of course, be approximated on an outdoor grill. The flavors of the ingredients are incredible and the aromas wafting around perhaps even more so.

ESTOFADO (STEWED): As I mentioned before, I have seen this method of cooking tomatoes and tomate verde in the valley of Oaxaca. Cut the tomatoes into 8 pieces and put into a saucepan with 1 tablespoon of oil and ¼ cup (63ml) water for 1½ pounds (675g) of tomatoes. Cover the pan and cook over medium heat, shaking the pan from time to time to avoid sticking, until they are mushy, about 20 minutes.

RALLADO (GRATED): Cut the top off a round tomato and grate it by pressing, and thus flattening, the skin against your palm as you work it on a box grater. This is a method of preparing tomatoes that I have seen only in northern Mexico—actually in both Sonora and Nuevo León.

Tomate Verde

MEXICAN GREEN TOMATOES

A distinctive, indigenous ingredient in Mexican cooking is the *tomate verde (Physalis ixocarpa)*, known in the United States as the *tomatillo*. It has various regional names in Mexico: *tomate de hoja* in the Sierra de Gorda, Queretero; *miltomate* in Oaxaca; *tomate milpero* or *tomate de capote* in Colima; *fresadilla* in Nuevo León. The list continues.

There are very small, miniature tomate verde that grow wild, no larger than the tip of a little finger; the largest and juiciest, called *tomate manzano*, are cultivated in the state of Mexico and are distinguished not only by their size but also by their bright, shiny green surface, which is patched with yellow.

Tomate verde are not juicy and heavy so there is a surprisingly large number—about twenty-two medium-size ones (about 1½ inches/4cm in diameter)—to the pound.

While tomate verde are usually prepared for sauces by cooking in one of several ways depending on the cook or the region, they are very occasionally used raw—for example, in a rustic sauce to accompany the pit-barbecued mutton in the state of Mexico, or quite exceptionally in a salad (see *My Mexico*, page 110).

Whichever method you are using to prepare them, the papery husk has to be removed and the tomate rinsed of some of the slightly sticky substance around the base. Of course, there is one exception: a Oaxacan cook told me of one recipe in which the husk is left on and the tomate is cooked in hot ashes for a special sauce. The husk itself contains certain acidic properties that, when infused in water, provide a rising agent often used by traditional cooks to leaven their tamales sometimes, but not always, combined with tequesquite (see page 165).

PREPARATION

ASADO: With husk removed, place the whole tomate on an ungreased comal or griddle and cook over medium heat until fairly soft and the skin is patched with brown. The tomatoes are not skinned, but ground for a table sauce usually with garlic and chiles.

COOKED IN WATER: This is the most common method of cooking tomate. Cover with water and simmer until soft, about 10 minutes, taking care that they do not boil and burst open. They are then partially drained and blended for either table or cooked sauces. I have seen cooks from the valley of Oaxaca cutting the tomate verde into small pieces and stewing them in very little water until soft.

TOMATES VERDES *ASADOS.*

WILD GREENS

There are many wild greens, or *quelites,* now cultivated on a large scale, that are important in the regional cuisines of Mexico. There are many borderline herbs, and vice versa, but I have included them here if they are an important part of a particular dish. I have included colorín flowers here because they are gathered in much the same way as wild greens.

Chaya

The leaves of chaya *(Cnidoscolus chayamansa)* are used in many dishes in the southern states of Mexico (Yucatán, Campeche, Chiapas, and Tabasco). It is a native plant of tropical America and was cultivated by the Maya from wild plants whose leaves can give you a nasty sting

A small paperback, *El Libro de los Guisos de Chaya,* was published under the auspices of the governor of Quintana Roo in 1974, who recognized the value of this plant in the daily diet and had it analyzed. It was determined that 100g (about $3\frac{1}{2}$ ounces) of fresh leaves contained 9 percent protein, 2 percent oils, 7 percent carbohydrates, and significant amounts of calcium with phosphorous, iron, vitamin A, niacin, vitamin C, and very small quantities of vitamins B_1 and B_2. At that time many families were encouraged to grow it domestically in order to have a continuous supply.

The leaves are used in soups and stews, and in tamales; also for wrapping tamales (see Dzotobichay in *The Art,* page 78), as well as cooked with eggs, meats, and other vegetables. The leaves are soft and silky to the touch when tender and young, but tough when mature. They have a dark green, matte surface; the underside is lighter green and

Chaya con Huevo

CHAYA LEAVES WITH EGGS

Chaya con huevo, in Mayan chay-he, *is one of the popular snacks served free in the cantinas of Mérida (in the hope that you will go on drinking!). Although not traditional, I have added a touch of chile. If a fresh habanero is not available, then substitute a serrano.*

SERVES 4 AS AN ENTREE, 6 AS AN APPETIZER

6 ounces (180g) chaya, spinach, or Swiss
    chard leaves
3 tablespoons lard or vegetable oil
3 tablespoons finely chopped white onion
2 garlic cloves, peeled and finely chopped
1 medium green bell pepper, seeds
    removed and cut into small squares

½ habanero chile, seeds removed and
    finely chopped, or serrano with seeds
    included (optional)
Sea salt to taste
3 plum tomatoes, finely chopped,
    about ¾ cup (about 190ml)
6 large eggs, lightly beaten with salt to
    taste

Cut off the tough little stems of the chaya, or trim the spinach or chard, rinse, shake dry, cover with boiling water, and cook over fairly high heat until just tender, 10 minutes for chaya and chard, and 6 minutes for spinach. Drain, discarding the liquid, and squeeze the greens as dry as possible. Chop fine; you should have about 1 cup (250ml) firmly packed. Set aside.

Heat the lard or oil in a large, heavy skillet. Add the onion, garlic, and pepper (and optional chile) with a good sprinkle of salt and cook over medium heat, stirring from time to time, until the onion is translucent, about 3 minutes. Add the tomatoes and continue cooking over medium heat, stirring to avoid sticking, until the juice has evaporated, about 4 minutes. Add the chaya and continue cooking over a fairly high heat until well incorporated and beginning to look shiny and dryish, about 5 minutes more. Gradually stir in the eggs and continue stirring over medium heat until thoroughly set, not creamy. Adjust the seasoning and serve immediately with corn tortillas or totopos.

This dish may be prepared about 1 hour ahead, up to the point of adding the eggs, and finished off at the last minute. I don't recommend freezing.

shiny. An average leaf measures about 6 inches (15cm) across and about 5 inches (12.5cm) from base to tip.

When cooked, chaya has a rich green flavor from the iron—akin to spinach—but with a touch of sweetness. When chaya is not available, many recipes tell you to substitute spinach, but especially in the case of tamales, I prefer to use (green) Swiss chard. I particularly like chaya leaves cooked with scrambled eggs, which is often served as an appetizer in Yucatán or as an entree before the main course.

Flor de Colorín

Colorín Flowers

The early chroniclers were amazed at the importance that flowers played in the everyday life of the Aztecs: they were in their botanical gardens, as carpets of flowers for ceremonies, to decorate the temples, and carried by the dancers. Men of distinction would never appear in public without carrying flowers. And they were eaten! Yellow squash flowers, white yucca buds, pink petals of cocohuite, the pastel-shaded plumeria (cacalasuchil), and the bittersweet cream-colored strands of palm buds (pacayas and tepejilotes) are a very few of the flowers that are prepared in different regions in different ways.

The first spring I was living in Mexico I was delighted by the colors of the tree-lined streets: the purple-blue of the jacarandas and the red of the coral trees, known as zompantle. The maids used to collect the red flowers from the coral trees to make *tortitas de flor de colorín*—or *pitos,* or *gazparitos,* by whatever name they knew them. First was the job of removing the yellow pistils—they are bitter—then cooking the flowers in water; sadly, the color changes to a dull purple. They are mixed with beaten egg and fried in small fritters, and served in a thin tomato sauce—or sometimes they are cooked and added to a meat stew. In some areas, cooks prefer the immature, brownish colorín buds, which remain crisper to the end, while others wait until they turn a brilliant red, but the taste is much the same.

Guajes

I am encouraged to see so many more of the rarer Mexican ingredients, among them guajes (*Leucaena* spp.), being imported now and sold in many areas where there is a sizable Mexican community. Guaje—the word means a "pod"—is indeed a large, flattish pod, on average about 6 inches (15cm) long and about ¾ inch (2cm) wide. The pod contains a number of flat seeds resembling beans that when fresh have a strong odor.

There are many species of this decorative tree, which grows wild in poor soil in tropical areas at many altitudes in Mexico, generally below 6,000 feet. Not only are the seeds eaten raw when mature, but so are the new shoots with their closely furled leaves and small crisp green balls (which are the unopened flowers).

You will usually see two types of pods, either a light green or a deep red, but the flavor is essentially the same. The seeds are used either raw with guacamole or made into a sauce; they can also be cooked in fritters or ground up with tomatoes and other ingredients for a *guaxmole*. When dried the seeds turn brown and become brittle; they are then toasted and salted and, as *cacalas*, eaten as a snack (see *My Mexico,* pages 234–236).

Huauzontles

Visitors to markets in Mexico are always fascinated by the bunches of long-stemmed greens topped with sprigs covered with little hard green seeds, although these are actually the flowers and the part that is eaten. The huauzontle (*Chenopodium berlandieri* spp. *nuttalliae*) is a native plant of central Mexico, and although it is considered to be at its best in spring and is a popular Lenten food, it is now cultivated and available the year round. I was delighted to see that it is available in parts of the United States (I have seen it at least in New York and Texas), since it is one of my favorite greens with its intense "green" flavor and interesting texture.

Tortas de Huauzontles

The light egg batter tends to absorb a lot of oil. It is therefore, as with chiles rellenos, best to prepare them an hour or so ahead and reheat in a 350°F (180°C) oven on trays lined with absorbent paper. Much of the oil will seep out. So as not to waste oil, I always choose a smaller rather than larger skillet.

MAKES 6 SERVINGS

3 long stems of huauzontles, about
    1 pound (450g)
About 4 ounces (115g) Mexican
    Chihuahua or U.S. Muenster cheese,
    cut into square bars about 3 inches
    (7.5cm long)

Vegetable oil, for frying (not canola)
3 large eggs, separated
Sea salt
About ¼ cup (63ml) flour

Have ready a tray lined with two layers of absorbent paper. Have also ready a saucepan with boiling salted water. Remove the small, flower-laden stems from the main stalks, add to the pot, and cook over high heat until just tender but not soft, 5 to 8 minutes depending on how mature they are. Strain, pressing down well to remove excess water. Form the sprigs into small bunches, about six in each, and again squeeze well. Insert a strip of the cheese into each bunch.

Fill a medium skillet with about 1 inch (2.5cm) of vegetable oil and set it over medium heat.

Meanwhile, beat the egg whites until they form firm peaks and do not slide around in the bowl. Gradually beat in the yolks with salt to taste.

When the oil is hot enough to fry in, lightly pat one of the bunches with flour (do not flour all of them in advance or the flour will become soggy). Dip the torta into the egg batter so it acquires a good coating and lower it gently into the oil. Fry the tortas on each side until the beaten egg is a crisp golden brown. Strain in a perforated spoon over the pan and drain on the prepared tray. Until you have a lot of practice, don't fry more than two at a time.

If you are serving with a salad, make sure the tortas are well drained of excess fat, and serve immediately with a red or green tomato sauce on the side. If you are serving with the pasilla sauce (page 134), add the tortas to the hot sauce and let heat through for about 5 minutes. If you want to serve them later, see note above.

The "flower" sprigs are usually boiled, squeezed into small bunches, then fried in beaten eggs like chiles rellenos. To make them a little more substantial, a piece of cheese is put in the middle of the greens and it melts with the frying. These *tortas de huauzontles,* as they are called, are usually served in a light tomato or pasilla chile sauce. However, there is an exception and once again I give an example from the eastern part of Michoacán. Here, they are served hot but with a crisp accompaniment of shaved raw cabbage mixed with tomato and onion and seasoned with lime juice and salt—a great pairing! Pass either a tomato or tomatillo sauce separately.

I give the recipes for the tortas as well as the cabbage relish and a pasilla sauce because the real aficionados and curious cooks will want to try them.

FROM TOP: FORMING BUNCHES OF COOKED HUAUZONTLES; LIGHTLY PATTING WITH FLOUR; DIPPING IN BEATEN EGG; FRYING THE TORTAS.

Pasilla Chile Sauce

This is the simplest of sauces, and I am sure some cooks will want to add more ingredients. But I am giving you the traditional, very simple thinnish sauce, which allows the subtle flavor of the greens to come through.

MAKES ABOUT 3 CUPS (750ML)

7 pasilla chiles, veins and seeds removed
3 cups water (750ml)

1 tablespoon vegetable oil
Sea salt

Put the chiles into a small saucepan, cover with water, and bring to a simmer. Continue simmering for about 3 minutes, then set aside to soak for 5 minutes more. Drain the chiles and transfer to the blender jar with 1½ cups (375ml) of the water and blend until smooth.

Heat the oil in a medium skillet, add the sauce, and fry over high heat until reduced and seasoned, about 3 minutes. Add the rest of the water with salt to taste and bring to a simmer. Simmer for 5 minutes more—the sauce should have a medium consistency and lightly cover the back of a wooden spoon. Add the tortas and heat through for about 8 minutes more.

Cabbage Relish

This is a very simple salad, but the crispness combines very well with the fried tortas.

MAKES 6 SERVINGS

4 cups (1L) finely slivered cabbage
3 medium tomatoes, each cut into 6 small
  wedges

1 medium white onion, very thinly sliced
Fresh lime juice to moisten
Sea salt to taste

Toss all the ingredients together just before you start frying the tortas.

Quintonil

Several species of the amaranth family of plants are known as *quintonil* (*Amaranthus* spp.), and while they are one of the wild greens known as quelites, they are also cultivated both for the produce markets and to complement cattle feed. The wild ones are gathered in the spring when they appear profusely in irrigated fields throughout central Mexico. Without doubt this is the time when they are at their best and their rather strong iron flavor is more pronounced. They should be gathered when still tender and before the spiky flower characteristic of this family of plants appears.

The leaves and tender stems are used. Although many local people here in Michoacán first cook them in water, it is far better to cook them *al vapor*. That does not mean steaming in the usual sense: sauté a little chopped onion, serrano chile, and garlic in a skillet, then add the rinsed and drained greens with a little salt to taste. Cover the pan and let them cook, with no additional water, until tender—about 5 minutes depending on how tender they are. If they have exuded a lot of juice, cook uncovered over high heat for a minute or so until still moist but not dry. Stuffed into a freshly made corn tortilla they make a delicious, healthy taco. Quintoniles can be used in recipes calling for spinach, and I have even made ricotta gnocchi with them with great success.

Another quelite, called *cenizo (Chenopodium berlandieri)*, is also at its best in spring and early summer. The tender ash-green leaves and spiky flowers are prepared in the same way as quintonil.

Romeritos

These stringy little greens *(Suaeda torreyana)* grow wild in poor sandy soil, but to meet the demand growers are now cultivating them the year round. According to a 1991 census (INEGI), surprisingly the largest crop in both spring and autumn is grown in the Federal District—Mexico City—which accounted then for 92 percent of the total yearly crop for the country.

Romeritos grow in bunches of narrow, round, juicy leaves about 1½ inches (4cm) long. They are grayish-green in color and while they do not have an aroma, they are acidic like nopales.

Romeritos lend their name to a Lenten dish of dried shrimp fritters served in a mole with vegetables, both of which vary according to the area of the country. In central Mexico, however, romeritos are an absolute must for this dish, which is also prepared for the Day of the Dead at the beginning of November and for Christmas Eve supper—alongside that most Mexican of dishes, Bacalao a la Vizcaina.

Verdolaga

Verdolaga *(Portulaca oleracea)* is a wild green native to North America. Known as purslane in the United States, it is often found in farmers' markets and now in markets and stores catering to a Mexican public. In Mexico it is often gathered wild, but it is also cultivated the year round. The small, round, fleshy leaves are acidic, and although they are sometimes eaten raw as a salad, they are most often cooked in a stew, especially with pork (see *Essentials,* page 271).

MEAT,
POULTRY,
AND
SEAFOOD

Beef, Cooked and Shredded

Beef that has been cooked and shredded, either alone or seasoned with a sauce, is a popular filling for tacos and enchiladas, or for a topping for tostadas or other *antojitos*. It is best to buy a cut of meat that is easy to shred, like flank or skirt steak; these cuts also have a lot of flavor.

To prepare the beef

Makes scant 2 cups (500ml)
1 pound (450g) skirt or flank steak, cut into 1-inch (2.5-cm) cubes
1 small white onion, roughly chopped
1 garlic clove, roughly chopped
Sea salt to taste

Put the beef and other ingredients into a saucepan, cover with water, and bring to a boil. Lower the heat and simmer the meat, covered, until tender, about 40 minutes. Take care not to overcook because the cooking process will continue as the meat cools off. Set aside for the meat to cool off in the broth, then strain, reserving the broth for a soup or another dish.

When cool enough to handle, shred the meat—not too finely—discarding any gristle or connective tissue.

This meat could be frozen for about two weeks.

Pork, Cooked and Shredded

Cooked and shredded pork, either alone or seasoned with a sauce, is a popular filling for tacos and enchiladas, a topping for tostadas and other *antojitos*, or a stuffing for chiles rellenos. It is best to buy stewing pork, with some fat for flavor. When shredding take care not to make it too fine, as many Mexican commercial cooks do; remember what is lost in texture is lost in flavor.

To prepare the pork

Makes about 2½ cups (625ml), tightly packed
2 pounds (900g) boneless stewing pork with some fat
½ medium onion, roughly chopped
2 garlic cloves, roughly chopped
5 peppercorns
Sea salt to taste

Cut the meat into 1-inch (2.5-cm) cubes, put it into a saucepan with the rest of the ingredients, cover with water, and bring to a boil, then lower the heat and simmer, covered, until tender, about 35 minutes. Do not overcook because the cooking process will continue while the meat is cooling in the broth. Set aside to cool. Strain, reserving the broth for another dish.

When cool enough to handle, shred the meat roughly, discarding any excess fat, connective tissue, or gristle. For stuffed chiles, chop the meat to a medium texture.

I don't recommend freezing because the flavor is impaired.

Chorizo

The Spaniards introduced pigs and the making of pork products, including chorizo, to Mexico early on in the colonial period, but the Mexican chorizo bears little resemblance today to its Spanish forebears.

In writing more fully about chorizos in *The Art of Mexican Cooking*, I was guided by a delightful little book on the subject written by Alfonso Sanchez Garcia, *Toluca del Chorizo*. While the chorizos made around the Toluca area are still renowned today, other regions have their versions that vary slightly in the type of seasoning or the texture of the meat. In and around Toluca and Mexico City, and in fact in other parts of central Mexico, the name *longaniza* is usually applied to chorizos made with inferior cuts of meat, sometimes including beef, and stuffed into one long length of pork casing. In Yucatán, a large proportion of achiote seeds are ground with the spices and the long, very thin longanizas are smoked. The longanizas in Emiliano Zapata, Tabasco, are seasoned with purer achiote, spices, and bitter orange juice (see *My Mexico*, page 332) and they are not smoked.

In fairly recent years a novel green chorizo has appeared and become very popular (see *The Art*, page 268). The following is a recipe (with slight changes) for a red chorizo that I particularly like from Huetamo in the hot country of Michoacán, which was first published in *The Art of Mexican Cooking*. The chorizos should be left to mature in flavor and dry for several days before eating. If you grind the meat at home, then check the size of the holes in the attachment to your electric mixer; ideally they should be ¼ inch (75mm). If they are larger, then push the meat through very fast. And don't skimp on the fat. You need it for texture and flavor; it will seep out in cooking, anyway.

Red Chorizo

MAKES ABOUT 15 3-INCH (7.5-CM) LINKS

2 pounds (900g) ground pork, medium
   grind

8 ounces (225g) pork fat, medium grind

35 guajillo chiles

About 2 cups (500ml) mild white
   commercial vinegar

6 garlic cloves, roughly chopped

2 Mexican bay leaves, or 1 ordinary,
   broken up

Leaves of 4 sprigs fresh thyme, or scant
   ½ teaspoon dried

Leaves of 4 sprigs fresh marjoram, or scant
   ½ teaspoon dried

1 rounded teaspoon dried Mexican
   oregano

10 black peppercorns, crushed

6 whole cloves, crushed

3 whole allspice, crushed

2 tablespoons coarse sea salt

7 feet (2.10m) narrow pork casings, cut
   into 3 lengths

Thin string or shredded dried corn husks
   for tying the sausages

Start the day before stuffing the chorizos. Mix the ground meat and fat together in a glass, enamel, or nonreactive bowl and set aside. Remove the stems, if any, from the dried chiles; slit open and remove the seeds, but leave the veins for heat. Put the chiles into a saucepan, cover with water, and bring to a simmer. Remove from the heat and let soak for about 5 minutes. Then drain, discarding the water. Cover the chiles with 1½ cups (375ml) of the vinegar and let soak for about 1 hour.

Put the remaining vinegar into a blender jar, add the garlic, herbs, spices, and salt, and blend until smooth. Stir into the meat. Drain the chiles and put the vinegar in which they were soaking into the blender jar. Add the chiles a few at a time and blend thoroughly after each addition until you have a smooth purée—or as smooth as possible. Add to the meat in the bowl through a fairly fine strainer, pressing out the debris (there always is some when you are using the tough-skinned guajillos) to extract as much juice and flesh as possible. Mix the meat, spices, and chiles very thoroughly—it's best to do this with your hands, which is messy but most effective. Cover the bowl and set in the refrigerator to season overnight, stirring the mixture from time to time while you are still awake.

The following day, rinse and drain the lengths of casings (see page 142 for preparation) and tie a double knot at one end of each. Now you may either use the stuffing attachment to your electric mixer and follow the instructions or stuff by hand, which is far more therapeutic unless, of course, you have 100 pounds of chorizos to make! Slip

OPPOSITE: ADDING PURÉED CHILES TO GROUND PORK. FROM TOP: TESTING CASINGS FOR BREAKS; HAND-STUFFING THE CASINGS; TYING CHORIZO LINKS WITH SHREDDED DRIED CORN HUSKS.

the open end of one length of casing over the tube of the stuffing funnel, and gather up the rest, easing it into tight folds and leaving about 6 inches (15cm) from the knotted end loose for the first sausage.

Half-fill the funnel with some of the meat mixture, and with either your fingers or a dowel, force it down into the casing. Sometimes air bubbles form in the base of the casing; if this happens carefully squeeze the air out to the top of the funnel. Continue stuffing so that the casing is firm to the touch, neither too stretched nor too slack, smoothing the sides of the stuffed casings evenly as you progress. Leave about 4 inches (10cm) of casing unstuffed at the top. Now start from the bottom to form the links, each about 3 inches (7.5cm) long. Give a double twist to form the link and tie tightly. (At this point if you have overstuffed the casing and/or there is a weak point in it, it will split open and the mixture will ooze out. It is so frustrating! But you just tie another knot farther up and start again.)

Now squeeze out any stuffing that has backed up into that 4 inches (10cm) of slack and tie a firm knot. Then attach a double length of string to that end so that you can hang the chorizos up to dry in a very airy, dry place. Be sure to put a pan underneath to catch the dripping vinegar and hang them well out of the way of normally perfectly well-behaved cats and dogs (during the years both of mine have proved their *mexicanidad* and consumed the whole lot raw at one go with no ill effects). The drying time will depend very much on your climate. In a damp atmosphere they can take about five days. You do not want them to delay longer, so put an electric fan near them for several hours each day until they feel dry to the touch but not shriveled up. At this stage they can be refrigerated and kept for another week. After that it is best to rub the surface with a little lard and freeze them.

When you want to skin chorizos and find that the casing is too dry, moisten your hands with water and rub them for a few seconds. The casing will, or should, become detached from the meat filling.

CHORIZO CASINGS

In Mexico the small intestines of the pig are used for chorizos. They are packed in sea salt and kept in the freezer (although they never freeze with the high salt content). They become a dull grayish brown and look unappetizing. Never buy plastic casings, which do not allow the meat to breathe, let alone taking into account the detrimental effect of grease on plastic; besides, it is so unaesthetic!

Always prepare the casings well ahead of making the sausages. Cut off lengths of about 4 feet (122cm), rinse them twice in cold water, drain, and then cover with fresh water—adding 1 tablespoon of strong vinegar for 4 cups water—and let soak for at least 1 hour or overnight. Drain well and rinse the casings once more.

To test to make sure there are no punctures, take one length of the casing, submerge it in water, and let the water run through from one end to the other. It will balloon up unevenly. This procedure also helps to open up the casing, making it easier to stuff. Tie a double knot at one end of each length, then let them drain for about 15 minutes.

Chorizo y Papa
CHORIZO AND POTATO FILLING

A mixture of chorizo and potato makes a popular filling not only for molotes but also for tacos, quesadillas, sopes, gordas, and even garnachas.

MAKES 1 ROUNDED CUP (APPROXIMATELY 280ML), ENOUGH FOR 12 MOLOTES (DOUBLE THE QUANTITY FOR 12 OTHER TYPES OF ANTOJITOS)

Approximately 1 tablespoon lard or
   vegetable oil
1 Mexican chorizo, about 3 ounces (85g)
6 ounces (170g) waxy new potatoes, diced
   and cooked al dente, about 1 rounded
   cup (280ml)

1 chipotle en adobo, chopped (optional)
Sea salt to taste

Melt the lard in a small skillet. Skin and crumble the chorizo, add to the pan, and cook over low heat until the fat has been rendered out. Add the potatoes and chile, if using, and continue cooking over medium heat, scraping the bottom of the skillet from time to time to avoid sticking, until well seasoned, about 8 minutes. Season with salt. Set aside to cool a little before using.

Chicharrón

CRISP-FRIED PORK RIND

As you enter the meat section of any local Mexican market you will be struck by the piles of unevenly curled sheets of richly browned chicharrón—crisped pork skin. The skin is first dried, often in the sun, and fried in lard. It is gently cooked in the beginning and then at a hotter temperature so that it puffs up—somewhat like honeycomb—and is completely crisp.

There are two types of chicharrón: one thinnish and totally crisp; the other—from the part of the skin covering the stomach area—is thicker and lined with a layer of browned fat. Both are delectably greasy and addictive and provide one of Mexico's favorite snacks.

CHICHARRÓN, WITH
RED AND GREEN
LONGANIZA.

Chicharrón, cooked in a green or red sauce—it loses its crispness—provides a traditional dish for *almuerzo,* the hearty breakfast. It can be broken into small pieces to serve as a topping for some pozoles, guacamole, salads, and so on. Crumbled, it can be used as a filling or mixed with masa for gorditas.

Chicharrón prensado is small pieces of browned fatty chicharrón pressed together in large batches and sold as such again for snacks and *antojitos.* The very small pieces of skin and fat that sink to the bottom of the vats of lard in which the chicharrón has been fried are sold as *migajas* or *asiento,* or *zorrapa* in the Isthmus of Oaxaca, among other regional names. In central Oaxaca, asiento, mixed with rather dark lard, is sold to spread on the favorite snack, *tortillas con asiento,* or added to masa to form the little dumplings or Chochoyotes (see page 173).

Chicken, Poached and Shredded

Chicken that has been poached and shredded is used for fillings for tacos and enchiladas, as a topping for tostadas and other *antojitos,* or even for stuffing poblano chiles or adding to soups.

You could certainly cook a whole chicken and use the white and dark meat, but it is probably more practical to use chicken breasts. For the best flavor buy a large, whole, unskinned breast on the bone. There is nothing more unappetizing than a boneless, skinless breast, especially if it has been frozen to death beforehand. I like to poach the chicken in a well-flavored chicken broth to enhance the flavor and then salt it well before using to balance the blandness of the tortilla.

To prepare the chicken

Makes about 2½ cups (625ml) shredded chicken

5 cups (1.250L) chicken broth or water (if using water, add a small piece of onion, a garlic clove, and salt)

1 large whole chicken breast, about 1½ pounds (675g), halved

Salt to taste

Bring the chicken broth to a simmer, add the chicken, cover the pan, and cook over low heat until just tender, about 25 minutes. Don't overcook because the cooking process will continue as the breast sits in the broth. Set aside to cool off in the broth. Strain, reserving the broth for a soup or stew.

When cool enough to handle, remove skin and bone and shred the meat—not too finely or you will lose flavor. Add a little bit of the skin and season well.

Caldo de Pollo

CHICKEN BROTH

A good chicken broth is absolutely indispensable for many Mexican soups, rice, and stews; no canned or powdered substitutes should be seen in the kitchen of a cook who prides herself on her food. After all, it is easy enough to buy lots of chicken pieces, cook them a long time, and then freeze for future use. Some people, like the microwave crowd, protest they don't have time. It's like breadmaking: you don't have to sit and watch! You can even use a slow cooker and leave it all night on low.

When I first went to Mexico in 1957 we could buy, in any market, good fat hens that made the most delicious, strong chicken broth. That's where I learned to draw the chicken and use all its parts (except the liver): intestines, head, feet, and unlaid eggs included. Now Mexico has followed the practices of its neighbor to the north, and the flavor of the chickens is not what it used to be. There are, of course, some exceptions. When I last went to Campeche, very large, fat—and whitish, not yellow—hens were still available for the local fortified stews. Of course, in the United States there are organic chickens like those from Sonoma, and I am sure other parts of the country, but the main supermarket chicken is pretty soft and tasteless. But you have to make the best of it. So use a very large quantity of giblets, backs, and wings instead of a large boiling fowl—if such a thing still exists! This is a basic white stock, the simpler the better.

How to make chicken stock

Makes about 14 cups (3.5L) chicken broth
5 pounds (2.5kg) chicken carcasses, trimmed of excess fat
1 pound (450g) giblets, trimmed
1 medium white onion, roughly chopped
3 garlic cloves, unpeeled, roughly chopped
Sea salt (optional)

Crack the main bones of the chicken, chop the carcasses into pieces, and put into a stockpot with the giblets, onion, and garlic. Cover with plenty of water; it should come at least 5 inches (13cm) above the level of the bones. Bring to a boil, lower the heat, and simmer for about 4 hours. (If you are in a hurry, then use a pressure cooker with less water and cook at low pressure for 1 hour). Set aside to cool. It is better to leave the bones in overnight to increase the gelatinous content, providing you have a very cold place or room in the refrigerator.

Strain the broth, add the optional salt, bring to a boil, cool, and skim off the fat. Use as necessary or measure into ice-cube trays and freeze. When the cubes are solid, pack into freezer bags and store marked with the amount in each package and the date the broth was made.

Jaiba

CRAB

The delicate flesh of the small blue crab caught in the Gulf of Mexico is very much appreciated and used in many different ways: stuffed, in chilpachole, as a filling for empanadas, as a topping for tostadas, or made into a thin savory cake, among other uses. The large whitish crab, *cangrejo*, is found farther down the coast and used particularly in the cooking of Tabasco and Campeche. The only disadvantage of the blue is that it is time-consuming to clean, particularly if you take care to use all the parts that enrich the white flesh: the crab fat and eggs.

Female crabs can be distinguished by the orange tip on the claws and are preferable, providing they are not caught in the closed season when they reproduce. You can also distinguish them by the heart-shaped breastplate, as opposed to the long skinny one on the males.

You should always buy crabs while they are still alive and kicking; they deteriorate very quickly, especially in hot weather. Kill the crabs by immersing them in boiling, salted water; continue cooking for about 5 minutes only. To check for doneness, break one open and see if the flesh is opaque and flakes. Strain them immediately. (I do not believe in cooling them off in cold water because this impairs the flavor.)

Clean the crabs over a bowl to catch the juices. Pry off the main shell. Scrape out the creamy fat. Remove the orange-colored eggs and save. Pick out the body meat, then crack the thick part of the claw and remove the meat. Discard the blackish colored sac.

Octopus

When buying a fresh octopus, or one that has been frozen, choose one that is less than 2 pounds (900g). It will, generally, require less cooking, depending, I am told, on where it has been fished.

You can buy octopus already cleaned, but never buy one that has been precooked—it usually means overcooked. Of course, it is more interesting to learn what the animal is all about and clean it yourself, providing you are not cooking for three hundred people. You will need a firm grip and a razor-sharp knife. In the center, at the base of the tentacles, you will see the beak—a transparent, tortoise shell-like piece. Make a slash across and squeeze it out, along with the hardish ball underneath, called *piedra,* or "stone," in Mexico. It is said that if you leave it in, the octopus will remain tough despite any amount of cooking.

Then cut out the eyes and discard. Then either turn the body inside out or cut it open and carefully peel out the membranous sac that holds the interior organs of the animal. If you want to save the ink, carefully cut open the slimy mass and find the roundish ink sac. Pierce it over a small bowl containing 2 tablespoons mild white vinegar.

To test for cooking time, cut off a small piece of a tentacle and the body and toss them into hot olive oil. If after a few minutes they are crisp-tender, then proceed with the recipe. If they are still very hard, then add liquid to the pan, cover, and cook over low heat, checking from time to time until you have the desired texture, about 20 minutes.

Dried Shrimp

The most popular use for these delicious dried shrimp is for making the Lenten dish *romeritos,* fritters of powdered dried shrimp in beaten egg. They are served in a mole or other regional sauce. Also popular in central Mexico is a strong and pungent broth made of dried shrimp; it is served at the beginning of a meal and also recommended in the morning for a hangover.

In the Isthmus of Tehuantepec, where the majority of these shrimp are caught, cooked briefly, salted, and partially dried in the sun, they provide an indispensable part of the local diet—used as a snack; in soups, rice, and tamales; with beans; in a pipián; or as *guetavingui* (baked cakes of corn masa). In the markets there, in the city of Oaxaca, and in parts of neighboring Chiapas, they are an appetizing orangey color and are still moist. However, those sent to other parts of the country and exported are completely dried and highly salted.

To prepare the shrimps, remove the head and discard the black eyes, which are very hard. The heads are full of flavor and can be ground and used to flavor dishes that include the shrimps. Then remove the legs and, if you are very fussy, the tail, but leave the skin intact. Soak the shrimp very briefly in cold water; if left too long, the flavor is lost.

I don't recommend buying packages of preground shrimps, because they have such a high percentage of salt. Nor do the little bare shrimps packed in Asia—with an attractive orange color—begin to compare in flavor with the Mexican product.

See recipes in *My Mexico:* pozole, page 56; molito, page 414; *guetavingui,* page 407; rice, page 392; and tamales, page 415. In *Essentials: consomé,* page 134; and fritters, page 22. In *The Art:* broth, page 113; fritters, pages 202, 203, and 205; with white beans, page 112.

RICE
AND
PASTA

Arroz

RICE

Rice was introduced into Mexico quite early in the colonial period, brought from the Philippines to Acapulco on the famous trading galleon, the *Nao de China*. An important crop in Mexico, it forms an integral part of the everyday diet.

A long-grain rice is always used in Mexico for the most popular of the *sopa secas*—a serving of rice—which is served as a separate course, usually between the soup and main dish, like pasta in Italy. It is often accompanied by a tomato, green tomato, or chile table sauce. Do not use converted or precooked rice in these recipes, or for any Mexican rice dish. These types of rice will never produce the right texture.

The method of cooking rice would seem rather complicated for those used to steaming it only, but it has a very special flavor, almost addictive. The most popular of all is rice seasoned with a tomato purée. In parts of the south, and the coastal areas, it is more usual to have white rice, and then one comes across the occasional green rice, flavored with chiles and herbs.

When cooking these recipes with different brands of rice in other countries, it is best to be conservative about the amount of liquid until you know just how much the type of rice you are using will absorb. I like to cook and serve rice in a Mexican cazuela, but that is not possible for most cooks. Make sure you have a heavy-bottomed pan because the rice tends to stick and scorch unless you are very careful. I have given dimensions for pots here because the shape is important: too deep a pot and the rice will likely be mushy; too wide and the rice will cook too quickly and not be tender.

All the rice dishes can be prepared several hours ahead and reheated. Leftovers can be frozen for a couple of weeks without losing flavor. But do not thaw before reheating; put the frozen rice directly into the pan so you do not lose the flavor in the melting juices.

Arroz a la Mexicana

MAKES ABOUT 6 SERVINGS

1½ cups (375ml) long-grain white rice
¼ to ⅓ cup (63–83ml) vegetable oil
8 ounces (225g) tomatoes, roughly
    chopped, about 1½ cups (375ml)
1 tablespoon roughly chopped white
    onion
1 garlic clove, roughly chopped

About 3½ cups (875ml) chicken broth
1 small carrot, trimmed, scraped, and
    thinly sliced (optional)
2 tablespoons peas (optional)
1 large sprig parsley (optional)
2 serrano chiles, left whole (optional)
Salt to taste

For this quantity you will need a flameproof pan about 4 inches (10cm) deep and 9 inches (23cm) across. Pour hot water to cover over the rice and let soak for about 5 minutes. Strain, rinse in cold water, and strain again. Be sure to shake the strainer well to remove any excess water. Do not do this step ahead of time or the rice will become too damp.

Heat the oil in the pan and stir in the rice—it should sizzle as it touches the oil. Stir until the grains are evenly coated and continue frying over medium heat until they sound brittle and are just starting to turn golden, about 10 minutes. Tip the pan to one side and drain off the excess oil.

Meanwhile, put the tomatoes, onion, and garlic into a blender jar and blend until smooth. Stir the purée into the rice and continue frying over fairly high heat, scraping the bottom of the pan to avoid sticking, until the mixture has been absorbed, about 5 minutes.

Add the broth and the optional ingredients; stir the rice well, adjust the salt, cover the pan, and cook over medium heat until all the broth has been absorbed—airholes will probably form. Carefully dig to the bottom of the rice with a fork to see if any moisture remains; if so, then continue cooking over low heat for a few minutes more. Set aside, still covered, to give the rice a chance to continue steaming evenly for about 15 minutes.

When serving, gently stir the rice from the bottom with a fork because the seasonings tend to sink to the bottom.

NOTE: *Mexican cooks never stir the rice when it is cooking—they say it will become mushy and stick to the bottom of the pan.*

BELOW, FROM TOP: FRYING RICE WITH THE PURÉE; ADDING LIQUID; THE FINISHED RICE.

ABOVE, FROM TOP: STIRRING AND FRYING THE RICE; ADDING TOMATO PURÉE.

Arroz Blanco

WHITE RICE

White rice can be made with chicken broth, and with peas and carrots added for color and crunch, but in the tropical coastal areas it is much more likely to be cooked with water and served with some fried plantain on top. A typical central Oaxacan custom is for it to be served with slices of a raw, fruity banana eaten raw, known as plátano de seda.

Some cooks blend the onion and garlic with a little water and add to the rice in the frying stage so that the flavors are evenly distributed, while others follow the more usual way of sautéing them, finely chopped, with the rice at the beginning.

With notable exceptions this rice is served alone as a sopa seca, *or accompanied by a table sauce. Like most rice dishes, this can be prepared ahead and reheated, or kept frozen for about two weeks without losing too much texture and flavor.*

MAKES 6 SERVINGS

1½ cups (375ml) long-grain white rice
¼ cup to ⅓ cup (63–83ml) vegetable oil
1 tablespoon finely chopped white onion
1 garlic clove, finely chopped
About 3½ cups (875ml) water or chicken
  broth

1 small carrot, trimmed, scraped, and
  thinly sliced (optional)
2 tablespoons peas (optional)
1 large sprig parsley or cilantro (optional)
2 serrano chiles, left whole (optional)
Sea salt to taste

For this quantity you will need a flameproof pan about 4 inches (10 cm) deep and 9 inches (23cm) across. Pour hot water over the rice and let it soak for 5 minutes. Strain, rinse in cold water, and strain again. Be sure to shake the strainer well to remove any excess water. Do not do this step ahead of time or the rice will become too damp.

Heat the oil in the pan and stir in the rice—it should sizzle as it touches the oil. Stir until the grains are evenly coated and continue to fry over medium heat for 5 minutes. Add the onion and garlic and continue frying until they sound brittle, just before they turn golden, about 10 minutes. Tip the pan to one side and spoon out the excess oil.

Add the water or broth and optional ingredients along with the salt. Cover the pan and cook over medium heat until all the liquid has been absorbed—small holes will appear in the rice. Carefully dig to the bottom of the rice to see if any moisture remains; if so, then continue cooking over low heat for a few minutes more. Set aside still covered to give the rice a chance to steam and swell for about 15 minutes.

When serving, gently turn the rice over with a fork from the bottom, where the seasoning tends to sink.

NOTE: *Mexican cooks never stir the rice when it is cooking—they say it will become mushy and stick to the bottom of the pan.*

Arroz Verde

GREEN RICE

There are various recipes for green rice—that is, rice cooked with a purée of greens and mild chiles (see The Art, *page 123;* My Mexico, *page 300; and* Essentials, *page 163), although it is not as popular as the normal tomato-flavored or white rice. While inventive cooks add other flavors—puréed cilantro or epazote—arguably the cooks of Oaxaca add more intriguing flavors to their rice with the use of herbs, either chepil, hierba de conejo, or piojito (see pages 82, 85, and 90)—which are not puréed.*

Follow the instructions for Arroz Blanco (opposite), adding 1 cup puréed herbs and chiles after the first stage of frying and reduce over high heat as you would the tomato purée in Arroz a la Mexicana (page 150).

Morisqueta

According to the dictionary, the word morisqueta *could mean "a Moorish trick," a "grimace," or "plain boiled rice"—enough to make some people grimace! But it makes a great foil for a rather strong seasoning (see* The Art, *pages 125, 260, or 343). Of course, a rice cooker would be fine, but, being a traditionalist, I cook my morisqueta in a small Mexican clay pot, an olla. It has a reduced neck and broad shoulders, which allow the steam to fall back into the pot and help keep the rice moist.*

MAKES 2½ TO 3 CUPS (625–750ML)

8 ounces (225g) long-grain white rice	Small pinch of sea salt (optional)
2 cups (500ml) cold water	

Put the rice into a bowl. Cover with hot water and leave to soak for about 5 minutes. Rinse in cold water and drain well.

Put the 2 cups water into the pot and stir in the rice (and optional salt). Cover the pot, bring the water to a simmer, and continue cooking over low heat until all the water is absorbed, about 15 minutes. With a fork, carefully fluff it up from the bottom, re-cover the pan, and set aside off the heat for the rice to absorb every bit of moisture, about 15 minutes more.

NOTE: *Every type of rice is different, so you may have to adjust cooking time and amount of water. The rice may stick together in lumps. If so, let it get cold and separate with a fork before reheating.*

Pasta

Italian-type pasta was introduced into Mexico by the Spaniards quite early on in the colonial period, according to researchers Cristina Barros and Marco Buenrostro. One of the early references is in a cookbook by Fray Geronimo de San Pelayo, written in 1780 in Mexico but not published there until 2000. In a Spanish cookbook dated 1611 by Sebastian de Covarrubias, there is a description of *fideos* and *macarrones,* saying that the former word came from the Latin *fides, fidum* referring to the thin strings of a string instrument.

In the earliest days it was probably eaten only in more affluent homes and later in elegant restaurants. Today, however, pasta is everyday food, both popular and economical. It is prepared as either a *sopa seca*—served as a pasta course would be in an Italian meal—or a *sopa aguada,* a soup. The former would most probably be angel hair pasta, *fideos,* which is fried and then cooked in a tomato sauce until almost dry; or spaghetti, *espagueti,* or elbow macaroni, *codos,* cooked in water and served with cream and cheese, a tomato sauce, or both. For a soup, *fideos* or little figures like stars, *estellitas,* and alphabet, *letras,* shapes are fried and then put into a broth seasoned with tomato. (The frying part scandalizes my Roman priest neighbors!) A few recipes for these pastas can be found in *Essentials,* pages 121 and 160; *The Art,* pages 128, 129, and 130; and *My Mexico,* page 519.

SPICES, AROMATICS,

AROMATICS,

AND

SWEETENERS

Spices (as well as aromatic herbs and leaves) have been used for flavoring and coloring food in Mexico since pre-Columbian times. The earliest were the seeds of achiote and allspice, various chiles, and the dried narrow pod of the vanilla orchid—all natives of Mexico and tropical America. After the Spanish invasion, cloves, cinnamon, and pepper were brought into Mexico through the voyages of the famous *Nao de China* (a Spanish merchant galleon), which traveled between the Philippines and the Pacific port of Acapulco. Coriander, saffron, and, later, cumin were introduced from the Mediterranean.

I have also seen wizened roots of ginger that are used sparingly in some moles in Oaxaca and Chiapas and in *tatemado,* the regional dish of Colima. In the mountains of San Luis Potosí another small, wizened root, brown-skinned and with pale orange-colored flesh—camote de azafran (*Curcuma longa,* a native plant of India)— is used in a local stew called *caldo loco.*

Generally speaking, spices are used very sparingly in Mexico so that their flavors do not overpower those of the other ingredients. For instance, when a Mexican cook is describing a recipe, she will specify four peppercorns or two cloves, and hold up her fingers to show you how much cinnamon bark to use. And those quantities may be for a mole or cooked sauce for six or eight servings. One of the great failings of commercial Mexican food in the United States, whether in restaurants or frozen or canned, is that the spicing is uneven and far too strong. Undoubtedly, commercial powdered spices have been used for convenience' sake but with far too liberal a hand.

Ideally, whole spices should be bought and stored in airtight containers in a dry environment (except, of course, for baking, unless you do as I do and periodically grind a fresh batch of whole spices for that purpose only). Their fragrance and strength will last at least two years, and even then, toasting them slightly in a small skillet over medium heat for a minute or so will work wonders apart from adding an enticing aroma to your kitchen.

When adding spices to a blender jar with other ingredients for a sauce, like a mole, I crush them roughly first in a small molcajete or mortar. Or when feasible, you may add the crushed spices, with garlic or whatever, and blend them first with a small quantity of water before adding the more bulky ingredients. Of course, there is always an exception to whatever generalization you care to make, and in the spectrum of Mexican regional cooking, Yucatecan seasonings provide that exception. Their seasoning pastes, which are known as *recados* (as opposed to *recaudos,* which is a different mixture of ingredients), consist of spices ground together in a concentrated form and diluted, generally but not exclusively, with the juice of bitter oranges. Small quantities may be added to broths, or spread over meats or fish, and left to season.

SPICES

Achiote

The annatto seed (of the tree *Bixa orellana*), called *achiote* in Mexico, is used for coloring and flavoring certain regional dishes in the south and southeast parts of the country. This small tree, a native of tropical America, produces a brown, rough-skinned, oval husk about 1½ inches (3.75cm) long, the inside of which is packed with very small seeds covered with a layer of matte red pigment (see photo above). There is another varietal of this tree that gives a slightly larger, smoother brown husk with seeds that are orange rather than red. However, I have never seen this used with great enthusiasm.

There are two ways in which this seed is used. In the Yucatán Peninsula, the whole seed is ground together with other spices and formed into a reddish seasoning paste, called *recado rojo* (see page 164). In Chiapas, Tabasco, and the Isthmus of Oaxaca, the achiote is used in a much purer, more concentrated form. The seeds are boiled in water for some hours until the water has evaporated, leaving a concentrated red dye. This form of achiote is much more expensive, but naturally gives a deeper color and stronger flavor to the food.

Allspice

The allspice berry comes from a very graceful tree *(Pimenta dioica),* which belongs to the myrtle family and is indigenous to tropical America. The tree grows wild in the lowland areas bordering the Gulf of Mexico. Its highly aromatic, elongated leaves—a shiny mid- to dark-green in color—are also used to flavor dishes in Veracruz, Tabasco, Campeche, Yucatán, and Chiapas—much as Mexican "bay leaves" are used farther north. The berries are picked and dried when they are mature but not fully ripened. When dried they are mid- to dark brown in color, and while they can vary considerably in size, an average one is less than ¼ inch (5–6mm) in diameter.

The allspice berry is known by various regional names in Mexico: *pimienta gorda* (fat pepper), *pimienta de Jamaica* (Jamaican pepper), or, in Tabasco, *pimienta de la tierra* (native pepper). Its Nahuatl name is *xocoxochitl.* It is used either ground with other spices as a seasoning paste or whole in pickles or stews.

If stored in an airtight container, the berries can last for years without deteriorating.

Aniseed

The seed of the anise plant *(Pimpinella anisum), anís* as it is known in Mexico, is generally used whole to flavor dessert syrups or the dough of certain types of semi-sweet yeast rolls, for cakes, and in some regional liquors. One particularly interesting use of these seeds can be found in Hidalgo, where they are often added to both the corn masa and the beans for the bean filling of savory gordas (see *My Mexico,* pages 201–202). A small quantity of the ground seeds is used in some recipes for the sophisticated moles of Puebla and Oaxaca. Curiously, a recipe from a San Luis Potosí cookbook calls for a small quantity of the whole seeds to be used when cooking cauliflower, probably less for flavor than for its carminative properties.

The small stems and feathery leaves of wild anise, or *anise del campo (Tagetes micrantha),* are also used for flavoring more indigenous dishes: atoles in Michoacán, a fresh corn pozole in Guerrero, and to cook with ears of fresh corn in Hidalgo, among other uses.

If stored in an airtight container, the aniseeds may be kept for a few years without deteriorating.

Cinnamon

Cinnamon, or *canela* as it is called in Mexico, is the flaky bark of a tree *(Cinnamomum verum,* formerly *zeylanicum)* native to Sri Lanka and southwestern India. Small pieces of the rolled cinnamon bark are used whole with cooked fruits, in dessert syrups, or in café de olla. Ground with other spices, cinnamon is used in very small quantities for seasoning meats and stews, and in moles. Powdered, it is sprinkled over the surface of desserts and sweetmeats.

Nobody in Mexico would consider using the hard-barked cassia that often passes for cinnamon in the United States, for it is less aromatic, more difficult to grind, and darker in color. The real cinnamon is not difficult to find; most supermarkets now carry it—just make sure you buy the right type. Spice shops specializing in ingredients from Ceylon and India often have large sacks with impressively thick, long pieces of cinnamon sticking out. But you can always find it marked "canela" in Mexican markets in the United States. But beware—even then the wrong type can creep in and be incorrectly labeled.

Properly stored in airtight containers, cinnamon bark will last for several years without deteriorating.

Cloves

Cloves are the aromatic dried flower buds of a tree *(Syzygium aromaticum)* indigenous to the Molucca Islands, grown in large quantities in the Caribbean and in Zanzibar. In Mexico, they are called *clavos,* or *clavos de especia* (to make sure you don't mean "nails," which they actually resemble). They are used whole for pickles, or cooked with fruit, but more often they are ground with other spices and sparingly used for seasoning moles and other cooked sauces.

Instructions in Mexican recipes are for adding two or three cloves, even for a rather large quantity of sauce.

Always buy whole cloves and keep them in tightly sealed containers.

Coriander Seeds

The small, round, light brown seeds of the coriander plant *(Coriandrum sativum),* *semillas de cilantro,* as they are known in Mexico, are used whole, mostly in pickling, or ground with other spices for some of the more sophisticated moles of Puebla and Oaxaca. According to cookbooks written at the end of the nineteenth century, coriander seeds were used much more frequently than they are today in recipes with decidedly Spanish roots.

The plant, a native of the Mediterranean, was introduced into Mexico by the Spaniards and the green leaves—cilantro—have become an indispensable part of many regional recipes.

Properly stored in airtight containers, the seeds can be kept for a few years without deteriorating.

Cumin

Small, slender, light-brown cumin seeds, known as *cominos*, are used ground—often with other spices—in small quantities in the cooked sauces and seasoning pastes of many parts of Mexico. In the north, especially Nuevo León, they are used much more liberally and their flavor sometimes predominates in sauces or bean dishes.

The plant *(Cuminum cyminum)*, a native of the Mediterranean, was cultivated by the Minoans as far back as the third century B.C. In Mexican recipes, the quantities given are for whole seeds, so always buy them whole, never ground, and store them in an airtight container. They will last for several years without deteriorating.

Garlic

Garlic *(Allium sativum)*, in Spanish, *ajo*, was brought to Mexico by the Spaniards. It is not, as many people would believe, used in great quantities in traditional dishes, except where those dishes have strong Spanish roots: chicken or seafood *en ajillo*, sopa de ajo, and the like. The most fragrant and delicate garlic are purple and have very small heads. In the more traditional markets of southern Mexico, they are usually sold with their long stalks tied in bunches of different sizes.

Of course, with influences from the United States, and the dictum "bigger is better," the larger producers—in the Bajio, for instance—that grow for export as well as the home market, are changing things. Garlic gets bigger and bigger, and there goes the flavor! Curiously enough, from my very early days in Mexico I remember a type of elephant garlic that was tied into a small circle with red and sold as a lucky charm. It was certainly not for eating.

Peppercorns

Mild black peppercorns known variously in Mexico as *pimienta negra, pimienta chica,* or *pimienta de Castilla* are used in cooking throughout Mexico, but are rarely used as a condiment as, for example, in Europe and the United States. Peppercorns are the fruit of a climbing vine *(Piper nigrum)* native to Madagascar, South India, and Sri Lanka and were introduced into the cuisines of Mexico soon after the Spanish invasion in the sixteenth century.

They are always purchased whole and used whole in pickles and for some meat or fish broths. Peppercorns in small quantities are ground with other spices to season moles and other cooked sauces. However, they are used in much larger amounts for the pungent seasoning pastes, *recados,* of the Yucatán Peninsula (see page 162).

Recados

Yucatecan Seasoning Pastes

The seasoning pastes of Yucatán, known as *recados,* were in years gone by prepared from scratch by each cook, and I have never come across two cooks who give the same quantities for the same *recado.* When I first visited Mérida, the capital city of Yucatán, in 1958, I was intrigued to see market stalls displaying an array of little balls of different colors. There was one for *cochinita pibil,* another for *bifstek,* one called *chilaquil* only for tamales, and yet another for a hearty brothy stew called *salpimentado.* Not much has changed: in one area of Mérida's central market, you can still see those *recados* prepared in front of you and order what you need for the dishes you are cooking that day. The spices are ground, moistened with water, vinegar, or the juice of bitter oranges, and formed into cakes or balls of various sizes and prices.

Cooks outside Yucatán have always had to content themselves with packaged *recados* of inferior quality and flavor owing to substitutes and preservatives. But take heart: you can prepare your own for any particular dish; two variations are given here. But first I want to mention one that I am always asked about, that extraordinary black seasoning paste called *chilmole* (not to be confused with the totally different *chilmole* of Tabasco), popular in Yucatán but virtually unknown or appreciated elsewhere. It is made of a combination of dried local chiles, *chiles secos yucatecos,* burned black and ground with other spices. Commercial pastes are smoothed out with additives, but the real stuff tends to be very slightly gritty.

Chilmole is most famously used for turkey in *relleno negro.* The paste is diluted with bitter orange juice and spread lightly over the skin of the turkey. The turkey is then stuffed with ground pork seasoned with the same paste. I do not have a recipe for this dish, but for the curious cook who wants to season a turkey with it, I suggest you buy the commercial *chilmole,* because the burning of the Yucatecan dried chiles in alcohol, the principal ingredient, should be left to the experts or the most intrepid of aficionados (having nearly choked to death when I attempted to do it).

Here are some general points to remember:

Since relatively large quantities of peppercorns are used for these recipes, make sure you have mild ones—the strong Pondicherry or Egyptian ones will overpower the other seasonings and leave you gasping.

The fragrant "oregano" of Yucatán has a large leaf and is always used dried. It is usually sold when it has been toasted to a medium brown color. If it is not available, substitute the more common Mexican oregano.

These basic seasoning pastes are very strong and should be used diluted, and even then in small quantities: for instance, a very thin smearing on fish and meat that is to be fried or grilled. If possible, season the ingredients well ahead of time or overnight to enhance the flavors.

Always make more than you need of the basic seasonings. Store the rest in the freezer, ready for emergencies; I have kept some up to two years in this way.

Grinding spices, particularly achiote seeds, in these quantities is hard on the blades of an electric spice grinder, so I suggest that you first crush them roughly in a mortar or molcajete, or soak them overnight in a small amount of water, and then grind them in a blender.

When *recados* that contain achiote are diluted in a liquid, they increase in volume as they stand, so you may have to thin them a bit with more liquid before using.

Recado de Toda Clase

The recipe for this basic all-purpose seasoning paste was given to me years ago by Señora Isela Rodriguez in Mérida. You make it in a concentrated form, season it with crushed garlic and salt, and dilute with bitter orange juice or fruit vinegar and achiote when called for by the recipe.

MAKES ½ CUP (125ML) FIRMLY PACKED

4 tablespoons mild peppercorns, crushed
12 whole cloves, crushed
12 whole allspice, crushed
2½ inches (6.5cm) thin cinnamon stick,
    roughly broken

½ teaspoon cumin seeds
4 tablespoons crumbled oregano,
    Yucatecan if possible
Approximately ⅓ cup (83ml) water

Put the spices into an electric coffee or spice grinder and grind as thoroughly as possible. Strain and grind the residue once again. Transfer to a small bowl and add just enough water to mix to a thick paste.

To use Recado de Toda Clase

A portion of this base recipe makes a *recado* that, when diluted, will season about 2½ pounds (about 1kg) chicken pieces, 6 large pork chops, or 6 small steaks.

2 tablespoons *recado de toda clase*
4 garlic cloves, crushed
3 tablespoons bitter orange juice (or use Bitter Orange Substitute, page 110) or
    fruit vinegar (pages 270–271)
Salt to taste

Mix the ingredients together well and smear in a thin layer over the meat and chicken. Set aside to season for several hours, or overnight.

Simple Recado Rojo

This is a simpler recado *for* cochinita pibil *and* pollo pibil *(see* Essentials, *pages 277 and 344). This quantity is sufficient for about 8 pounds (3.6kg) of pork or 4 large chickens.*

MAKES APPROXIMATELY ⅓ CUP (83ML)

4 rounded tablespoons achiote seeds, lightly crushed

2 teaspoons crumbled dried oregano, Yucatecan if possible

1 teaspoon cumin seeds

½ teaspoon mild peppercorns, lightly crushed

12 whole allspice, crushed

Approximately 3 tablespoons water

First grind half the achiote seeds as finely as possible, strain, and grind the residue again. Repeat for the remainder of the seeds. Grind the rest of the spices and mix with the achiote. Stir in the water and mix to make a thick paste. It can be stored in this form for future use. It will keep in the refrigerator for a couple of months, but it is best to freeze it.

To use Simple Recado Rojo

Season 4 pounds (1.8kg) of pork or 2 chickens with half the above *recado* and
10 small garlic cloves, peeled and crushed
Salt to taste
⅓ cup (83ml) bitter orange juice or substitute (page 110)

Spread the diluted *recado* sparingly over the meat or chicken and set aside to season for at least three hours, or overnight.

Saffron

Saffron, or *azafran,* from the plant *Crocus sativus,* is called for in some recipes with strong Spanish influences. Because the price is prohibitive for many cooks, the orange-red stamens of safflower *(Carthamus tinctorius)* are used instead. While they color foods, they do not have the haunting flavor of the real saffron.

Salt

Although most cooks use the more convenient, free-flowing commercial salt, the more traditional ones insist on sea salt, various qualities and textures of which Mexico produces in abundance on the coasts of Baja California, Yucatán, Oaxaca, and elsewhere. And it is cheap. I suppose through NAFTA the sea salt is now being imported into the United States, and I have seen it sold at a much more reasonable price than other imported sea salts.

Mined mineral salts are also available but mostly used for commercial purposes, while a pinkish-hued salt *(sal de A)* is used for making cheeses in the hot country of Michoacán. There are also composite mined salts used in the cooking of parts of Oaxaca, Puebla, and Veracruz to counterbalance the acidity in sauces.

Tequesquite

Tequesquite is a gray mineral salt—combining chloride and sodium carbonate—that was used in pre-Columbian times, and still today by traditional cooks, as a leavening agent for tamales and buñuelos, or to add to the cooking water to soften dried beans and corn. When cooking nopales, cooks often add it to preserve the natural color.

Tequesquite forms a thin brittle crust on the edges of the highland lakes of the Central Valley of Mexico, and the inhabitants of those areas collect it and sell it in the local markets. It varies in quality and is classified accordingly, but the most commonly found resembles gray ash mixed with brittle flakes. Tequesquite can often be found now packaged in Mexican markets, but if you can't find it, use backing powder—referred to as "Royal" in Mexico—as nontraditional cooks in Mexico do.

For some types of tamales a Mexican recipe might call for *agua asentada de tequesquite.* Cooks have different methods of preparing this. My neighbors simply put a small quantity in cold water and leave it to soak. Gradually the particles sink to the bottom of the receptacle, leaving a grayish clear water. Another method is to simmer the tequesquite with the husks of tomatillos.

To prepare tequesquite

Makes enough for about 50 tamales

1 cup (250ml) water
1 rounded teaspoon powdered tequesquite
4 tomatillo husks (optional)

Put the ingredients into a small, nonreactive pan and bring to a boil. Set aside for the powder to settle, about 2 hours. Pass the clear water through cheesecloth.

SWEETENERS

Sugar

Mexicans in general have an enormous sweet tooth, which is reflected in the quantity of sugar, *azucar,* used in desserts, fruit pastes, and candies. Although in turmoil at the present time, the sugar industry in Mexico is capable of producing an enormous amount of sugar: the refined granulated white, a brown granulated known as *moscabada* (which is not very popular), and *piloncillo, panela,* or *panocha,* which are either cones or cakes of delicious, dark unrefined sugar.

Confectioners' sugar, *azucar glas,* is used mostly for decorating cakes and cookies. I, like other traditional cooks, grate the piloncillo and use it for atoles (see *Essentials,* page 455), maiz gruel, and cooking fruits en tacha (see *Essentials,* page 438), wherever possible to enhance flavors and nutritional values.

In tropical areas you can often come across small mills or *trapiches,* many still operated by one family, where a very dark brown, soft panela is made. These round, flattish shapes are sold either in pairs, known as *cabezas,* or in dozens, when they are secured together with broad strips of dried cane stalks. (I have written about one small trapiche near where I live in Michoacán in *My Mexico,* page 14.)

Honey

Mexico is a great producer of honey, and this is a favorite sweetener for a lot of people, especially for herbal teas of which there are innumerable varieties. Honey is also a base for a strong, sugary liquor made in Yucatán called Xbentun.

One of the most incredibly delicious honeys of Mexico—unfortunately named Jungle Honey—is from wild bees in the tropical forest Calakmul in the state of Campeche. The perfume of the flowering trees native to the area is encapsulated in this dark, liquid honey.

Friends of mine in Tabasco also lure and collect the honey of wild bees—one of the rare, naturally organic delights of this shrinking natural world.

MAKING
ANTOJITOS

A*ntojitos,* or "little whims," made of corn masa form an important part of the popular foods in Mexico. There is an enormous variety and most are intrinsically regional. In this chapter I provide a selection of the better known ones.

Antojitos can be so enticing and delicious, but if not properly made, they can be rubbery and bland. Here are some points to remember:

✳ A lot depends on the quality of the masa available (see the chapter on tortillas, page 238), but even with the best, it should be worked as much as possible to aerate it and thus make it more porous. It's impossible to overwork.

✳ If your masa is rather damp and heavy, you may have to add a small amount of baking powder (about 1 teaspoon for 1 cup/250ml masa) to try to leaven the dough a little.

✳ If you have to resort to one of the dry corn products for your masa (see page 218), and the dough cracks as you use it, you may have to add a little ordinary flour.

There is no evidence that in pre-Hispanic times any type of fat was used in corn masas, but adding a small percentage of lard does improve the taste, texture, and keeping qualities. They can also be reheated more successfully. Corn masa and pork lard have an affinity, and when you fry in lard both the flavor and the texture of the masa is enhanced. Obviously, you will use oil when expedient.

While without a doubt *antojitos* are best eaten as soon as they are made—pan-to-mouth food—I suggest in each recipe whether they can be reheated. Generally speaking, a fried *antojito* can be more successfully reheated on an ungreased comal or griddle, or in a toaster oven (it is not worth heating a large oven). If the *antojito* has not been fried but simply cooked on a comal, then it is best to warm through on a greased comal over low heat. *Never* use the microwave; it will toughen the dough and detract from the flavor.

When you are frying *antojitos*—for example, molotes—just put a minimum of lard or oil to cover the bottom of the pan and add more by degrees as necessary. When frying, set the *antojitos* well apart in the skillet so that they can brown evenly.

Most *antojitos* are not large in size, with the exception of the pellizcadas of Catemaco, Veracruz; the huaraches of Michoacán and the state of Mexico; the empanadas of Oaxaca; and some of the gordas of Aguascalientes.

For proportions, figure 1 cup (250ml) corn masa weighs between 9 and 9½ (255–270g) ounces. If you take 1 heaped cup, you should have enough dough for twelve 1¼-inch (3.25-cm) balls. However, if it is too nerve-racking, use 1½ cups (375ml) and have a little left over.

When making *antojitos*, divide the dough and form the balls first; while you are working with one, cover the rest with a slightly damp cloth to prevent a crust forming.

You will find it helpful to read the chapter on making tortillas (page 238) if you are a newcomer to corn masa. The techniques described there are essential to making *antojitos*.

CLOCKWISE, FROM FAR LEFT: GORDITAS, CHALUPAS, MOLOTES, AND QUESADILLAS.

Chalupas

"Little Boats"

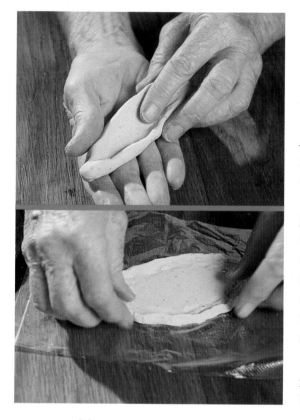

The antojitos *of tortilla masa called* chalupas, *or* chalupitas, *were probably named for the little canoelike boats that were used in the narrow waterways or chinampas, the floating gardens in Xochimilco, not far from Mexico City. In fact, they are either flat and oval or canoe shaped and often filled with shredded chicken and seasoned with a green sauce, topped with chopped onion and crumbled queso fresco.*

There are two ways of forming them: either by pressing out an oval shape and pinching up the edge to form a ridge or making a canoe shape in thicker masa. But there are always exceptions, and it is curious that in Puebla, about 125 km to the southeast, chalupas are round, probably an influence from Chilapa, Guerrero, where they are small, concave circles of crisp dough.

FORMING CHALUPAS: METHOD ONE (TOP) AND METHOD TWO.

MAKES 12 CHALUPAS

1 heaped cup (280ml), about 10 ounces (280g), Tortilla Masa (page 241)
Melted lard or vegetable oil, for reheating

THE TOPPING
1½ cups (375ml) loosely packed, cooked and shredded chicken (page 144)

¾ cup (188ml) Salsa Verde (page 204)
About ⅓ cup (83ml) finely chopped white onion
About ⅓ cup (83ml) crumbled queso fresco

Work the masa well until it is soft and smooth and divide into twelve equal parts. Roll each part into a ball about 1¼ inches (3.13cm) in diameter and cover with a damp cloth.

recipe continues on next page

METHOD ONE: Warm an ungreased comal over medium heat. Taking one ball of the dough, roll into a cylinder about 3 inches (7.5cm) long. Press out in a tortilla press lined with plastic bags, but not too hard, until you have a thin oval shape about 4 inches (10cm) long. Remove the top plastic bag, and as though you were making a tortilla, placing the dough on the fingers of your left or right hand, peel off the second bag. Place the dough carefully onto the warmed comal and cook over medium heat until the underside of the dough is opaque and speckled with brown, about 2 minutes. Turn the chalupa over and cook on the second side until speckled with brown, for 4 minutes, and then remove and pinch up a ridge around the edge. Replace on the comal with the first side down and continue cooking until the dough is firm, about 2 minutes more.

The dough will be soft inside with a thin crusty surface. Fill with the shredded chicken and dress with the sauce, onion, and cheese.

METHOD TWO: Warm a lightly greased comal over medium heat. Roll a ball of the masa into a cylinder about 3 inches (7.5cm) in length, and with your index finger (as shown), press down to form a hollow in the center of the masa and tapering at the end like a small canoe. Place on the warmed comal bottom down and cook until the masa is opaque and slightly speckled with brown, about 4 minutes. Turn the chalupa over and cook on the hollowed side for a further 4 minutes, or until the dough is cooked but soft inside with a slightly crusty surface.

Fill and dress the chalupas; you will need half the quantities given in the list above.

NOTE: *Like all masa antojitos these are best eaten the moment they are cooked, but this may not be practical. So make them ahead of time and keep them covered— unfilled—with a damp cloth. Reheat gently in the melted lard or oil and then fill and serve. I do not recommend freezing (although some people do it) because it tends to toughen the masa or it disintegrates when defrosted.*

Chochoyotes

Small Dumplings

Chochoyotes *is the name given to small dumplings of central Oaxaca that have a deep indentation in the masa to ensure even cooking. They are enriched either with asiento, which gives a nice crunch and flavor to the masa, or pork lard and added to some soups, moles, or beans to give more substance and calories. In part of Veracruz they are formed in the same way and referred to graphically as* ombligitos, *or "little belly buttons."*

There are some regional variations for these "dumplings": in Emiliano Zapata, Tabasco, the masa is colored with achiote and shaped like an elongated snail (see photograph in My Mexico*), which belies their name* bolitas—*"little balls." In a dish of beans typical of Xico, Veracruz,* xonequi, *the little round balls of masa—true bolitas—are enriched with lard and seasoned with epazote and sometimes onion. And in Chiapas, a soup of chipilin (or chepil; see page 82) traditionally includes bolitas that are fried before adding to the broth, to name a few examples. I am giving here the simplest recipe in which chochoyotes are included, but do refer you to Sopa de Guias in* My Mexico, *page 401, and Amarillo and Chichilo Negro, both in* The Art, *pages 232 and 300, for other options. If you are using asiento, try it first, because it may be fully salted and extra salt in the masa may not be necessary. No, I am afraid there are no acceptable substitutions for the fat. Oils or vegetable lard just won't do it.*

MAKES ABOUT 18 1¼-INCH (3-CM) CHOCHOYOTES

1 cup (250ml), about 9½ ounces (270g), Tortilla Masa (page 241)

2 tablespoons asiento (see page 31) or lard
Sea salt to taste

Mix the masa, asiento, and salt well and divide into about eighteen small pieces. Roll each into an even ball about 1 inch (2.5cm) in diameter. Taking one of the balls in the palm of your hand, rotate the index finger of your other hand until you have formed a round indentation in the center—this allows for more even cooking of the dough. Set aside, covered with a damp cloth, while you form the rest. They are now ready for cooking in one of the dishes mentioned.

Frijoles Negros con Chochoyotes

BLACK BEANS WITH DUMPLINGS

For many campesino *families this is served as a main dish with corn tortillas, but it can also be a soup course, or even to accompany some grilled meat. The black beans for this Oaxacan recipe are often flavored with hierba de conejo (see page 85), but also epazote or avocado leaf (see pages 84 and 87).*

MAKES 6 SERVINGS

⅓ cup (83ml) water
6 sprigs hierba de conejo or epazote,
    or 4 avocado leaves, the latter toasted
    until crisp
2 chiles pasilla de Oaxaca, seeded and
    toasted, or 4 chipotle mora, toasted
    with seeds
3 garlic cloves, toasted and peeled

2 tablespoons lard or vegetable oil
3 thick slices medium white onion
About 3½ to 4 cups (875ml to 1L) (with
    broth) Frijoles Negros de Olla
    (page 97)
1½ cups (375ml) water
Salt to taste
1 recipe Chochoyotes (page 173)

Put the ⅓ cup (83ml) water into a blender jar, add the herbs, and blend well with the chiles and peeled garlic.

    Heat the lard in a small skillet and fry the onion until golden. Add the blended ingredients and fry to reduce and season for about 2 minutes. Add to the cooked beans with the remaining 1½ cups (375ml) water. Adjust the seasoning and bring to a simmer; continue simmering for about 5 minutes. Gradually add the chochoyotes, making sure that the beans do not begin to boil or the masa of the chochoyotes will disintegrate. Simmer until the chochoyotes float to the surface and are cooked through, about 15 minutes. Serve the soup in deep bowls with plenty of broth.

NOTE: *You can cook the whole dish well ahead up to the point of adding the chocho-yotes. But if you cook and season the beans a day ahead, the broth will thicken considerably and you will need to dilute it with extra water. The seasoned beans and broth can be frozen for about one month.*

Gorditas

"LITTLE FAT ONES"

There are so many masa "fantasies," as I like to call antojitos, *named* gordas *or* gorditas *that it would be impossible to give them all here. But the better known ones are those that are like fried inflated tortillas, often seasoned with black bean paste from Veracruz—akin to the salbutes of Yucatán and Campeche. Then there are the small disks of dough stuffed with beans from the Coatepec area of Veracruz (see* My Mexico, *page 293) and the better known thick disks of dough from farther north, in Michoacán and Aguascalientes, among other places, that are cut open and stuffed with shredded meats or chicharrón, with the indispensable chopped onion and cilantro.*

Here is a recipe from Michoacán. (One of my helpers, Guadalupe, makes them small and almost delicate—rather like little flying saucers.) They should be really well stuffed as their name implies.

MAKES 12 3-INCH (7.5-CM) GORDITAS

1 pound (450g) Tortilla Masa (page 241),
   about 2 scant cups (480ml)
1 tablespoon lard
Sea salt to taste
Melted lard or oil, for reheating

THE STUFFING
2½ to 3 cups (625–750ml) cooked and
   shredded beef (see page 138)
½ cup (125ml) finely chopped
   white onion
⅔ cup (166ml) loosely packed, roughly
   chopped cilantro
Sea salt to taste
⅔ cup (166ml) Salsa de Jitomate (page
   200) or Salsa Verde (page 204)

Mix the masa, 1 tablespoon lard, and salt well, working it as much as possible to aerate the dough. Divide the dough into twelve pieces and roll each into a ball 1¾ to 2 inches (about 5cm) in diameter.

Warm an ungreased comal over low heat.

Flatten one of the balls into a cake about ¼ inch (6mm) thick and about 3 inches (7.5cm) in diameter, and cook on

FROM TOP: FORMING A GORDITA; COOKING GORDITAS
AND TLACOYOS.

recipe continues on next page

the comal until the underside is opaque and speckled with brown, about 4 minutes. Turn the gordita over and cook on the second side for a further 4 minutes, then back again for 2 minutes on each side until the dough is cooked through but still soft; the outside should be slightly crusty. Slit the gordita horizontally about three-fourths of the way through and proceed with shaping and cooking the rest of the gorditas.

When all the gorditas are cooked, heat a little lard, just enough to lightly cover the bottom of the skillet, and heat the gorditas through on medium for about a minute on each side.

Mix the shredded meat, onion, cilantro, and salt to taste and stuff each one with about ¼ cup (63ml)—it should be very well stuffed. Add about 2 teaspoons of the sauce and serve immediately—you will most probably need both hands to eat it.

NOTE: *Like the other* antojitos, *ideally these should be eaten as soon as they are made, but this is not always practical. If you make them ahead, keep them—unstuffed—under a damp towel and reheat in the melted lard. Then stuff and serve them. I don't recommend freezing them, as the thickish dough tends to be tough and may disintegrate when defrosted.*

Molotes

Molotes are bobbin-shaped antojitos *typical of part of the Sierra Norte de Puebla, the north of Veracruz, and the valley of Oaxaca.*

In the Sierra, they are made of a tortilla dough enriched with very little pork lard and seasoned with salt. These molotes are either filled with shredded beef or chorizo with potato, then fried and served in a light tomato sauce, with shredded lettuce and a dry, regional cheese from the Huasteca, queso de palma—the name comes from the palm frond in which it is wrapped for sale in the markets. In the Papantla area of Veracruz, molotes are filled with cooked and chopped pork seasoned predominantly with oregano.

In Oaxaca, molotes are made with a slightly richer masa and filled with chorizo and potato. They are fried and served (you are given a choice) with either a guacamole or a thickish sauce of beans flavored with avocado leaf, shredded lettuce and radish, and a touch of chile de árbol or pasilla (de Oaxaca) sauce.

I am giving here the recipe for those from the Sierra Norte de Puebla.

MAKES 12 4-INCH (10-CM) MOLOTES

1 heaped cup (280ml), about 10 ounces (280g), Tortilla Masa (page 241)
1 tablespoon pork lard
Sea salt to taste
Approximately 1 cup (250ml) cooked and shredded beef (see page 138) or Chorizo y Papa (page 142)

Melted lard or oil, for frying
1 cup (250ml) Salsa de Jitomate Cocida (page 201) diluted with $\frac{1}{2}$ cup (125ml) meat broth
1 cup (250ml) finely shredded lettuce
$\frac{1}{3}$ cup (83ml) grated dry cheese (añejo or romano)

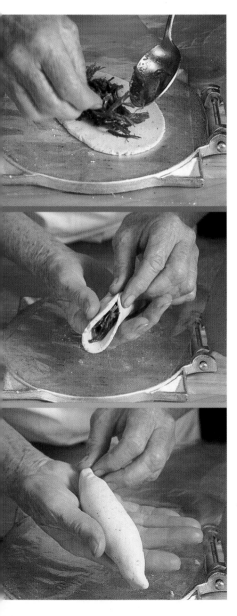

FROM TOP: FILLING, CLOSING, AND FORMING A MOLOTE.

Mix the masa, lard, and salt until smooth and cohesive. Divide into twelve balls about 1¼ inches (3.13cm) in diameter, and cover with a damp cloth so that they do not dry out. Take one of the balls and roll between your hands into a cylinder about 2¼ inches (5.63cm) long and ¾ inch (1.88cm) wide. Press out in a tortilla press lined with plastic bags to a slightly elongated oval.

Put 1 scant tablespoon of the meat down the center, leaving a little space at both ends. Using the plastic bag, or your hands, press the edges together lengthwise and seal to cover the filling completely. Remove the bag and roll the molote between your hands as shown to form a bobbin shape. Proceed with the rest of the balls. They can be prepared several hours ahead up to this stage and kept under a damp cloth until you are ready to fry them.

In a heavy skillet, heat the lard, which should thinly cover the bottom of the pan, and fry over medium heat a few molotes at a time, turning from time to time, until they are lightly browned and crusty, about 8 minutes. Drain on paper towels and serve immediately sitting in a little of the sauce and topped with the lettuce and cheese.

NOTE: *Obviously, it is much better to serve as soon as the molotes are made, but that may not always be practical. So if you have fried them ahead, reheat in a toaster oven for about 10 minutes (to conserve energy, it is not worth heating up a large oven unless, of course, you are baking or cooking something else in it). Or put the molotes into an ungreased skillet, covered, over medium heat until sizzling slightly, about 8 minutes.*

Panuchos

There are many regional antojitos *that combine corn masa with beans, but these panuchos from Yucatán come high up on the list of favorites. They are small inflated tortillas stuffed with a paste of black beans and a slice of hard-cooked egg. They are fried and then traditionally topped with shredded Cochinita Pibil, Pollo Pibil, or Pollo en Escabeche Oriental (see* Essentials, *pages 277, 344, and 345) and topped with onion rings pickled in bitter orange juice. All the crunchy textures and contrasting flavors make for a simply delicious and addictive mouthful. These are usually served as an evening snack in Yucatán. This sort of recipe—if you don't want to be strictly traditional—lends itself to many adaptations. Any leftover cooked meats, or fish for that matter, can be shredded and used. But be sure to make them luscious!*

Surprisingly, once the panuchos are made but not fried, they freeze very well for about two months. Just defrost and fry.

If you want to avoid the frying part of the recipe, then brush the panuchos, made but untrimmed, with a liberal coating of lard or oil and bake them at 375°F (190°C) until slightly crisp around the edge and golden, about 10 minutes.

MAKES 12 PANUCHOS

1¼ cups (313ml), about 11 ounces (300g), Tortilla Masa (page 241)
12 medium-thick slices hard-cooked egg
About ¾ cup (190ml) Frijoles Colados Yucatecos (page 99)

Melted lard or vegetable oil, for frying
About 1½ cups (375ml) cooked and shredded meat (page 138)
1½ cups (375ml) Cebollas Encurtidas para Panuchos (page 180)

Divide the masa into twelve pieces and roll each into a ball about 1¼ inches (3.25cm) in diameter. While you work with the first balls keep the rest covered with a damp towel. Follow the instructions for making a tortilla on page 244—it will be about 4 inches (10cm) in diameter—trying to ensure that it inflates. Immediately, with a small paring knife, slit about one-third of the way around the circumference of the surface dough to form a pocket. If the tortilla doesn't puff up, or just partially, take a small paring knife and carefully slide it under the top thin layer of masa.

Put a slice of egg in the pocket, holding it to the top layer while you insert a tablespoon of the bean paste in the bottom. Press down lightly, spreading the bean paste out a little. Set the panucho aside while you do the rest.

Have ready some tongs, a spatula, and a tray covered with two layers of absorbent paper. Heat the lard or oil to the depth of ¼ inch (63mm) in a skillet and fry

the panuchos until they are golden and slightly crisp around the edge. Drain, dress with the meat and onions, and serve immediately. This is pan-to-mouth food.

NOTE: *If you are making a great number of panuchos, then put them in one layer on baking sheets lined with absorbent paper—without the meat and onion—and heat them through in a 350°F (180°C) oven for 8 to 10 minutes. Then garnish and serve.*

FROM TOP: CUTTING A POCKET IN A TORTILLA; PUTTING IN THE EGG; ADDING THE BEAN PASTE; FRYING THE PANUCHO. BELOW: DRESSING THE PANUCHO.

Cebollas Encurtidas para Panuchos

PICKLED ONIONS FOR PANUCHOS

Nowadays you see purple onions pickled in a slightly different way on top of panuchos, but Señora Berta, who taught me, says this is the traditional way of preparing them. Of course, if you can use bitter (Seville-type) oranges, so much the better. The oranges grown in Yucatán are picked green—some never change color—and are sweetish compared to those grown here in Michoacán. You will need sharp white Mexican onions.

MAKES ABOUT 2 CUPS (500ML)

3 cups (750ml) finely sliced white onion rings
4 cups (1L) boiling water
About ½ cup (125ml) bitter orange juice or substitute, or mild white vinegar

½ cup (125ml) water
1 tablespoon dried Yucatecan oregano, toasted and crumbled, or ½ tablespoon dried Mexican oregano
1 habanero chile, finely sliced, with seeds

Put the onions into a colander and immerse them in the boiling water for a few seconds. Drain and put into a glass or other nonreactive bowl. Add the rest of the ingredients and mix well. Set aside to season for about 2 hours before using.

These onions will keep for about ten days in the refrigerator.

Quesadillas

When I first moved to Mexico in 1957, the most popular quesadilla was a small, uncooked tortilla of corn masa doubled over a filling of Oaxaca cheese, a strip of poblano chile, and some epazote leaves cooked on an ungreased comal. In the rainy season we made fillings of cooked squash flowers or cuitlacoche, and little mushrooms called clavitos. *Now too often it consists of a flour tortilla folded over a semisoft cheese and heated through until the cheese melts—which is simple and pleasant, but compared with the traditional . . .*

Quesadillas can also be fried crisp. They are traditionally served alone, hot from the pan.

MAKES 12 4½-INCH (11.25-CM) QUESADILLAS

1 heaped cup (about 300ml), about 10 ounces/285g, Tortilla Masa (page 241)
About 1½ cups (375ml) cooked cuitlacoche or squash flowers; or the traditional filling of:

About 5 ounces (140g) Oaxaca string cheese, Chihuahua, or Muenster, cut into strips about 2½ inches (6.25cm) long and ½ inch (1.25cm) wide
12 strips poblano chile
24 epazote leaves

Warm an ungreased comal over medium heat.

Divide the masa into twelve pieces and roll into balls of about 1¼ inches (about 3cm); cover those you are not using with a damp cloth.

Put one of the balls into a tortilla press lined with a plastic bag and press out to a tortilla about 4½ (11.25cm) in diameter. You will note that the dough will be slightly thicker than that of a tortilla because it has to contain the filling. Remove the top bag.

Place a tablespoon of the cuitlacoche or squash flowers, or a strip of cheese, a strip of poblano chile, and 2 epazote leaves, in the center of the dough and, supported by the plastic bag, fold the dough in half to cover the filling. Seal the edges together well.

Place on the comal and cook until the underside is opaque and speckled with brown, about 5 minutes. Turn the quesadilla over and cook for another 5 minutes. The surface will be slightly crusty and the inside dough soft but cooked through. Serve immediately; I do not recommend reheating or the dough will be very dry and leathery.

NOTE: *To fry a quesadilla, heat lard or oil to a depth of about ¼ inch (63mm) in the skillet and fry the quesadillas on both sides until crisp and lightly browned, about 3 minutes on each side.*

FROM TOP: FILLING A QUESADILLA; FRYING QUESADILLAS.

Sopes

Sopes, *as well as* picadas *or* pellizcadas, *are untranslatable regional names given to* antojitos *that are, generally speaking, small disks of masa with the edge pinched up to form a slight ridge—presumably so that the sauce on top will not run down your chin. Quite often they are spread with refried beans and topped with either shredded meat or just a* picante *sauce and crumbled cheese, chopped onion, sometimes shredded cabbage or lettuce, and cream.*

Pellizcadas, or "pinched ones," are slightly different in that the surface of the dough is pinched up, forming little ridges. The most substantial are those made in and around the Catemaco area: they can be about 6 inches (15cm) across and topped with strips of broiled meat—not my favorite. But sopes are—and I warn you—addictive.

MAKES 12 3½-INCH (8.25-CM) SOPES

1 heaped cup (about 300ml), 10 ounces/
   285g, Tortilla Masa (page 241)
Melted lard or oil, for reheating
½ cup (125ml) Frijoles Refritos (page 98)
   (optional)
1½ cups (375ml) Chorizo y Papa
   (page 142)

½ cup (125ml) Salsa de Jitomate (page
   200) or Salsa Verde (page 204)
1 cup (250ml) finely shredded lettuce or
   cabbage
½ cup (125ml) finely chopped white onion
⅓ cup (83ml) finely grated añejo cheese
   or crumbled queso fresco

Work the masa until very soft and smooth, and divide into twelve equal parts. Roll each into a ball about 1¼ inches (3.13cm) in diameter and cover with a damp cloth while you work. Warm an ungreased comal over medium heat.

Take one of the balls and press out gently in a lined tortilla press or by hand to a disk about 3½ inches (8.25cm)—it will be thicker than a tortilla, about ¼ inch (63mm). Place carefully on the comal and cook over medium to low heat until the underside is opaque and speckled with brown, about 2 minutes. Turn the sope over and cook on the second side for a further 2 minutes. Remove from the comal and immediately (although you may burn your fingers a little) pinch up the dough around the periphery of the sope, return it to the comal, and cook briefly until the dough is firm and cooked through, about 2 minutes more. Continue with the rest of the balls.

Heat a very small amount of the lard or oil in a skillet and let the sopes heat through for about ½ minute on each side. Spread with the bean paste and top liberally with the rest of the ingredients. Serve immediately.

NOTE: Antojitos *of masa are always best eaten as soon as they are made, but this is not always practical. So make them ahead, cover with a damp cloth, and then heat them through in the fat and garnish just before serving. I do not recommend freezing the sopes; the dough tends to crack and disintegrate when defrosted.*

FROM TOP: PINCHING UP THE EDGES OF THE DOUGH; FILLING THE SOPE; THE FINAL TOPPING.

Tlacoyos

Tlacoyo *is the common name, a variation of the Nahuatl words* tlatlaoyo *and* claclaoyo, *given to an* antojito *typical of central Mexico: corn masa formed into a flattish elongated oval and stuffed often with ricotta, requeson, or a paste of fava beans. They vary enormously in size from very large—about 5 or 6 inches (13–15cm), in Santiago Tianguistenco, Estado de México—to medium—about 4 inches (10cm) in Xochimilco—to very small—about 3 inches (7.5cm) in Sierra Norte de Puebla. Most traditional tlacoyos do not have lard and salt in the masa, and if not eaten the minute they are cooked they become very tough and dry, even when reheated.*

Here is a recipe from the Sierra Norte de Puebla for the best I have tasted. Señora Hortensia Fagoaga, who gave me the recipe, said that her sister, a great expert, insists that the masa should be worked as much as possible so it becomes aerated and the lard distributed well. They can be eaten either alone or with the suggested topping.

MAKES ABOUT 12 TLACOYOS

2 cups (500ml), 18 to 19 ounces/about 510g, Tortilla Masa (page 241)
2 tablespoons softened lard
Sea salt to taste
About 1 cup (250ml) bean paste (either black or dried fava) or well-drained ricotta

THE TRIMMINGS

About ½ cup (125ml) finely chopped white onion
About ⅓ cup (83ml) finely grated queso añejo, or ½ cup (125ml) crumbled queso fresco
1¼ cups (313ml) Salsa Verde (page 204) (optional)

Work together very well the masa, lard, and salt—the longer the better—until it is well aerated and very smooth. Divide into 12 equal pieces and roll each into a ball about 1½ inches (3.75cm) in diameter. While you work with one, keep the rest of the balls covered with a damp cloth.

Heat an ungreased comal over medium heat.

Roll the ball into a cylindrical shape about 2½ inches (6.25cm) long and 1

ROLLING THE MASA INTO A CYLINDRICAL SHAPE.

inch (2.5cm) wide. Place the dough in a tortilla press lined with a plastic bag (as if making tortillas) and press out, not too hard, to an oval shape about 3 inches (7.5cm) wide and about 4 inches (10cm) long. Place a scant tablespoon of the bean paste or ricotta in the middle of the dough and fold the sides over to cover the filling. Then pat out a flattish oval about ¼ inch (62mm) thick. Place the tlacoyo on the warmed comal and cook over medium heat until the underside is opaque and shows dark brown speckles. Turn the tlacoyo over and cook on the second side, about 8 minutes on each side. The dough should be cooked through, but still soft, with a slightly crispy crust.

Sprinkle with the onion and cheese, and serve with the optional sauce.

NOTE: *Like all* antojitos *of masa, ideally tlacoyos should be eaten right away, but this is not always practical. Once cooked, keep them under a damp towel and when ready to serve heat through gently, covered, on a warm comal. Then garnish and serve.*

FROM TOP: PRESSING INTO AN OVAL FORM; CLOSING THE FILLED TLACOYO; THE FINAL SHAPING.

MAKING
MOLES

The word *mole* conjures still in many people's minds a "chocolate sauce." Of course, it isn't. The most commonly known moles of Puebla and Oaxaca have a very small quantity of chocolate in proportion to the chocolate-colored dried chiles used. They are by far the most complicated in terms of ingredients and are *the* food for celebrations. But the everyday regional moles, or molitos, are much simpler sauces: for instance, in the eastern part of Michoacán people abhor sweet moles and would never dream of putting sugar or chocolate in them. Then there are, of course, the colored moles: *verdes* (green), the *amarillo, colorado,* and *chichilo negro* (yellow, colored, and black chichilo) of Oaxaca. Again, in the provinces the word *mole* is widely used to cover very simple sauces with perhaps only one type of dried chile and a few scant spices like peppercorns, cloves, and perhaps cinnamon, all blended together with a little onion and garlic.

The word is generally believed to have come from the Nahuatl *molli,* meaning a "mixture of ingredients ground together." In fact, moles are cooked sauces—except, of course, when it comes to guacamole. There are *moles de olla* (generally but not exclusively from central Mexico), which are soupy stews seasoned with dried chiles; *guaxmole* (from Puebla), a tomato-chile sauce with very strong-flavored guajes; *tesmole* (from the southeast part of Puebla), made with the *picante* little chiltepec; *clemole* (also from Puebla) and *ayamole* (from Guerrero), made with pumpkin, among many other such sauces mostly from central and southern Mexico.

Curiously, in the seven recipes for turkey mole in *La Cocinera Poblana* (published in Puebla in 1877), the ingredients are much the same as the moles poblanos of today, yet not one of them calls for chocolate! In the same book there is one recipe for *mole prieto* that does list *una tablilla de chocolate* and, I am told by researchers Cristina Barros and Marco Buenrostro that a recipe for "mole prieto oajaqueño" (*sic*) appeared in a cookbook published in Puebla in 1849, which also included the same amount of chocolate. So the search goes on for the very first indication of chocolate in a cooked sauce.

In some of those "original" recipes the turkey was fried and then cooked in the sauce, or cooked first in water and the broth added to the chiles, but often a pork knuckle and some boneless pork were added to the mole with the turkey.

I must confess that in the following recipe I have deviated from the norm because, although the turkeys today are much more tender, they lack the flavor of the natural birds of bygone days. If you sauté and then braise the turkey as I have done, the pan juices will give the sauce a wonderful flavor.

Mole Poblano

There is not much subtlety in cutting up a turkey for serving in mole at a village fiesta. It is cut rather unceremoniously into about six pieces and put either raw into the chile sauce or precooked in broth.

If you are making this mole, use a small turkey about 10 pounds (4.5kg). If you are making a very large quantity, then use two or three small ones rather than one huge one. Cut off the wings and remove tips (add them to the broth), then cut off the legs, separating them from the thighs. Cut the breast into four pieces and then proceed with the recipe.

If you decide to use chickens, choose two of the largest and firmest possible, 4 to 5 pounds (1.8–2.25kg) each, if possible. Cut up in the same way and add either raw to cook slowly in the mole to absorb the flavors, about 40 minutes, or poach for 15 to 20 minutes in a strong chicken broth before adding to the mole and continue cooking until tender and well seasoned with the sauce, about 15 minutes more (the timing is for U.S. chickens).

There are no general techniques that apply to all the regional moles, but it is important to prepare the ingredients as indicated to bring out the authentic flavors and textures.

MAKES ABOUT 10 SERVINGS

THE CHILES

Approximately ¹⁄₂ cup (125ml) lard
8 mulato chiles, seeds and veins removed
5 ancho chiles, seeds and veins removed
6 pasilla chiles, seeds and veins removed
(reserve 1 heaped tablespoon of the
chile seeds for step 4)
1 cup (250ml) turkey broth

THE BROTH

The turkey giblets
1 carrot, trimmed and sliced
1 medium white onion, roughly chopped
6 peppercorns
Sea salt to taste

THE TURKEY

Approximately ¹⁄₃ cup (83ml) pork lard
1 small turkey (8 to 10 pounds/4–4.5kg),
cut into serving pieces, or 2 of the
largest chickens or capons you can find
Sea salt to taste

INGREDIENTS FOR MOLE POBLANO.

THE EXTRA SAUCE

1 tablespoon reserved chile seeds
¹⁄₄ teaspoon coriander seeds
¹⁄₄ teaspoon aniseeds
7 tablespoons sesame seeds
4 whole cloves
10 peppercorns
¹⁄₂-inch (1.25-cm) piece of cinnamon stick
Approximately ¹⁄₄ cup (65ml) lard
2 tablespoons raisins
20 unskinned almonds
2 ounces (60g) raw, hulled pumpkin seeds,
about ¹⁄₃ cup/83ml
1 dried corn tortilla
3 small slices dry French bread
7 cups (1.6L) turkey broth
3 small tomatoes, *asado* (see page 125)
3 garlic cloves, *asado* and peeled
1¹⁄₂ ounces (45g) Mexican drinking
chocolate
Sea salt to taste

recipe continues on next page

PREPARE THE CHILES: Have a large bowl of water ready. Heat a little of the lard in a skillet and start frying the chiles, a few at a time, on both sides, pressing them down as you turn them, until the inside flesh turns a tobacco brown. This takes a few seconds on each side; take care not to let them burn. Drain each one of excess oil over the pan and put them into the water to soak. Only add a little more of the lard as you go along.

Leave the chiles to soak for about 1 hour, no longer, unless you are cooking mole for five hundred. Do not attempt to skin the chiles. Drain them and set aside until you want to blend them.

Preheat the oven to 325°F (165°C).

PREPARE THE BROTH: Put the giblets, carrot, onion, peppercorns, and salt into a saucepan, cover well with water, and bring to a simmer. Continue simmering until the giblets are very soft, adding more water if necessary, about 1½ hours. Strain the broth and set aside. Discard the giblets or save for the dog.

MEANTIME, PREPARE THE TURKEY: Heat the lard in a Dutch oven, add the turkey pieces a few at a time, and fry until the skin is golden. Drain off excess fat and reserve for frying later. Return all the turkey pieces to the Dutch oven, season with salt, cover, and cook until the meat is almost tender, 35 to 40 minutes. Pour off the pan juices, skim, and add to the giblet broth. Make up with water to 8 cups (2L) of liquid.

Put 1 cup (250ml) of the broth into a blender jar and blend the chiles, a few at a time, to a thick, slightly textured consistency. You will need to be constantly loosening the chile paste as it tends to clog the blades. You may have to put a little more liquid to loosen the blades but not too much because you need to fry the paste in a concentrated form to bring out the full flavor of the chiles.

Put the reserved frying lard into a heavy, flameproof casserole and fry the chile paste over medium heat for about 10 minutes, scraping the bottom of the casserole frequently to avoid sticking. Set aside.

PREPARE THE EXTRA SAUCE INGREDIENTS: In a small skillet toast briefly—and separately—the following ingredients, shaking the pan so that they toast evenly and do not scorch: the reserved chile seeds, the coriander seeds, the aniseeds, and the sesame seeds. Set them aside to cool. Grind in an electric coffee/spice grinder as finely as possible the cloves, peppercorns, cinnamon, and all the toasted ingredients except for the sesame. Reserve 4 tablespoons of the sesame seeds for serving the

mole; grind the rest as finely as possible, and add to the spice mixture. Set aside.

Add a small portion of the lard to a small skillet and begin to fry the following ingredients separately, putting them into a strainer to drain off any excess fat: the raisins until they plump up, the almonds until well browned, the pumpkin seeds until they swell (take care since they tend to explode and jump), the tortilla and bread until crisp. Only add a little more lard at a time or it will all be absorbed, especially by the tortilla and bread. Crush the almonds, tortilla, and bread roughly (to help your blender). Put 1 cup (250ml) of the broth into the blender jar, add the tomatoes (unskinned) and peeled garlic, and blend until smooth. Gradually add the spice mixture and blend well. Then add another 1 cup (250ml) of the broth and gradually blend the fried ingredients to a slightly textured paste. Try not to add more liquid (unless your blender motor is heating up or smoking) but constantly release the blades with a rubber spatula.

Reheat the fried chile paste, add the blended ingredients, and fry over medium heat, scraping the bottom of the pan very often to avoid sticking. Continue frying until the mixture is very thick, about 8 minutes, then add the chocolate, broken into small pieces with yet another 1 cup (250ml) of the broth and continue cooking and scraping the bottom for another 5 minutes. Add the remaining 4 cups (1L) of the broth and continue cooking over medium heat— the mixture should be bubbling and splattering—for

recipe continues on next page

FROM TOP: FRYING THE BLENDED CHILES; ADDING THE BLENDED INGREDIENTS; ADDING THE CHOCOLATE; ADDING THE BROTH.

about 25 minutes. By now pools of oil should be forming on the surface (a requisite to show that the sauce has been well cooked). Add the turkey pieces and any more juices that they have exuded, and adjust salt. Cook for another 15 to 20 minutes.

To serve, place pieces of the turkey on warmed plates with plenty of the sauce. Top with a good sprinkling of the reserved sesame seeds and a lot of warm corn tortillas. This mole can be made well ahead up to the point of adding the turkey pieces. Leftover sauce can be kept very successfully in the freezer for about six months. When reheated it will probably have to be diluted with more broth and freshly cooked chicken (you won't want to do the turkey thing again), or better still used for chicken-filled enchiladas.

THE FINISHED MOLE WITH CHICKEN.

Mole Verde

GREEN MOLE

Every region has its version of mole verde, which reflects local tastes because of what is easily available year round—or perhaps the reverse is true. Many are lighter than this very substantial and textured green mole given to me by a neighbor, Señora Severa, which is one of my favorites. It is a very typical dish of the eastern part of Michoacán around Zitacuaro, which is a focal point for transport of products from the hot country to the west. Among them is the winter crop of ajonjoli, or sesame. Until about fifteen years ago there was even a mill there to extract cooking oil from the sesame seeds; but tastes have changed and it is no longer in operation.

While this mole is best eaten soon after it is made, to appreciate the flavor of all the fresh greens, it can be prepared ahead up to the point of blending and adding the greens. Heat varies very much according to taste, so the number of serranos is optional. Typically this mole has a thickish texture and thickens more as it stands so it may require diluting.

For all dishes of this kind, the larger and more compact the chicken the better—no fryers please. And adding extra giblets for a stronger broth is not a bad idea. This mole verde is also popularly made with espinazo, the backbone of the pig, which gives it a delicious flavor. I often make the mole with country-style spareribs cut into pieces.

MAKES 6 TO 8 SERVINGS

INGREDIENTS FOR MOLE VERDE.

THE MEAT

1 large chicken (3^1/$_2$–4 pounds/1.575 to
    1.8kg), cut into serving pieces, or
    4^1/$_2$ pounds (about 2kg) country-style
    spareribs, cut into 2-inch (5-cm) pieces
1 small white onion, roughly chopped
2 garlic cloves, roughly chopped
Water or light chicken broth to cover
Sea salt to taste
1 pound (450g) giblets (optional)

THE SAUCE

5 ounces (140g) sesame seeds, about
    1 cup (250ml)
1^1/$_2$ ounces (45g) raw hulled pumpkin
    seeds, about ^{1}/$_3$ cup (83ml)
3 whole cloves
3 peppercorns

3 allspice berries
About ^{1}/$_3$ cup (83ml) lard or vegetable oil
2 garlic cloves, roughly chopped
6 ounces (180g) tomate verde (about
    8 medium), roughly chopped
2 poblano chiles (unpeeled), seeds and
    veins removed and roughly chopped,
    about ^{1}/$_2$ cup (125ml)
6 to 8 serrano chiles, roughly chopped
8 romaine lettuce leaves, roughly chopped
5 green Swiss chard leaves, stems removed
    and discarded, leaves roughly chopped
1 large bunch cilantro, trimmed of thick
    stems and roughly chopped, about
    1^1/$_2$ cups (375ml) tightly packed
1 small bunch flat-leaf parsley, roughly
    chopped, about ^{1}/$_2$ cup (125ml) tightly
    packed

recipe continues on next page

Put the chicken pieces, onion, and garlic into a large saucepan; add water or chicken broth to cover and add salt. Add the optional giblets if you are making this with water. Bring to a simmer and cook over low heat until the meat is almost tender but still firm, about 25 minutes. (A lot will depend on the quality of the chicken.) If using pork, cook for about 20 minutes longer. Strain, reserving the broth. Reduce or add water to make up to 6 cups (1.5L).

Put the sesame seeds into an ungreased skillet over medium heat, stirring them constantly until they become a deep golden color, about 5 minutes. Take care not to let them burn. Spread them out on a tray to cool. Put the pumpkin seeds into the pan and stir them until they begin to swell and start to pop around, about 3 minutes. Set aside to cool. When the seeds are cool, grind the sesame first with the cloves, peppercorns, and allspice to a slightly textured powder. Then grind the pumpkin seeds to the same texture. Transfer both to a bowl and stir in 1 cup (250ml) of the reserved broth to make a thick paste.

Heat about 3 tablespoons of the lard or oil in a heavy casserole, add the seed paste, and fry over medium-low heat, scraping the bottom of the pan constantly to avoid sticking—if necessary add a little more fat—until dry, shiny, and a rich deep golden color.

Unless you have a large blender jar you may need to blend the greens in two batches, but try to use the minimum of liquid. Put 1 cup (250ml) of the broth into the blender jar and add the garlic, tomate verde, and chiles and blend fairly smooth. Gradually add half of the greens and blend as smoothly as possible. Add the rest of the greens little by little, with just enough of the broth to enable the blades of the blender to work efficiently.

Gradually stir the blended ingredients into the fried seed paste over medium heat, stirring the mixture well after each addition. Continue cooking over medium heat, stirring frequently, until the sauce starts to reduce and thicken, for about 10 minutes. Add the remaining broth and cook for a further 10 minutes—pools of oil will form around the periphery. Add the meat, adjust salt, and cook for a further 10 minutes. Dilute with more broth or water if desired. Serve with corn tortillas.

ADDING THE BLENDED GREENS.

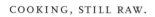

COOKING, STILL RAW.

THE FINISHED MOLE.

MAKING
TABLE
SAUCES

The fresh flavors and crisp textures of Mexican salsas, and the variety of colors and piquancy lent by chiles, fresh, dried, or smoked, seem never-ending. When referring to *salsas,* I mean sauces that are put on the table, as a condiment as it were; this word does not apply to sauces that are part of a cooked dish. There are many regional salsas in my other books, so here I shall just give the very basic ones used primarily, but not exclusively, in central Mexico, of fresh chiles with tomatoes and tomates verdes and two of my favorite sauces of dried chiles. The former are, of course, best eaten as freshly made as possible—except where indicated; there is nothing so disappointing as a sauce with tomatoes that have been cut too far ahead or stored too long in the refrigerator or have been frozen so that the sauce is discolored or separated and watery. Salsas made of dried chiles, although they may include grilled tomatoes, can be kept for two or three days in the refrigerator.

Points to remember:

* Unless you have a lot of guests, make these table sauces in small quantities; many don't keep well.
* Any acidic sauce should be kept and served in nonreactive bowls—acid attacks the glaze of the traditional low-fired Mexican pottery and other similar bowls.
* Dried chiles that are not soaked before blending should be wiped clean before toasting.
* Do *not* peel or remove seeds from serrano chiles.

You may note that I have included a new, improved method for making dried chile sauces in the blender (why I didn't think of it before escapes me): grind the toasted chiles, garlic, and salt first dry. The resulting texture and flavor are far better.

Salsa Mexicana

In some areas this is called pico de gallo *and is perhaps the best known of all table sauces. Certainly it is the most ubiquitous. There are occasional regional differences that can be found in my other books.*

Chop evenly and carefully; there is nothing so unattractive as unevenly chopped ingredients in this sauce. A serrated knife for the tomatoes is almost indispensable. The balance of ingredients is variable according to taste.

MAKES ABOUT 2 CUPS (500ML)

8 ounces (225g) tomatoes, finely chopped, about 1½ cups (375ml)
½ cup (125ml) finely chopped white onion
3 serrano chiles, or to taste, finely chopped (not seeded)

⅓ cup (83ml) finely—but not too finely—chopped cilantro
Sea salt to taste
¼ cup (63ml) water (optional)

Mix all the ingredients and serve at room temperature.

Although best served as soon as possible, this sauce will keep for a few hours without losing its crispness and fresh cilantro flavor. Obviously this is not a sauce for freezing.

CLOCKWISE FROM LEFT: SALSA MEXICANA,
SALSA DE JITOMATE, SALSA VERDE.

Tomato Sauces

Tomato sauces differ very slightly from region to region; while the techniques are essentially the same, the chiles used may vary. I give here four variations of the better known and used sauces. See also Salsa para Mochomos (Sinaloa) (*Essentials*, page 21); Salsa de Jitomate Sonorense (*Essentials*, page 239); and Salsa de Jitomate Veracruzano (*Essentials*, page 240).

Salsa de Jitomate

RAW TOMATO SAUCE

This simple fresh sauce is better eaten the day it is made. It is so important to have really ripe, juicy tomatoes. Of course, it is so much better when made in a molcajete, but if you are making it in the blender, then do not overblend—it is meant to be a rustic, textured sauce.

This sauce, with slight regional variations, is a salsa because it is often used almost like a condiment: it is there on the table and used principally on antojitos *and tacos, rice, omelets, or with grilled meats.*

MAKES ABOUT 2 CUPS (500ML)

2 garlic cloves
4 serrano chiles, *asado* (see page 56) and
   roughly chopped
Sea salt to taste
1 pound (450g) tomatoes, *asado*
  (see page 125)

About ⅓ cup (83ml) finely chopped white
  onion
About ⅓ cup (83ml) roughly chopped
  cilantro

Crush or blend the garlic, chiles, and salt to a paste. Gradually add the tomatoes (unpeeled), grinding well after each addition. The sauce should be textured and the skin will never all completely disappear.

Sprinkle the top with the onion and cilantro and serve.

Salsa de Jitomate Cocida

COOKED TOMATO SAUCE

A cooked tomato sauce is used for certain dishes: Uchepos (Essentials, page 106, or The Art, page 86), Bocoles de Frijol Negro (My Mexico, page 28), Pintos (The Art, page 53), Molotes (page 174 or The Art, page 44), among others. Some cooks use tomatoes that have been simmered with the chiles in a little water, while others use char-grilled tomatoes—which I prefer for better flavor.

MAKES ABOUT 1½ CUPS (375ML)

1 pound tomatoes, *asado* (see page 125)
2 garlic cloves, *asado*, peeled, and roughly chopped

4 or more serrano chiles, *asado* (see page 56) and roughly chopped
2 tablespoons vegetable oil
Salt to taste

Put two of the unskinned tomatoes into a blender jar with the garlic and chiles and blend to a fairly smooth texture. Gradually add the remaining tomatoes, blending again to a slightly textured purée.

Heat the oil in a medium skillet, add the sauce, and cook over fairly high heat until reduced and seasoned, about 5 minutes. Add salt to taste.

This sauce is served hot with uchepos, room temperature with bocoles and pintos, and reduced with a little broth and served warm with molotes (see page 176). It can be made ahead of time and will keep in the refrigerator for about three days, and frozen for about one month. After defrosting it is better to blend briefly before reheating.

Salsa Ranchera

This sauce is prepared with a slightly different technique again. It is of course best known when prepared with eggs for Huevos Rancheros (Essentials, page 171).

MAKES ABOUT 1½ CUPS (375ML)

1½ pounds (675g) tomatoes, *asado* (see page 125)
2 garlic cloves, peeled and roughly chopped
4 serrano chiles, *asado* (see page 56) and roughly chopped

2 tablespoons vegetable oil
2 heaped tablespoons finely chopped white onion
Sea salt to taste

Put two of the unpeeled tomatoes into a blender jar, add the garlic and chiles, and grind to a fairly smooth texture. Gradually add the remaining tomatoes and blend to a medium texture.

Heat the oil in a medium skillet. Add the onion and cook over medium heat until translucent, about 2 minutes. Pour in the sauce and cook over fairly high heat until reduced and seasoned, about 5 minutes. Add salt to taste.

Keep the sauce warm until ready to use. It can be prepared several hours ahead and reheated. It can also be frozen for about one month, but when defrosted you may need to blend it briefly before reheating as it tends to separate.

Salsa de Jitomate Yucatecan

YUCATECAN TOMATO SAUCE

This is a more usual version of the rustic chiltomate simply made with tomatoes that have been char-roasted on the hot stones of the pit barbecue (called a pib*), and crushed with chile habanero and onion. The frying process, which is optional, helps bring out flavor and reduce the juice of the tomatoes.*

MAKES ABOUT 1¼ CUPS (313ML)

1 pound (450g) tomatoes, *asado*
  (see page 125)
1 tablespoon vegetable oil
2 thin slices white onion, cut into strips

Sea salt to taste
1 chile habanero, with a cross cut at the
  bottom

Blend the unpeeled tomatoes to a slightly textured purée.

Heat the oil in a small skillet, add the onion, and fry for a few seconds until translucent; do not brown.

Add the blended tomatoes, salt, and whole chile and cook over fairly high heat until reduced to about 1¼ cups (313ml), about 5 minutes.

The sauce will keep well only for about two days in the refrigerator; it can also be frozen but should be blended after defrosting, as it tends to separate, and before reheating.

Salsa Verde

MEXICAN GREEN TOMATO SAUCE

A sauce made with tomate verde, known as tomatillos *in the United States, is unique to Mexico. It is an uncooked table sauce, as I call it, as opposed to a green sauce in which meats, vegetables, or chicharrón are added, or as a component of, say,* budin azteca, *or tamales.*

Of course, the sauce is more flavorful when made in a molcajete, although the tomato skins are rather tough to grind for the unpracticed or the cook in a hurry. With minor exceptions, the tomatoes are cooked.

MAKES ABOUT 2 CUPS (500ML)

1 pound (450g) tomate verde, husks
  removed and rinsed
3 or more serrano chiles, finely chopped
½ cup (125ml) loosely packed, roughly
  chopped cilantro, plus 2 tablespoons
  for the top

1 garlic clove, roughly chopped
2 tablespoons roughly chopped
  white onion
Sea salt to taste

Put the tomatoes whole in a small saucepan, barely cover with water, and bring to a simmer. Lower the heat and continue cooking until soft but not falling apart, about 5 minutes depending on size. Drain, reserving the cooking water.

USING A MOLCAJETE: Mash and grind together the chiles, ½ cup (125ml) cilantro, the garlic, onion, and salt. Add the tomatoes a few at a time, crushing and grinding well after each addition and adding a little of the cooking liquid until you have a textured sauce of medium consistency. You will probably need about ½ cup (125ml) or even more of the cooking liquid.

USING A BLENDER: Put ⅓ cup (83ml) of the cooking water into the blender jar. Add the chiles, ½ cup (125ml) cilantro, the garlic, and the onion and grind to a paste. Add the tomatoes a little at a time, blending with about ⅓ cup (83ml) more of the cooking liquid until you have a textured sauce of medium consistency. Add salt to taste.

Although this sauce is much better eaten the same day on which it is made, it could be kept for a second day but I do not advise freezing. To serve: sprinkle the top with the extra cilantro.

NOTE: *When tomate verde sauce is a component of a dish (and not a table sauce), use the same proportion of ingredients (although the cilantro is not always used) and cook the tomates with* whole *serranos. Drain, roughly chop the chiles, and blend all the ingredients with about 1 cup (250ml) of the cooking water until you have a fairly smooth sauce. Heat 1 tablespoon of vegetable oil in a skillet and fry the sauce over medium heat, scraping the bottom of the pan to avoid sticking. Continue cooking until the sauce has reduced and thickened to about 1½ cups (375ml). This sauce will keep in the refrigerator for about three days and can be frozen for about one month. It tends to separate after defrosting, so give it a whirl in the blender.*

Salsa de Chile de Árbol

CHILE DE ÁRBOL SAUCE

The very picante *dried chile de árbol combines well with tomate verde to make this rustic, textured table sauce. For traditionalists, the sauce is better when ground in a molcajete, but it is hard work; thank goodness for the blender! A food processor will not work in this case.*
If the chiles have stems attached it is easier to turn them on the comal.

MAKES ABOUT 1¼ CUPS (313ML)

8 ounces (225g) tomate verde (about 11 small ones), husks removed and rinsed
8 chiles de árbol, wiped clean and left whole with stems (if any)

1 garlic clove, roughly chopped
About ⅓ cup (83ml) water
Sea salt to taste

Put an ungreased comal or griddle over low heat and cook the whole tomatoes, turning them from time to time until they are soft and slightly charred, about 15 minutes.

Place the whole chiles—if there is room—to one side of the comal and toast them whole, turning them around from time to time and taking care not to let them burn—this will take a few seconds. When cool you should be able to crumble them easily into a blender jar (discard the stems). Blend dry to a textured powder, then add the garlic and cooked tomate and blend to a roughly textured sauce. Dilute with the water and add salt to taste.

This sauce can be kept in the refrigerator for two to three days, but I do not recommend freezing.

Salsa de Chile Costeño

CHILE COSTEÑO SAUCE

This very thin picante *sauce of dried chile costeño (either red or yellow) is very much an acquired taste, but you can really appreciate the flavor of these thin-fleshed, pungent chiles. This is a favorite sauce of mine especially to eat with rice cooked with dried shrimp, or the breakfast masa and egg pancake in* My Mexico *(page 426).*

As with most table sauces, this has even more flavor when ground in the molcajete, but the blender does an acceptable job for all but the die-hard traditionalists. The chiles should be wiped clean before toasting (this applies to any dried chile that is not soaked in water before blending). They should be very lightly toasted, not browned to a crisp. This preserves both flavor and the brick-red color of the sauce. Abigail, the famous Zapotec cook, says the chiles should be calentado, *heated through, preferably in hot ash. It may sound absurd, but try it next time you have a grill going with good wood or charcoal ash. Only shake the chiles; do not wash off the fine residue of ash—it adds flavor. Do not remove the seeds; they add bulk and flavor.*

MAKES JUST OVER ¾ CUP (ABOUT 195ML)

12 costeño chiles, either red or yellow, wiped clean and left whole	Salt to taste
1 garlic clove	About ¾ cup (190ml) water

Place the whole chiles, with stalks if any, on a preheated comal over low heat and toast very lightly, turning them from time to time until the surface just begins to turn color and hardens very slightly. Tear into small pieces and add them with their seeds to a blender jar. Add the garlic and a little salt and blend dry as fine as possible. Scrape down the surface of the jar, which will be speckled with minute pieces of chile. Then add the water and blend for about 30 seconds, or until you have a very slightly textured purée. Add more salt to taste and set aside to season for a minimum of 1 hour before using. It should have a medium consistency, neither thick nor watery.

This sauce will thicken as it stands because the chile will rehydrate, so dilute with a little more water if desired.

It is the type of sauce best left to mature for several hours before serving. It will keep for several days in the refrigerator and even freezes well—but after defrosting give it a whirl in the blender.

MAKING
TAMALES

Recently a renowned academic and researcher on the subject of tamales reported that she knew of at least 350 different tamales and acknowledged that there must be many more. Indeed, the variety is bewildering and perhaps infinite (discounting the latest nouvelle innovations). There are even great variations on a given theme: tamales with beans, for instance. There are certainly marked regional differences, but bean tamales can vary from one village to another, and not surprisingly even from one cook to another.

The treatment of the corn and the type of masa for tamales can differ; the leaves in which they are wrapped vary depending on local tastes and what is available in the area—many give a special flavor to the masa. The fillings, the textures, the shapes, and the occasions for eating certain tamales are very much dictated by local customs and lore. Not all tamales are made with a corn masa: there are some made with wheat flour (and I don't mean whole wheat), like the Tamales de Espiga from Michoacán (*My Mexico,* page 10) and Tamales Canarios with rice flour (*The Art,* page 91); some also from Michoacán are made of pinole of black corn and toasted corn silk. The name *tamale* is also loosely applied to any food wrapped and cooked in corn husks: small fish, nopales, or brains, especially in central Mexico.

I have briefly listed and described a variety of tamales in my other books, and given recipes for some fascinating and even lesser known ones, but nothing could really do the subject justice short of a very large volume on that subject alone. Here I have described the methods for making some of the better known tamales, following recipes that have appeared in my other books.

Making tamales is time-consuming, but like the preparation and serving of so many delectable foods, much depends on planning and organization. As I have said elsewhere, making some of the more difficult ones, tamales colados, for example, is a fascinating culinary exercise, almost like putting a jigsaw puzzle together—but then you can't eat jigsaw puzzles!

Although I am always unpopular saying this, you have to use a good pork lard. One of the happiest of marriages occurred in colonial times when pork lard was introduced to corn! The description of some of the different tamale wrappers can be found starting on page 211. In most cases, tamales are served in their wrappers. The tamale steamer and substitute are described on page 300. The description and preparation of different masas, when not detailed in the recipe itself, start on page 216.

Wrappers are not usually eaten, although there are minor exceptions when they are wrapped in Swiss chard and chaya (*The Art,* pages 80 and 78) or in hoja santa. Some tamales are eaten with a sauce (the uchepos and corundas of Michoacán, among a few others), but most are not. It is very difficult to generalize, and of course there are no hard-and-fast rules about when you can eat a tamale, but they are not a snack food like a taco. Traditionally they are eaten with atole in the evening or often reheated on the comal for *almuerzo.* Some bean or unfilled tamales were often served with a mole poblano, although you don't come across that so much these days. There are tamales made for specific occasions like those for the Day of the Dead, notably *muk-bil pollo* of Yucatán or those like *pan de milpa,* a type of tamale with nine or thirteen layers prepared for the blessing of the cornfields in Campeche, *han-li-cool,* among many other examples.

When steaming tamales some cooks put salt in the water, but I find this does not make a significant difference and the water always seems to dry up faster (totally unscientific, I fear!). Some cooks put the olote, or core of the cob, below the tamales to increase the flavor of fresh corn tamales. I usually forget until it is too late. Some types of tamales are cooked vertically, held upright by divisions in the top section of the tamale steamer. They should not be packed too tightly or there will be no room for the dough to expand. If the tamales are stacked vertically in the steamer it is best to cover them with a piece of toweling to absorb the moisture that collects and drips from the lid.

If the recipe calls for tamales, usually the flat types, to be laid horizontally in the steamer, the bottom layer should be cooked first for about 10 minutes for the dough to start firming up. If they are all stacked on top of each other from the beginning the bottom ones tend to get flattened. When laid horizontally they should be in overlapping layers and not stacked one on top of the other, to allow the steam to circulate and cook them evenly.

Tamales should be cooked as soon as possible after assembling so that the masa retains its sponginess and the sauce does not make it watery or leak out. Always have a pot of water heating on the side because once the water level goes down it has to be topped up with hot and should not go off the boil; if this does happen the tamales will tend to be heavy.

Most tamales, with the notable exception of Colados (page 223), once cooked can be frozen very successfully, but note when reheating they should not first be defrosted but go still frozen straight into a very hot steamer for about 15 minutes. Another method of reheating is to place them, still frozen in their wrappers, on a comal over low heat for about 20 minutes, turning them once. The wrapper will become slightly charred and if left long enough on the heat the lard will give a golden crust to the masa.

WRAPPERS

The following descriptions include only some of the better known wrappers for tamales and how to prepare them. They comprise leaves, fresh and/or dried, that are folded, and sometimes tied, not only to provide a waterproof wrapping but also to define the form of the masa and its filling.

Chaya leaves, described on page 128, are used for a Yucatecan tamale Dzoto-bichay (*The Art,* page 78); hoja santa, described on page 86, is used for a flat tamale included in the unique barbecue of Tezoatlan, Oaxaca (see *Essentials,* page 315); and a large-leaf *Calathea lutea,* called *hoja de to* in Tabasco and *hoja blanca* in the southern part of Veracruz, also provides an ample and completely waterproof wrapping for the regional tamales of those entities. Other types of leaves, like those of the *Canna indica* and of plants of the ginger family, are used in tropical areas of Oaxaca, Veracruz, and Puebla. In the Jalapa area of Veracruz a tamale called *xoco,* or sour, is made of soured black corn masa and wrapped in a toughish leaf called caballero (*Oreopanax echinops*). I have also seen avocado leaves, described on page 87, used for rustic tamales in Morelos and a remote area of Puebla (see *My Mexico,* page 273).

Dried Corn Husks

Dried corn husks (*totmoxtles,* as they are known in central Mexico, from the Nahuatl *totomochtli,* but more generally *hojas para tamales* or *hojas de doblador* in Chiapas) are by far the most commonly used wrappers for tamales. When the corn cobs are mature they are left to dry in the fields, on the stalks and in their husks. At harvest time the husks are put aside either for the cattle or for tamales and the whole grains of corn are shaved off, *desgranado.* The advantage of these husks in Mexico is that they are left whole with the cupped end intact; this protects the tamale dough. Those sold commercially in the United States have been machine cut; therefore, they have no cupped end and tend generally to be rather tough. When using the latter it is rather tedious to close the top by bending it over and tying.

The husks usually come tightly pressed together. Loosen them, cover with water, and leave them to soak until they become pliable—at least one hour, longer if they are very tough. If you are in a hurry, cover them with hot water and simmer for a few minutes, but be sure to let them cool off before you start spreading the inside with the masa. One advantage of dried corn husks as a wrapper is that they absorb the excess fat in masa or let it transpire into the water.

Shake the husks dry, flatten them a little, and stack until you are ready to use them. Leaves are torn in half for the slim tamales of Nuevo León (see page 235). If you are going to tie your tamales, tear some of the husks into thin strips. For longer ties, knot two or three of the strips together.

Fresh Corn Husks

Fresh, green corn husks are used for wrapping either sweet or savory fresh corn tamales; not only do they provide an efficient waterproof casing but they add a delicate flavor of their own to the dough. The leaves are cut as near to the base of the cob as possible to get a slightly cupped end, and unfurled with great care so that they do not split. The outer husks tend to be rather thick and usually are too tough to be used as wrappers; these could be used to line the top section of the steamer and as a final layer to cover the stacked tamales.

Please note that fresh husks are generally used without softening. I know of one exception, however, for the uchepos de cuchara of Michoacán, made of ground, strained, and cooked fresh corn; these husks are wilted briefly in hot water.

Hoja de Milpa

The Cornstalk Leaves

The word *milpa* derives from the Nahuatl words *milli* and *pa*, referring to a plantation of corn. The long leaf of the corn plant—cut fresh—is used as a rather more complicated wrapping for tamales in some areas, notably parts of Michoacán, Oaxaca, and Chiapas. It adds a yellowish hue and a distinctive, delicate flavor to the masa. I have also seen this leaf dried and stored in Oaxaca for use when there are no fresh leaves available, but they don't impart the same flavor.

A mature leaf suitable for wrapping is ideally about 3 feet (92cm) long and about 3 inches (7.5 cm) wide. The leaf turns from light to a dark green as it matures; it is tough and has a slightly abrasive, ridged surface. For assembling tamales, the masa is spread on the smoother underside of the leaf. When using these leaves for corundas, some Michoacán cooks remove the tough lower part of the rib, stripping the leaf into two. Apart from wiping the leaf clean no other preparation is necessary.

Hojas de Carrizo

Reed Leaves

Leaves of the reed *Arundo donax*, a native of the Mediterranean, are used primarily for basket making in certain areas of Mexico, but are used in Michoacán for wrapping Corundas (see *The Art,* page 70) when fresh corn leaves are not available—or by choice. They do not impart any particular flavor or color to the dough.

In the eastern part of Michoacán the corundas resemble rubbery yellowish pellets. The pieces of raw dough are set out at regular intervals along the surface of the leaf (which is slightly smoother than the ribbed back of the leaf) and folded over in concertina fashion for cooking. In and around Morelia the more refined, spongy corundas are wrapped in reed leaves—only when fresh corn leaves are not available—with more intricate turns.

An ideal leaf is about 2 feet (61cm) long and about 3 inches (7.5cm) wide, ending in a sharp, elongated stringy point. The leaf is tough, a dull green in color, with a matte, finely ribbed surface. Apart from wiping them clean, no other preparation is necessary.

Banana Leaves

In tropical and semitropical areas of Mexico there are always some types of tamales that are wrapped in banana leaves, which both provide an effective waterproof covering and lend a certain delicate flavor to the dough. It is best to use the more tender flexible leaves, but if you have no choice, even the toughest will become more flexible when heated. I have seen cooks who make large quantities of tamales commercially, tying a bunch of the leaves together and boiling them in water to soften them. While this is very effective it does detract from the flavor.

If you have access to or grow a banana plant, cut the leaf off with some of the stem (take care as the sap it exudes is a strong brown dye that does not wash out). Holding the stem firmly, and using a very sharp knife, cut the leaf off on both sides of the stem starting from the top. The thick, pithy stem can then be shredded to make ties for tamales or wrapped meats. Cut the leaves carefully, or they will split, into the sizes you need for the tamales you are making. One by one, hold them over a medium flame or hot plate of an electric stove for a few seconds. The surface of the leaf will turn a bright shiny green and become soft and flexible. Let them cool before assembling the tamales. If the heat of the stove is too high, the green will turn to a dark brown; you can still use them but take care not to let them burn.

When assembling the tamales, the dough is always placed on the smoother underside of the leaf.

Many fruit markets and specialty stores in the Southwest carry fresh banana leaves already stripped from the center rib. In other areas of the United States where these are not available, Asian groceries and produce stores carry packages of frozen leaves. They tend to be rather tough and dark in color, but are fine to use for tamales. Wipe them clean with a damp cloth, cut them into the required sizes, and wilt them as explained above. They will take a little longer to soften.

There is only one example of a specific type of banana leaf called for that I know of. The tamales de mole of central Oaxaca have the thinnest layer, or rather a smearing, of masa on the leaves and multiple folds that require a wide and tender young leaf that is a yellowish green color. (I was told many years ago by a Yucatecan tamale maker that the leaves of the delicious and fruity-flavored plátano manzano should be used for tamales—an esoteric nicety in tamale lore.)

Ties for tamales can be made, as I have mentioned, of the fibrous stalk and rib, or by tearing one of the leaves into thin strips and then tying some together for the required length.

The type of corn masa used for tamales may differ from region to region, and even within a region, depending on the type of tamale. Flavors may vary with the type of corn used and textures will depend on how that corn is prepared. I give here the better known methods of preparing dried corn for five different masas, with recipes to illustrate their use.

The preparation of fresh corn for tamales is straightforward and only requires grinding like that for Uchepos (page 232).

Masa para Tortillas
TORTILLA MASA

The simplest masa is that made of dried corn prepared and ground for tortillas (see page 241). Two pounds (900g) of dried corn will yield about double its weight in masa, about 4 pounds (1.8kg) depending on how damp the air is; see the recipe for Tamales Oaxaqueños de Frijol (page 228). This masa should keep in the refrigerator for about two days without souring. Then it is best to freeze it; it will keep satisfactorily for about a month.

Masa Refregado y Martajado
TEXTURED WHITE MASA

Masa para tamales—a textured tamale dough—is prepared and sold in most *tortillerías* in the United States, but be sure not to buy *masa preparada,* or prepared masa, which has already been mixed with lard—or whatever fat they use. I hope you will want to mix your own, beating up the lard and masa to aerate it and make lighter tamales. The problem with making it yourself is finding an efficient machine to grind wet doughs. The dry dough that follows can be ground in simple grinders like that illustrated on page 300. If it comes down to the crunch, substitute one dough for another and apologize to your guests.

Masa refregado y martajado is literally rubbed hard and coarsely ground. The dried corn is prepared in a solution of lime following the recipe for tortilla masa, but after soaking overnight the corn is rubbed as clean as possible (with your hands) of every bit of skin and rinsed until quite white—except for the pedicel, where the kernel was attached to the cob, which remains a dark yellow color. It is then sent to the local corn mill or *tortillería* to be ground coarsely, and as dry as possible.

This masa should be kept no longer than two days in the refrigerator. It can then be stored frozen for about three months. Two pounds (900g) of dried corn will yield about 3½ pounds (1.680kg) masa.

Masa Molida en Seco
Dry-Ground Masa

I don't really know what to call this method, which produces a superb, crumbly masa that can be prepared at home if there is someone around who has both patience and a strong arm. You need a metal corn grinder like that illustrated here and on page 300 with the grinding disks set fairly, but not too, close together.

Prepare the corn with cal in the usual way. The following day rub all the kernels (with your hands) as clean as possible of every bit of skin, rinse well in several changes of water, and strain off as much of the water as possible. Then grind twice without adding a drop of water and pass the mixture through a medium, not fine, strainer to sift out the tough pedicels. The corn is now ready to be used for many types of fine tamales. For a rougher-textured tamale omit the sifting step.

Store in the refrigerator for no more than two days. It will keep satisfactorily in the freezer for three to four months. Two pounds (900g) of dried corn will yield about 1½ pounds (675g) masa.

FROM TOP: GRINDING THE SEMIDRY CORN MASA; THE GROUND MASA.

Masa Colada

STRAINED MASA

The most traditional cooks that I have come across in Tabasco and Campeche make their "strained" masa for tamales colados of local whitish corn prepared without lime. But many Yucatecan cooks use just an ordinary masa para tortillas that has been cooked with lime. The masa is never as white and delicate. You have three options:

1. Prepare your own white corn and have it ground to a medium texture at the local *tortillería*, providing that it has a grinding machine.

2. Prepare your own white corn and grind it as finely as possible in the Mexican metal corn grinder illustrated in the photograph on page 300.

3. Use a tortilla masa from your local *tortillería,* making sure it is not made from one of the commercial dried corn flours mentioned below.

Harina para Tamales

TAMALE FLOUR

I always associate this method of preparing dried corn with the spongy white (masa) tamales typical of Mexico City and part of the central Bajio area. You can buy this textured flour of white (cachuazintle) corn in some stores where they still grind chiles and spices or in local neighborhood markets, but I have not seen it commercially packed for some years now. Do not confuse it with the flour sold for tortillas (like Maseca, Minsa, or Quaker Masa Harina).

To prepare this "flour" use the wide, white corn used for pozole and prepare it as if for tortilla masa (see page 241). After soaking all night, rub it well of all the skins and rinse in several waters until it is absolutely white, except for the pedicels. Set the corn out in one layer on trays in the sun—it will take about two days depending on the intensity of the sun—or dry for several hours in a very low oven until dried and almost brittle but not toasted. Then grind (dry) in a grain mill to a fine, but slightly textured consistency, and sift in a medium strainer to remove all the tough pieces of pedicel. Depending on the efficiency of your machine, principally the strength of the motor, you will probably have to grind and sift a second or even third time until all the pieces of corn are evenly ground. This is a lesson in patience.

See the recipe for tamales on the next page. Two pounds (900g) of dried corn will yield about 1½ pounds (675g) when sifted.

This flour can be refrigerated for 1 month, frozen for 6.

Tamales Cernidos con Rajas y Queso

TAMALES FILLED WITH POBLANOS AND CHEESE

This type was the very first tamale I tasted in Mexico, and it has become a favorite. I always prefer a cheese, bean, or vegetable filling; meat, with few exceptions, always seems so worn-ragged with the cooking. These tamales are eaten just as they are: no adornments!

Although the proportion of lard in the masa seems high, don't worry: it is absorbed by the husk and transpires into the water. Of course, if you must use vegetable shortening, try at least adding a small proportion of lard for flavor. Unless you are a glutton for punishment or you need a tough arm exercise, use an electric mixer for this masa. Some cooks add baking powder, but if the masa is sufficiently beaten, no leavening agent is necessary. To test this, put a small dollop of the dough onto the surface of a glass of water. It should remain floating on top. If it sinks, continue beating and test again.

Once cooked, any leftovers should be kept no longer than two days in the refrigerator as they tend to dry out. This tamale freezes very successfully for about three months. When reheating, do not defrost; put them still frozen into a hot steamer for 15 to 20 minutes, or reheat in their husks, covered, on a comal over medium heat, turning them from time to time until well heated through and spongy to the touch, about 10 minutes.

Most Mexican cooks make much more substantial tamales (of this kind) than I like, with rather thick masa. I put a very thin layer of the masa over the husk, remembering that it expands quite a bit in cooking. You will see from the photographs that I have used a U.S.-type husk and have not closed it completely at the top. If you do try to bend the top over, the tamale won't expand as much and be as porous.

MAKES ABOUT 36 TAMALES

About 40 dried corn husks, soaked and shaken dry

THE MASA

12 ounces (340g) pork lard

1½ pounds (675g) Harina para Tamales (opposite)

About 2 cups (500ml) lukewarm chicken broth

Sea salt to taste (you need plenty)

THE FILLING

2 cups (500ml) reduced Salsa Verde (page 204) made with 1 pound (450g) tomates verdes reduced until rather thick

2¼ cups (563ml) chile poblano strips

1 pound (450g) Mexican Chihuahua or Manchego, or Muenster, cut into small bars about ½ inch (1.25cm) square and 2½ inches (6.25cm) long

recipe continues on page 222

BALL OF MASA FLOATING
IN WATER.

FROM TOP LEFT: ADDING TAMALE
FLOUR TO LARD; THE TEXTURE,
WITH SOME BROTH ADDED;
ADDING ADDITIONAL BROTH.

FROM TOP: SPREADING MASA IN CORN HUSK; ADDING SALSA VERDE; ADDING THE FILLING OF CHEESE AND CHILE POBLANO.

BELOW: THE INITIAL AND FINAL FOLDS OF THE HUSK.

Have ready a prepared tamale steamer (see page 301).

Put the lard into the bowl of an electric mixer and beat at high speed until very white and fluffy, about 5 minutes. Gradually add the tamale flour alternately with the broth, beating very thoroughly after each addition. Add salt to taste and test the masa by floating a bit on a glass of water.

Put the prepared steamer over medium heat. Give the husks an extra shaking to dispel excess water.

Spread a large tablespoonful of the masa in a very thin layer over the top part of the husk and down about 3 inches (7.5cm) as shown. Put 1¼ tablespoons of sauce down the middle of the masa, two chile strips, and a piece of cheese. Fold the edges of the husk over so that the dough covers the filling (or almost; it may be unorthodox but I like a little bit of filling to show through the masa) and fold the spare part of the husk toward the back. Set the prepared tamales on a tray while you assemble the rest. Work as fast as you can so that the sauce is not absorbed by the masa.

By this time the water in the bottom section of the steamer should be boiling and the coins rattling around. Stack the tamales firmly but not too tightly, to allow for expansion in the top of the steamer. Cover with more husks, or a piece of thick toweling, and a tightly fitting lid and cook the tamales over a brisk heat for about 1¼ hours. To test for doneness, remove one of the tamales and tap lightly; it should feel spongy and resilient, and when opened up the dough should separate easily from the husk. Even thoroughly cooked, the masa will be slightly textured.

Tamales Yucatecos Colados

YUCATÁN TAMALES OF STRAINED MASA

These tamales are named for their corn masa, which is strained through cheesecloth, cooked with lard, and cooled to form a gelatinous dough. This recipe, which also appeared in The Art of Mexican Cooking, *was given to me as long ago as 1969, when I started serious research for my first Mexican cookbook,* The Cuisines of Mexico. *One of my first teachers was Transita, the traditional Mayan cook at the home of Joann Andrews at Quinta Mari in Mérida.*

The "strained" dough is, or should be, very delicate when the tamales are freshly cooked so it is better to let them cool off and "set" for about 15 minutes before serving in their banana-leaf wrappers. They are eaten alone! Don't be tempted to mess up the flavor with a sauce. Yes, these tamales are fussy to make, but they are so delicious. There is always a group of cooks who enjoy this culinary exercise and have the pleasure of eating them "homemade." But the sad part is that, while they can be kept for about three days in the refrigerator, they do not freeze well.

MAKES ABOUT 28 TAMALES

recipe continues on next page

2½ pounds (1.125kg) Tortilla Masa
(page 216) or masa made with
nixtamal, *refregado,* and *finely* ground
(see page 241)
Approximately 4 cups (1L) water
1 cup (250ml) melted pork lard
2 teaspoons sea salt, or to taste

THE CHICKEN FILLING

1 large chicken (3 to 3½ pounds
/1.35–1.575kg), cut into 8 pieces with
skin and bones
1 small head of garlic, or 6 cloves
1 teaspoon crumbled dried Yucatecan
oregano, or ½ teaspoon ordinary
Mexican toasted
3 tablespoons Simple Recado Rojo
(page 164)
1 tablespoon bitter orange juice
(page 110) or fruity vinegar
¼ teaspoon freshly ground black pepper
Sea salt to taste

THE ACHIOTE-FLAVORED GRAVY

The reserved masa (see above)
1½ tablespoons flour
3 cups (750ml) reduced broth from
cooked chicken

THE ASSEMBLY

The 28 masa squares
28 to 30 wilted banana leaves about
9 inches (22.5cm) × 7 inches (17.50cm)
The gravy
The cooked chicken
About 10 plum tomatoes, sliced
lengthwise into 56 slices
⅔ cup (165ml) roughly chopped epazote
leaves
Approximately 1½ cups (375ml) thinly
sliced purple onion
2 (15-inch/37.5-cm) ties of banana leaf for
each tamale

FOR THE MASA: Put 2 pounds (900g) of the masa into a large bowl, reserving the rest for the gravy. Add the 4 cups (1L) of water and mix until completely smooth. Pour the mixture through a fine strainer, pressing out any remaining lumps with a wooden spoon, into a wide, heavy pot. Discard the debris, which is called *shish* and integral to the Tabascan tamale called Socuco (see *My Mexico,* page 347); failing that, feed the chickens or the compost. Cook the mixture over medium heat, stirring and scraping the bottom of the pan as it will start to thicken almost immediately. Start stirring in the lard little by little; it should be absorbed completely before the next addition. When all the lard has been stirred in, season the mixture well with the salt and continue cooking until it is thick and shiny; it will shrink away from the sides of the pot and barely plop from the wooden spoon. This process should take 15 to 20 minutes.

Turn the mixture out into a Pyrex dish or mold about 11 inches (27.5cm) by 7 inches (17.5cm) and at least 1½ inches (4cm) deep, and smooth it evenly to a

recipe continues on page 227

FROM TOP: MIXING MASA WITH WATER;
TEXTURE OF THE DILUTED MASA; FINAL
SQUEEZE IN THE STRAINING PROCESS.

BELOW: THE THICKENED MASA; THE
FINISHED MASA.

BELOW: WILTING THE BANANA LEAF;
POSITIONING A PIECE OF DOUGH;
ADDING THE TOPPINGS. FROM TOP
RIGHT: THE PROCESS OF FOLDING AND
TYING THE TAMALE.

depth of about ¾ to 1 inch (2–2.5 cm) deep. Set aside to cool and become firm. Cut into 28 rectangular or square portions.

FOR THE CHICKEN: Put the chicken pieces into a pot and barely cover with water. Add the unpeeled garlic, oregano, *recado rojo,* bitter orange juice, and seasoning and bring to a simmer. Continue simmering until the chicken is just tender, about 25 minutes. Strain and set the chicken aside to cool. Return the broth to the pan and reduce over high heat to 3 cups.

When the chicken is cool enough to handle, strip the meat from the bones and divide it into fairly thick pieces, together with some of the skin for flavor.

FOR THE GRAVY: Put the masa and flour into a bowl and gradually stir in 1 cup of the hot broth, pressing out any lumps with the back of a wooden spoon (or put into the blender and blend until smooth). Gradually add the rest of the broth and strain again back into a saucepan. Cook over low heat, stirring and scraping the bottom of the pan to avoid sticking, until the gravy thickens to the point where it will cover, without slipping off, the back of a wooden spoon, about 5 minutes. Set aside to cool.

TO ASSEMBLE THE TAMALES: Set the prepared tamale steamer over medium heat and line the top section with any scraps of leftover banana leaves. Put a masa square on each piece of banana leaf and top with 1 tablespoon of the gravy, some chicken, two slices of tomato, some of the epazote leaves, and a few onion slices, topping them with a little more of the gravy. Fold the two longer edges of the banana leaf together securely, then the shorter edges and fold them toward the back to form a watertight package. Tie securely but not too tightly, and place in the top of the steamer horizontally in overlapping layers. Cover with more banana leaves or a cloth and a tightly fitting lid. Steam for about 1 hour. Remove from the steamer and allow them to cool a little and set before serving.

Tamales Oaxaqueños de Frijol

OAXACAN BEAN TAMALES

This recipe for tamales filled with a paste of black beans is typical of those made in the central valley of Oaxaca, but varies from those prepared in other parts of the state. In the Isthmus, the dough is textured and seasoned with epazote, chile, and crisp crumbs of chicharrón. In the Sierra Juarez and Usila, they are more elongated in shape, wrapped in a fruity flavored leaf of a wild plant of the ginger family—locally called cherimole *and* guaxmole, *respectively (Renealmia sp.). In the Sierras above the Pacific Coast the beans are sandwiched in between seven layers of masa, hence their name* tamales de siete cueros, *to give just a few examples of variations.*

These tamales can be wrapped in either a dried corn husk or a fresh or dried hoja de milpa, the long narrow leaf of the corn plant. When used fresh, the leaf gives a special flavor and color to the dough. The dough or masa for these tamales is finely ground; among the more traditional cooks no lard is added, and they are formed by hand. However, the method given here is practically foolproof as long as you don't forget to always line both *plates of the tortilla press with plastic bags.*

These tamales de frijol are often served with a chiles pasilla (de Oaxaca) sauce (see The Art, *page 342) or to accompany tasajo for almuerzo or comida. A local and delicious way of reheating these tamales is to spread the surface with a mixture of crushed garlic, oregano, and salt and brown them slightly on a liberally larded comal.*

MAKES ABOUT 15 TAMALES

About 15 dried corn husks or corn leaves, soaked until pliable and shaken dry, or 15 long fresh corn leaves
15 pieces hoja santa, about 3 inches (7.5cm) × 2 inches (5cm), or whole avocado leaves

THE BEAN FILLING
2 tablespoons pork lard
1 small white onion, thickly sliced
1/2 cup (125ml) water
1 medium chile pasilla de Oaxaca, wiped clean and lightly toasted

6 avocado leaves, toasted
6 garlic cloves, toasted and peeled
About 3 1/2 cups (875ml) Frijoles de Olla Oaxaqueños (page 97), with their broth
Sea salt to taste

THE MASA
2 ounces (60g) pork lard
Sea salt to taste
1 pound (450g) Tortilla Masa, about 2 cups (500ml) (page 216)

FROM TOP: TOASTING GARLIC AND AVOCADO LEAVES; FRYING ONION AND CHILES; BLENDING THE PREPARED INGREDIENTS WITH THE COOKED BEANS.

First make the filling and allow it to cool before assembling the tomales. Heat the lard in a deep skillet. Add the onion slices and fry to a golden brown. Spoon the onion into a blender jar (leave the lard in the skillet) and add the ½ cup (125ml) water. Tear the chile, seeds included, into pieces and add to the jar. Crumble the avocado leaves in with the rest of the ingredients, discarding the stalks and tough ribs. Add the garlic and blend to a smooth consistency. Gradually add the beans and their broth, blending well after each addition, adding more water only if needed to release the blades of the blender.

Reheat the lard in the skillet and add the blended mixture. Cook over medium heat, stirring and scraping the bottom of the pan from time to time to avoid sticking until you have a thick paste, about 10 minutes. Adjust the salt and set aside to cool, covered, to prevent a crust forming over the surface.

Have ready a tamale steamer prepared with water in the lower section with four dimes or light coins and the base of the top section lined with dried corn husks. Put the prepared steamer over medium heat.

Work the lard and salt into the masa with your hands until evenly distributed. Divide the dough into about 15 portions and roll each into a smooth ball. Place one of the balls on the bottom plate of a tortilla press with both plates lined with plastic bags and flatten slightly with your hand. Press the top plate down, but not too hard, to obtain a disk of dough about 5½ inches (14cm) in diameter.

Lift up the top bag simply to loosen the dough, and turn the bags over, with the dough inside. Remove the top bag. Spread a generous tablespoon of the bean paste over the center of the dough, leaving a border of about ½ inch (1.25cm) all around. Then starting from the right (or the left if you are left-

recipe continues on page 231

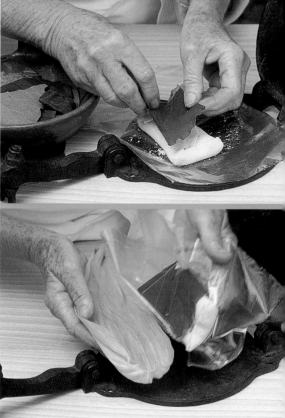

FROM TOP LEFT: SPREADING BEAN
PASTE ON THE MASA; FIRST FOLD
OF THE BEAN TAMALE; SECOND
FOLD; FOLDING THE ENDS. ABOVE:
PLACING THE HOJA SANTA LEAF;
PLACING TAMALE IN DRIED CORN
HUSK.

OPPOSITE, FROM TOP: FOLDING
THE HUSK; THE COOKED TAMALE.

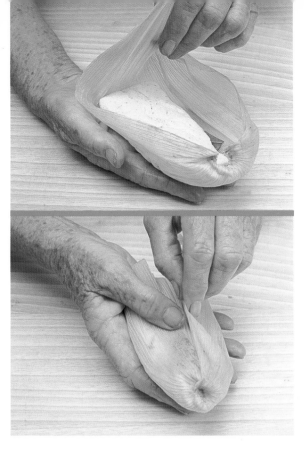

handed), gently lift up the bottom bag and fold the dough two-thirds of the way, covering the bean filling. Repeat on the other side so that the bean filling is completely covered. Then fold the dough at each end over about $\frac{1}{2}$ inch (1.25cm) to make a rectangular shape about $3\frac{1}{2}$ inches (9cm) $\times$ 2 inches (5cm).

Carefully transfer the tamale to whichever wrapper you choose to use, place a piece of the hoja santa on the surface, and fold the wrapper over to completely cover the dough. When all the tamales have been assembled, place them horizontally in overlapping layers in the top of the steamer, cover tightly, and cook over a fairly high heat—the coins should be jiggling around vigorously—for about 40 minutes.

If the tamales are properly cooked, the dough will separate cleanly from the wrapper. Eat immediately or store in the refrigerator for no more than two days. These tamales freeze very well for at least three months. Remember not to defrost before reheating in the steamer.

Uchepos

Fresh Corn Tamales from Michoacán

CUTTING THE BASE OF THE
FRESH CORN COB AND
UNFURLING THE LEAVES.

Of all the fresh corn tamales in Mexico, these uchepos—
the name derives from the Tarascan word uchepu,
*meaning bread—made in and around Morelia, in the
state of Michoacán, are the most delicate.*

*The varieties of fresh white corn grown in Mexico
are not, thank goodness, as sweet and soft as their
American counterparts. When mature, the starch content
is higher and they can be used successfully for fresh corn
tamales, budines, and so on. In the United States, one
would have to look for field corn destined for cattle feed.
When cooked, uchepos can barely be separated from their
fresh corn husk, so it is best to make them ahead and let
them cuajar, or set, well before reheating and serving.*

*This is one tamale that is turned out of its husk for
serving. The recipe is typical of the refined cooking of
Morelia, where I first learned how to make them in the
restaurant Los Comensales and with my friend, a one-
time restaurateur, Livier Ruiz de Suarez. Typically,
uchepos are served there with a tomato sauce, a slice of
queso fresco and/or crème fraîche.*

*For 5 cups (1.25L) of corn kernels you will need
about six large ears of white starchy field corn—always
buy a bit extra; in any case you can always use up any
leftovers in a soup—but get them with their green husks
intact. When choosing the corn, make sure that the
kernels are quite firm and mature but still a little bit
juicy. If they have passed that stage and are too hard and
dry, the tamales will be chewy and flavorless. If they are too immature and very juicy, the
tamales will never cohere and just fall apart when served.*

*Cut carefully around the base of the leaves, as near as you can to the stalk so that you
leave as much of a cupped end as possible to hold the rather runny dough. Carefully unfurl
the leaves and set aside for wrapping the uchepos. Rinse and shake dry.*

*You could use the corn grinder illustrated on page 300 to grind the fresh corn or the
metal blade in a food processor.*

MAKES 20 UCHEPOS

5 cups (1.25L) fresh corn kernels
¼ cup (63ml) whole milk, if necessary
1 tablespoon sugar
2 tablespoons unsalted butter
2 tablespoons natas (see page 29) or crème fraîche
1 rounded teaspoon sea salt
20 fresh corn husks

FOR SERVING
1½ cups (375ml) Salsa de Jitomate Cocida (page 201)
½ cup (125ml) crème fraîche
8 ounces (115g) queso fresco or substitute, cut into strips about ¼ inch (75mm) wide

Have ready a tamale steamer with light coins in the water of the bottom section, and the base of the top section lined with the tougher, outer leaves of the corn.

SHAVING KERNELS AND ADDING CREAM TO BLENDED CORN.

Put half of the corn kernels into a food processor and blend to a fairly smooth consistency—if they tend to be rather tough and dry, add the milk. Gradually add the rest of the corn, blending well after each addition until you have a finely textured consistency. Add the sugar, butter, natas, and salt and blend well. It should have the consistency of a thick, textured batter.

Fill the leaves immediately because the mixture tends to separate as it stands. Place a very generous tablespoon of the mixture down the center of one of the leaves, leaving space at the top and bottom. Fold the leaf—it is like rolling it—loosely over the mixture. Press the husk so that the mixture does not escape from the bottom and turn the end of the husk up toward the back.

Place a few of the uchepos in a horizontal layer in the top section of the steamer and steam over high heat for about 10 minutes or until the mixture is just beginning to set. This ensures that the bottom layer will not be squashed. Give the mixture a good stir before filling the rest of the husks. Each filled husk should go immediately into the steamer so that the mixture does not separate and ooze out. Steam over high heat for about 1 hour. When tested by opening up one of the uchepos, the mixture should be set and just beginning to separate from the husk.

recipe continues on next page

Serve two each of the uchepos on warmed plates with a little sauce—not smothered with it or you will lose the fresh corn flavor—a scant tablespoon of cream, and a small slice of slightly melted queso fresco.

Uchepos can be kept well for about three days in the refrigerator, but it is best to freeze any left over: they keep very well for about three months. But remember to reheat them in the steamer without first defrosting.

FROM TOP LEFT: FILLING THE FRESH CORN HUSK; ROLLING THE HUSK; TURNING THE END BACK; THE STEAMED TAMALES. ABOVE: A SERVING OF UCHEPOS.

Tamales Norteños

NORTHERN TAMALES

This recipe (given to me by a friend from Nuevo León, a legacy from his late mother) was published in The Essential Cuisines of Mexico. *I have included it here as a contrast to the others; these delicious tamales are small and slender, wrapped in a dried corn husk torn into half lengthwise. The masa is colored and seasoned with some of the sauce—with a pronounced flavor of cumin—used in both the meat or the bean filling. I have, however, used a slightly different masa from the original tamale masa prepared at the local tortillería in Monterrey.*

The original tamales were filled with everything a pig's head had to offer—rind, ears, and tongue for great textures and flavors, plus a little lean meat. However, you can use stewing pork but—please—with a little fat on it!

MAKES ABOUT 36 TAMALES

About 36 prepared halved corn husks, about 3 inches (7.5cm) at the top

THE MEAT FILLING
1 pound (450g) stewing pork with some fat, cut into $\frac{1}{2}$-inch (1.25-cm) cubes
Salt to taste
4 ancho chiles, seeds and veins removed
2 garlic cloves, peeled
1 teaspoon cumin seeds, crushed
4 peppercorns, crushed

THE MASA
1 pound (450g) Tortilla Masa (page 216), about 2 cups (500ml)
$4\frac{1}{2}$ ounces (130g) pork lard, about $\frac{1}{2}$ cup/125ml, plus 2 tablespoons
3 tablespoons reserved chile sauce
Salt to taste

Have ready a prepared tamale steamer.

FOR THE MEAT: Put the pork into a pan, cover with water, add salt, and bring to a simmer. Continue cooking until the meat is tender, about 35 minutes. Drain and set aside, reserving the broth. You will need about $2\frac{1}{3}$ cups broth (585ml) for the tamales, so either reduce to that amount over high heat or add water to make up to that amount.

Put the chiles and garlic into a small pan, cover with water, bring to a simmer, and cook for about 5 minutes. Strain and set aside.

Put $\frac{1}{2}$ cup (125ml) of the broth into the blender jar, add the cumin and peppercorns, and blend well. Tear the chiles into pieces and add to the blender with the

recipe continues on page 237

ABOVE: ADDING RESERVED BLENDED CHILES TO MASA AND LARD. FROM TOP RIGHT: SPREADING DOUGH ON A CORN HUSK; ADDING MEAT FILLING; FOLDING THE HUSK. OPPOSITE: THE COOKED TAMALE.

garlic and another ½ cup (125ml) of the broth. Blend to a fairly smooth consistency.

Put the meat into a skillet, add all but 3 tablespoons of the chile sauce and 1 cup (250ml) of the broth, and cook over medium heat, stirring from time to time until the sauce is slightly reduced to a medium consistency, about 15 minutes. Adjust the salt.

For the masa: In a large bowl, mix the masa, lard, the reserved chile sauce, and about ⅓ cup (83ml) of the remaining broth. Beat well together either by hand for about 5 minutes or in an electric mixer for a little less, until it is well aerated and spongy. Add salt to taste.

Line the top of the steamer with corn husks and place an inverted soup plate in the middle. Señora Hortensia, whose recipe this is, simply used two crossed forks on which to rest the tamales on a slant. Spread 1 rounded tablespoon of the dough in a very thin layer over the entire width of the top and for about 4 inches (10cm) down the halved husk. Place a few pieces of the meat and some of the sauce down the center of the dough and fold one edge of the husk over to completely cover the dough and form a very slender tamale. The overlapping leaf complete with masa will help to seal the husk securely. Double the point of the husk to cover the seam and make sure you do not flatten the tamales when wrapping them—most beginners do!

Stack the tamales in circular layers, the first layer supported by the upturned plate (or forks). Cover the steamer and cook over high heat for about 50 minutes. The tamale is cooked when the dough feels springy to the touch inside the husk and will separate cleanly from it.

These tamales are best eaten right away. They will keep for about two days in the refrigerator, but after that it is best to freeze them. Reheat either in a steamer or on the comal.

MAKING
TORTILLAS

The main indigenous staple of the Mexican diet is corn; and the indigenous bread, without which no meal is complete, is the corn tortilla. The tortilla is a thin round of unleavened, unseasoned dough called *masa.* The masa is made of mature, dried corn kernels that have been partially cooked in a solution of lime—in Mexican terms, *nixtamalizado*—and ground to a smooth consistency. Then patted by hand, or stamped out in a press, the tortilla is cooked on an ungreased griddle known in Mexico as a *comal.*

When properly made and eaten straight off the comal, a tortilla can be delicious: soft and mealy, subtle in flavor. Given time they become an addiction. The tortilla is a most versatile food. Most commonly it is eaten as bread with a meal, but it is also used as wrapping for tacos and enchiladas; for tostadas, it becomes a plate; with totopos, it is a scoop. For layered casseroles—budines—it resembles a type of pasta; when cut up stale, it is used for chilaquiles; dried and ground to resemble a textured flour, it is converted into gorditas or dumplings, among other uses.

As a diehard traditionalist, I think we ought to celebrate the tortilla as we know it while it is still alive and before it succumbs, alas necessarily, to the "tortilla of the new millennium" (*La tecnología de la tortilla, pasado, presente y futuro,* por Juan De Dios Figueroa Cárdenas y Jesús González Hernández, Ciencia y Desarrollo, Enero/Febrero 2001). The "improved" tortilla will be made with the entire corn kernel transformed by infra-red rays and ohmic heat through one long, waterless process into a highly nutritious tortilla with elevated quantities of its present nutrients: lysine, tryptophan, vitamins, minerals, and fiber. But what will it taste like? I don't trust those scientists: look what they have done to the tomato! Of course, this means a tremendous saving of water, fewer pollutants with the *nejayo* (limed cooking water), and energy—key factors with population overgrowth. This will also imply, again alas, genetically engineered corn incorporating genes from amaranth or soya to increase the lysine and tryptophan. This could come about as soon as fourteen years.

Today, sadly, there are now more bad tortillas than good ones, unless you happen to be in Oaxaca or other isolated places where the art of transforming mature, dried corn into masa, or dough, and then forming the masa into tortillas, is still very much alive—and a bad or indifferent tortilla made of the newish fast-track materials is not tolerated. If this is what's happening in Mexico, you can imagine what is happening elsewhere.

Some years ago there were some very good sources for delicious corn tortillas in the United States (and there still are—Harbar Corporation, for instance, in Jamaica Plains). When I was first traveling and teaching after the publication of *The Cuisines of Mexico,* I used to find some superbly made ones in small family-run *tortillerías* in Detroit and in the Central Market in Los Angeles, among a few others. Now, however, too many tortillas are made with a heavy, yellow masa that seems to be overcooked, or with too high a percentage of lime, which accounts for the yellow color and slightly bitter taste, although the purveyors insist that this extends the shelf life! And if they look deceptively white with no dark telltale specks of the kernels' germ, then they are probably made of a powdered corn product—one of the few that have monopolized the market.

Tortillas made of these products lack taste and texture, and they disintegrate when used to make dishes like chilaquiles or tortilla casseroles. On the other hand, there are some tortillas that are indeed made wholly or partially of corn, are deep yellow in color, are overly thin and as stiff as a board. Depending on where you live, you may have no choice but to make the best of what is available. Or buy in bulk by mail order and freeze the good ones.

If you want to make your own tortillas, then visit a local *tortillería* or tortilla factory—there are many now throughout the United States—buy their tortilla masa, and follow the instructions on the following pages. Or as a last resort, buy the powdered stuff and hope—I've given instructions on page 246. For dedicated aficionados, I give you the one method (that I use) for converting parched corn into masa for tortillas, although I have worked with cooks who vary their methods slightly.

OPPOSITE, FROM TOP: ADDING CORN KERNELS TO WATER WITH LIME; COOKED CORN, NOW YELLOW; WASHING SKINS FROM KERNELS.

Making Masa

Dried Corn Masa

MAKES ABOUT 3½ POUNDS (1.575KG), ABOUT 6¼ CUPS (1.75L)

**2 pounds (450g) dried corn, about
5 cups (1.250L)**

**1 tablespoon powdered lime (calcium
oxide; see page 243)**

Run the dried corn kernels through your hands and discard any bits of extraneous stones, chaff, etc. Then rinse in cold water and drain.

Put the corn into a nonreactive pot and cover with cold water to 2 inches (5cm) above the surface of the corn. Skim off any bits of skin or hollow kernels that float to the surface. Bring to a boil over medium heat. Meanwhile, dissolve the lime in about ½ cup (125ml) cold water and add it through a fine strainer to the corn. Stir well to distribute the lime evenly—the corn will turn a bright yellow color—and cook over medium heat, stirring from time to time to prevent the kernels from sticking to the bottom of the pan. Test by rubbing a few kernels between your fingers, and when the papery skin slides off the kernel easily, it is done. This should take about 15 minutes (see Note). Take care not to let the corn cook beyond this point. If it does, then you will find yourself with a gummy masa that cannot be used for tortillas.

Remove pan from heat, cover, and set aside to soak overnight. This is now called *nixtamal*. The following day, rinse the corn well—the water will be yellow and slimy with the softened skins—rubbing off the loose skins. Some cooks are not too diligent about this when making tortilla masa—after all, the skins provide some roughage—but most cooks in Oaxaca *refregar*, or rub

recipe continues on next page

well, until the kernels are quite white, except for the pedicel at the top of the kernel, which remains yellow.

Drain the corn, now *nixtamalizado,* and take it to a mill *(molino),* where traditionally it is ground—with no water added—between round, flat grinding stones to give it a smooth, soft texture. The resulting dough, or masa, is now ready to be used for tortillas or *antojitos* like sopes or gorditas, or for some types of tamales.

NOTE: *Weights will vary, of course, depending on how damp the masa is. Fifteen minutes is the amount of time needed to cook this amount of corn. Larger quantities of corn will take longer to cook, depending on your pot (a large amount will cook more quickly in a wide pot than in a deep pot). The exception is the small, flat local corn from the Isthmus of Oaxaca. These kernels may take as long as 45 minutes.*

SOME USEFUL TORTILLA MEASUREMENTS

1½ pounds (680g) corn tortilla masa makes about 2⅔ cups (666ml).
This quantity makes about 15 balls, each 1½ inches (4cm) in diameter.
Pressed out well, a ball makes a tortilla of about 5½ inches (14cm) wide.

Storing Corn Masa

Without a doubt, masa is best used right away or at least the same day. Do not leave it in a warm atmosphere for more than an hour or so because it will sour easily—not that soured masa is bad for you, but the slightly off taste masks somewhat the flavor of the corn. Refrigerate the masa until ready to use.

Don't forget to work the masa—kneading it a little—before you start making your tortillas. Some meticulous country cooks work the masa on the metate, or grinding stone, just to make sure it is completely smooth before starting.

If you have some masa left over, it can be frozen for up to one month. It can be kept for a longer period, but when defrosted it tends to lose its flexibility and breaks when pressed out for tortillas.

Corn Tortilla Rarities

In the highland areas of the state of Mexico, Michoacán, and elsewhere, you will see corn tortillas that are coarser in texture, dark in color, and generally thicker. They have been made with a proportion of wheat berries that are added to the soaked and strained corn, and ground with it. These tortillas are mainly sold toward the end of the year before the newly harvested corn is ready to be used and to eke out existing stocks, although you can find them occasionally at other times.

There's another very unusual instance of additions to the corn tortilla, this time in the rather poor rural area in the Mixteca Alta of Oaxaca. A certain proportion of cooked and chopped wild greens is added to the masa. They are nutritious and delicious to boot, especially when eaten with some cheese and a sauce (see *Essentials*, page 51). I have heard of other much more unusual additions, but not come across them personally—the roots of the banana trees, for instance!

Lime, or Cal

In Mexico, lime (calcium oxide) is principally used—and has been used for centuries—to convert dried corn into *nixtamal,* which is then ground into a dough, or masa, for tortillas or tamales.

In public markets in Mexico, lime is sold in solid lumps that have to be slaked to a powder before using. (Be careful not to get any of the powder near your eyes in this process.) To slake the lime, put a piece into a nonreactive bowl and sprinkle liberally with cold water, but do not let it sit in water. If the lime is fresh, it will immediately begin to crumble into a powder, sending off heat and a light steam. If the lime is very hard, this crumbling will take some time, but don't despair; it will slake eventually.

In the southeastern part of the United States, you can find powdered lime, ready to use, sold in small quantities as "pickling lime." It is used for a lye solution for preparing hominy. In Mexico, lime is also used for preparing fruits preserved in a heavy syrup. The soak in a lime solution ensures that the fruits do not disintegrate in the long cooking in syrup. Also, a paste of lime and water is used to "cure" the surface of clay comales, or even metal cooking surfaces, to prevent ingredients, especially masa, from sticking. A lime paste is also used to seal the pores in the outer surface of traditional clay cooking "bowls," cazuelas and ollas.

Corn Tortillas

MAKES 15 5½-INCH (14-CM) TORTILLAS

1½ pounds (675g) Tortilla Masa (page 216), about 2½ cups (625ml)

Water if needed

Work the masa well with your hands to make sure the moisture is evenly distributed and there are no lumps or whole corn kernels that have escaped the grinding stones.

Here's a warning to save you a lot of tears about the first impossible tortillas: if the masa is *too damp*, then you will never be able to get it off the plastic bags (in the press). If this happens, flatten the masa and leave in an airy place to dry until manageable. If your masa is *too dry*, then it will crack and crumble as you attempt to make tortillas. Add some water, working it in well a little at a time. (I know from experience that a little water goes a long way and you can easily make it too wet.)

Either divide the masa into the number of tortillas you are going to make—but cover them with a damp cloth so they do not dry out while you are working with the first balls—or with more practice, just take off lumps of the dough as you go along and keep the bulk of it covered while you work if the air is very warm and dry. Try to keep the balls as near the same size as possible. Mexican cooks are expert at this.

Heat the ungreased comal or griddle over medium heat. To test, the dough should sizzle slightly as it hits the hot surface. Line your tortilla press with two plastic bags, as shown in the photograph. Place a ball of the dough on the bottom plate of the press and flatten it a little with your hand. Close the top plate of the press down firmly—but don't put all your weight on it—and flatten the tortilla very thin. Open the press up, and remove the top bag.

Lift up the bottom bag with the dough, and resting the dough on the inside of your fingers (do not rest the dough on your palm because it will be difficult to transfer onto the comal), carefully peel back the plastic bag. Take care to lay the tortilla, as shown, on the comal and let it cook until the underside is just turning opaque and speckled with brown. Do not leave the tortilla to cook too much on the first side or it will be overcooked and inflexible.

Flip the tortilla over and cook a little longer on the second side. Flip it back again and continue for a few seconds more until the dough is cooked through and the top skin (ideally) puffs up. This will be the "face" of the tortilla, and since it is

recipe continues on page 246

BELOW: PLACING RAW TORTILLA ON THE
COMAL; COOKING THE SECOND SIDE;
TURNING THE TORTILLA.

FROM TOP: PRESSING BALL OF MASA
ONTO PRESS; CLOSING THE PRESS;
LOOSENING PLASTIC WRAP FROM MASA.

likely to flake off, it will always go inside when making a taco or an enchilada. (Note: Any traditional Mexican cook will tell you that a tortilla should never be turned more than twice.)

Unless you are going to eat it right away, place the freshly made tortilla immediately on top of the rest wrapped in a thick cloth, or a cloth-lined basket, to keep them warm and flexible. This process does need some practice until you become adept at recognizing what the masa should ideally feel like, just the right heat under the comal, and the timing of the turns. When you have those mastered, it is a soothing, therapeutic sort of job after a possible frenzied first attempt.

Wipe off the plastic bags and reserve them for a lot of other tortilla making. Make sure the inside plates of the tortilla press are clean and place a double layer of paper toweling between them when storing the press. Wipe the comal off with a slightly greased paper and store.

NOTE: *Tortillas can be made with Maseca, Minsa, or masa harina, but only use these dried corn products as a last resort. They do not have the same flavor or the texture of the real thing, and they tend to disintegrate when used for chilaquiles, tortilla soup, or casseroles. If you try to make tortillas right away without the waiting period, you will find the dough is not flexible and will tend to break and crumble.*

To make just over 1½ pounds masa (680g), or 2½ cups (625ml), use 12 ounces (340g) maseca or minsa, about 3 cups (750ml), and just under 2 cups (450ml) warm water. Put the powdered corn product into a large bowl and add most of the water, always reserving about ¼ cup (63ml) until you see how much the flour will absorb. Work well with your hands until smooth. Cover with a damp cloth and set aside in a cool spot for about 1 hour. This gives the starch particles time to swell and absorb the moisture thoroughly, giving more flexibility to the dough. Then follow the instructions for making tortillas on page 244.

Totopos

The word *totopo* is generally applied to small pieces of crisp-fried corn tortilla. *Totopo* is the abbreviated form of the Nahuatl word *totopotza*, meaning "to toast." (In Chiapas and parts of Tabasco, a *totoposte* is a large crisp tortilla with a hole in the middle so that it can be easily carried and strung up to dry out of reach of any predators). If totopos are triangular in shape, they are generally used as a scoop—for a guacamole, for instance, or for refried beans. Cut into narrow strips, they are used in a tortilla soup; cut into small squares they are mixed with scrambled eggs or used as a topping for soups, or for the unusual but delicious chilaquiles and minguichis of Michoacán (*The Art,* pages 328 and 331). (These should not be confused with the totopos from the Isthmus of Oaxaca.) I have had totopos, the size of tortillas, made with lard in the masa in Querétaro and Yucatán, and with rendered marrow fat in the Mixteca Baja of Oaxaca.

It is best to use a thinner tortilla for totopos; the thicker they are, the more oil they will absorb. It is also best to start the day before so that they dry out well before frying and will absorb less oil. Stack about four of the tortillas together and cut them into halves and each half into three triangular wedges, *or* cut off the rounded edges to form a large square and then cut into the size of squares you require for a recipe (use the edges for a soup or whatever, or throw to the chickens, dogs, or birds).

Set them out on a tray or cookie sheet in one layer to dry. At this stage you can decide if you are going to fry them or bake them crisp. If you are not in a hurry and are watching your energy bills, leave them in a warm airy place to dry off overnight. If you are in a hurry, put them into a 350°F (180°C) oven or toaster oven, turning them over from time to time until they are dried through, 20 to 25 minutes. You can continue to let them bake until crisp right through, or you can brush them well with oil and let them become crisp and slightly browned.

If you choose to fry the totopos, after first drying them, heat vegetable oil to the depth of about ½ inch (1.25cm) in a small skillet—so that you will use less oil—and fry in small batches until a deep golden color. Drain in a strainer over the skillet—so excess oil will drip back into the pan—and then spread on absorbent paper (brown shopping bags are great for this).

Totopos can be prepared well ahead and reheated if necessary in a 350°F (180°C) oven or toaster oven. If you have a lot left over, put them into an airtight container and freeze them since they tend to become rancid after a while.

Totopos Salados

This is a popular method of salting totopos, but it should be done in small batches with a small quantity of oil, which tends to break down with the liquid. It splatters horribly, too! Make a solution with 6 tablespoons of salt to 2 cups (500 ml) of warm water, stirring until the salt has completely dissolved. Quickly douse a small quantity of the tortilla pieces in the water and strain before throwing into the hot oil. Fry until crisp through.

Totopos Istmeños

The photograph at left shows totopos that are made exclusively in the Isthmus of Tehuantepec in the extreme southern part of Oaxaca. They are brittle disks of different sizes baked crisp, but not browned, on the sides of a globular oven of unglazed clay, a *comizcal*, which is used like the tandoor of India. The totopos are made of the local zapolote corn, which apparently has some gluten. This gives the masa its flexibility. Small holes are pierced in the uncooked dough so that it will remain flat and not inflate. These totopos are eaten to accompany a meal but most popularly as a snack. The corn masa is sometimes mixed with a black bean paste, giving it a dull brownish hue.

Tostadas

One of the most popular snacks in Mexico is a *tostada*, a crisp-fried corn tortilla topped with very simple ingredients. It might be mashed beans, shredded cabbage, chile sauce, and a sprinkling of cheese; or the tortilla is piled high with the most fanciful combinations of shredded meats or jellied pork, lettuce, tomato, cream, crumbled cheese, a chile sauce. Along the coast it would be shredded fish, or crab prepared in numerous ways, and again with lavish toppings.

There are no rules, except for the fact that the tortilla shouldn't be too big—about 4½ inches (11cm)—or you find the whole thing collapsing into a sorry mess in your lap, for this is finger food. Forget knives and forks! The attraction lies in crunching through layers of different textures and surprising contrasts of flavor.

Some of my favorite tostadas are from Apatzingan, Michoacán (*The Art*, page 26), and others in *Essentials*, pages 89 and 90, topped with Tinga Poblana (*Essentials*, page 272), Saragalla de Pescado (*Essentials*, page 381), or Salpicon de Jaiba (*Essentials*, page 16) as well as Minilla (*My Mexico*, page 303).

Raspadas

In the areas of northeast Michoacán, parts of Jalisco, Colima, and Nayarit, the evening pozole is served with *raspada*—very thin corn tortillas fried flat like tostadas. The difference is that the tortillas are half cooked on one side, and a layer of uncooked dough is removed with a short, thin, metal rolling pin. Raspadas are usually bought from women dedicated to making them daily, as a cottage industry, rather than made at home.

Tlayudas

If in Oaxaca you see a very large corn tortilla about 12 inches (31cm) in diameter, almost transparent and leathery to the touch and with an irregular surface, it is a *tlayuda*. They can be made of white, yellow, or blue corn.

The tortilla is stamped out in an extra-large usually wooden or metal press, given a little cradling by the expert hands of the tortilla maker, and cooked on a large clay comal over a wood fire. Once cooked it is set in slanted fashion around the edge of the comal until it is dried to a leathery consistency; it is not toasted crisp. In this fashion it is highly durable and portable.

Tlayudas accompany meals in central Oaxaca. They are put in the center of the table and large pieces are broken off and used as a shovel to lift the food or cooked sauces like moles, especially in country homes where knives and forks are rarely used. I am not suggesting you try to make them—I wouldn't!

Chilaquiles

A Mexican *almuerzo*, or brunch, would not be complete without a dish of chilaquiles. It is the simplest of dishes but so satisfying when cooked with care and good tortillas. (Please, if you respect your palate and stomach, never, never use a package of Fritos!) The word *chilaquiles* comes from the Nahautl words *chilli* and *quilitl*, the latter naming an edible wild green (although I have never known them made with wild greens). At some point, someone referred to them as a "broken-up old sombrero." I always think of them as a convenience food, using up the day before's tortillas and sauce.

Sometimes the tortillas are just torn into small pieces, but more often they are cut into six triangles: halved and then each half cut into thirds, but in Michoacán they are more often than not cut into small squares and fried extra crisp.

Always let the tortillas dry out the day before, but cut them to the required size before drying so that they will absorb less of the oil. Fry the tortillas in small batches in one layer with the minimum of oil.

Chilaquiles are either eaten alone or accompanied by beans or eggs, and sometimes topped with poached shredded chicken. They should be served immediately, otherwise the tortillas will become soggy. There are some fabulous recipes for chilaquiles in my other books, but I will give here another variation that I was once served in Puebla and loved.

Chilaquiles

MAKES 6 SERVINGS

12 5-inch (12.5-cm) corn tortillas, cut into 6 triangles and dried overnight

THE SAUCE
7 pasilla chiles, cleaned of veins and seeds
2 cups (500ml) water
2 garlic cloves
3 peppercorns, crushed
3 whole cloves, crushed
Sea salt to taste

ASSEMBLING THE CHILAQUILES
About ¼ cup (63ml) vegetable oil
The dried tortilla pieces
Salt to taste

THE TOPPING
⅓ cup (83ml) finely chopped white onion
½ cup (125ml) crumbled queso fresco
⅓ cup (83ml) thinned crème fraîche or sour cream
¼ cup (63ml) roughly chopped cilantro (optional)

Have ready a warmed serving dish or individual dishes and a tray lined with paper toweling.

TO MAKE THE SAUCE: Lightly toast the chiles, pressing them flat on the comal for a few seconds on each side, or until the inside of the chile turns an opaque tobacco brown. Put the chiles into a small pan, cover with water, and bring to a simmer. Remove from the heat and set aside to soak for about 5 minutes. If the chiles were very dry in the first place, leave them for 10 minutes. Strain, discarding the water.

Put ⅓ cup (83ml) of water into the blender, add the garlic and spices, and blend until smooth. Add the chiles and the rest of the water little by little, blending well after each addition. You should have about 3 cups (750ml) of a sauce that will comfortably coat the back of a wooden spoon.

recipe continues on page 252

FROM TOP: DRAINING FRIED TORTILLA PIECES;
ADDING SAUCE; STIRRING TO COAT TORTILLA
PIECES WITH SAUCE.

OVERLEAF: ADDING CHEESE TO COOKED
CHILAQUILES.

To ASSEMBLE: Heat a little of the oil in a medium skillet, add some of the tortilla pieces in one layer, and fry until golden and fairly crisp but not hard. Drain first in a strainer and then on paper toweling. Repeat with the remaining tortilla pieces, adding more oil if needed.

There should be 2 tablespoons oil in the pan: make up or remove to that amount. Heat the oil, add the sauce, and fry over fairly high heat until reduced a little and seasoned, about 5 minutes. Add salt to taste. Stir in the tortilla pieces, mixing them to cover them evenly with the sauce, and heat for a few seconds until bubbling. Cover the top lavishly with the onion, cheese, and cream—and cilantro if you want—and serve immediately.

Enchiladas

Enchiladas have become without a doubt one of the most popular Mexican dishes outside the country as well as in Mexico itself. While enchiladas are offered on a brunch menu—for businessmen—in more upscale restaurants, they would be on the lunch menus of more modest restaurants. At home, Mexicans would be more likely to eat them for supper. Enchiladas are served either alone or with some beans, de olla or refried.

Although the term *enchilada* is used rather loosely for some very different regional specialties, I give here two recipes for the better known enchiladas, each representing one of the two main methods of cooking, assembling, and serving them:

1. Whereby the tortillas are wilted in hot oil, then dipped into a cooked sauce.

2. Whereby the fresh tortilla is dipped into a raw sauce and then fried.

There are some basic things to remember:

✳ Work fast. There is nothing appetizing about a lukewarm, soggy enchilada.

✳ Any type of enchilada is best eaten immediately after cooking.

✳ If they are to be reheated, this should be done within a maximum of 20 minutes of preparing the enchiladas and put into a preheated 350°F (180°C) oven for no longer than 10 minutes, to prevent them from becoming a soggy mess of disintegrating tortillas—unless, of course, you have used those hard indestructible ones I mentioned before.

✳ When filling enchiladas, always remember that the face of the tortilla—the side that is cooked first with the thin layer of the dough that has inflated—should be on the inside. If not the enchilada will lose it appetizing coating of sauce.

✳ Use two instruments—tongs, but not the clawed type, and a broad spatula—when frying enchiladas so that you can turn them more easily and also ensure they do not break in midair when removing them from the pan.

✳ Always have warmed plates or a warmed serving dish ready.

✳ Have a tray or cookie sheet lined with a double layer of absorbent paper ready to blot the enchiladas as they come out of the pan.

✳ To ensure less greasy enchiladas, use a small skillet into which the tortilla will just fit comfortably and use about 1 tablespoon of oil at a time, replenishing only when needed. As you are removing the fried tortilla, using tongs and a spatula, hold it for a few seconds to drip over the pan and then blot it on the next tortilla to be fried.

✳ Always have the fillings and toppings ready ahead of time.

✳ For Enchiladas Verdes (page 254), have your sauce waiting ready and very hot.

✳ Sauces should be well salted because the tortilla isn't.

One of the simplest fillings, and very tasty, is a sprinkle of añejo cheese or crumbled queso fresco, and some finely chopped onion. Other popular fillings are cooked and shredded meat (pages 138 and 144), lightly fried potatoes with chorizo (page 142) or with strips of poblano chile (page 50), or mixed vegetables—the variety is endless depending on regional tastes or whatever you have on hand.

There is also a countless number of enchilada sauces in Mexico depending on local tastes and what chiles are available, so I give here one simple example for each of the two methods.

Enchiladas Verdes

MAKES 12 ENCHILADAS

About $\frac{1}{3}$ cup (83ml) vegetable oil, for
  frying
12 corn tortillas, about $5\frac{1}{2}$ inches (14cm)
  in diameter
2 cups (500ml) Salsa Verde (page 204), of
  medium consistency, kept warm
2 cups (500ml) shredded and well-salted
  cooked chicken (page 144)
1 cup (250ml) poblano chile strips
  (page 50) from about 5 chiles

THE TOPPING
About $\frac{2}{3}$ cup (166ml) thin sour cream
About $1\frac{1}{2}$ cups (375ml) tightly packed,
  finely shredded lettuce
About $\frac{1}{2}$ cup (125ml) finely grated queso
  añejo, cotija (Pecorino in the U.S.), or
  crumbled queso fresco
About $\frac{1}{2}$ cup (125ml) finely chopped
  white onion

Have ready a warmed serving dish and a tray
lined with a double layer of absorbent paper.
Heat about 1 tablespoon oil in a small skillet,
preferably about 6 inches (15cm) in diameter.
Using tongs and a spatula, fry one of the tortillas lightly on both sides, turning it twice so
that it heats through thoroughly but does not
become crisp around the edge, about 50 seconds. Blot the excess oil onto the next tortilla
to be fried. Dip the tortilla into the warmed
sauce: it should have a good coating. Put a generous portion of the chicken and chile strips on
one-third of the tortilla and roll it up loosely.
Proceed with the remaining tortillas.

Pour the remaining sauce over the top and
serve immediately, topped with the sour cream,
shredded lettuce, cheese, and onion.

Enchiladas can be served in individual
portions (of two) or on a warmed serving dish.
Serve immediately after assembling, alone or
with soupy or refried beans.

FRYING THE TORTILLA AND DIPPING IT
INTO COOKED SAUCE.

LEFT AND BELOW: ROLLING THE
FILLED ENCHILADA.

A SERVING OF
ENCHILADAS VERDES.

Enchiladas Rojas

This simple recipe illustrates the second main method for preparing enchiladas, whereby a freshly made corn tortilla is dipped into an uncooked sauce and then fried. After frying, it is filled with a little cheese and onion and topped with vegetables. This is the type of enchilada that one finds in Michoacán and the central Bajio area of Mexico. It is often served with a piece of chicken; alone these enchiladas make a good vegetarian dish.

If you want a more picante *sauce, use 6 guajillos and 6 puyas. Start by preparing the vegetables and then the sauce.*

MAKES 12 ENCHILADAS

THE VEGETABLES

3 medium carrots, trimmed, scraped, and cut into small cubes
1 teaspoon sea salt
4 small red-skinned or other waxy potatoes, peeled and cut into small cubes
⅓ cup (83ml) mild white vinegar

THE GUAJILLO CHILE SAUCE
(MAKES ABOUT 1⅔ CUPS/416ML)
9 guajillo chiles, seeds removed but not the veins
About 1½ cups (375ml) water
2 garlic cloves, roughly chopped
2 peppercorns, crushed
2 whole cloves, crushed
¼ teaspoon dried Mexican oregano
Sea salt to taste

ASSEMBLING THE ENCHILADAS

About ⅓ cup (83ml) vegetable oil, for frying
12 corn tortillas, about 5½ inches (14cm) in diameter
The chile sauce
8 ounces (225g) fresco or grated cotija cheese (you can substitute Pecorino)
About ⅔ cup (165ml) finely chopped white onion, salted

FOR SERVING

Chiles Jalapeños en Escabeche (page 46)
About 1½ cups (375ml) finely shredded lettuce or cabbage
About ½ cup (125ml) crumbled fresco or cotija cheese
About ½ cup (125ml) finely chopped white onion

TO PREPARE THE VEGETABLES: Put the carrots into a small pan, barely cover with water, and add the salt. Bring to a boil, covered, and continue cooking for about 5 minutes. Add the potatoes and cook until still a little al dente, about 10 minutes more. Drain and transfer to a glass or nonreactive bowl. Barely cover with cold water, add the vinegar, and set aside while you prepare the chile sauce.

FROM TOP: FRYING VEGETABLES
WITH CHILE SAUCE; FRYING
TORTILLA DIPPED IN SAUCE;
FILLING AN ENCHILADA.

To MAKE THE SAUCE: Flatten the chiles as much as possible and toast lightly on a comal over medium heat for a few seconds, taking care not to let them burn. Transfer the chiles to a small pan, cover with water, and bring them to a simmer; continue cooking for about 5 minutes. Set them aside to soak for another 10 minutes; by this time they should be rehydrated and fleshy. Strain the chiles, discarding the water, and tear them into small pieces.

Put ½ cup (125ml) of fresh water into a blender jar, add the garlic, peppercorns, and cloves, and blend as smooth as possible. Gradually add the chiles and the rest of the water, blending well after each addition. It is important to blend the chiles as much as you can because the skins are very tough. Transfer the sauce to a bowl through a fairly fine strainer, pressing as hard as you can to extract as much of the flesh as possible. Discard the debris of tough, stubborn pieces of skin. (This step is not necessary if you are using anchos and most other chiles that have a much softer skin.) Add the oregano and salt to taste and set aside.

Preheat the oven to 350°F (180°C), as you need to keep the enchiladas hot as you fry and fill them and fry the vegetables. Heat a serving dish or individual plates.

To ASSEMBLE THE ENCHILADAS: Heat about 2 tablespoons of the oil in a small frying pan, about 6 inches (15cm) in diameter over medium heat; the oil should not be too hot or the sauce will burn. Dip one of the tortillas into the sauce to lightly coat it, and supporting it with tongs and a broad spatula, fry for a few seconds on

recipe continues on next page

each side—the tortilla should not become crisp around the edge. Hold it over the pan to drain off excess oil, then sprinkle some of the cheese and onion down the center of the "face" (see page 244) of the tortilla, roll loosely, and place on a serving dish. (You could fry all the enchiladas, then fill them, but the chilied surface tends to stick to the paper toweling or whatever you are working on.) Add more oil, a little at a time as necessary, and prepare the rest of the tortillas. When all the enchiladas have been fried there should be some chile sauce left over. Add the remaining oil and heat it, then add the rest of the sauce and the drained vegetables and fry them until the sauce has reduced and seasoned the vegetables, about 5 minutes. Pass them through a strainer to drain off any excess oil and spread over the enchiladas.

Top with the serving ingredients and serve immediately.

Enfrijoladas

While enchiladas are tortillas dipped in a chile sauce, enfrijoladas are tortillas immersed in a purée of beans. There are regional versions of enfrijoladas, but to my mind the best are those prepared in Oaxaca, where the main elements—corn tortillas and little black beans—are so delicious. Because this is such a simple dish it relies on the very freshest tortillas and well-seasoned beans. Some cooks just immerse warmed tortillas in a sauce of cooked and puréed beans, but if you season that purée by reducing it in a little lard (or oil), you will have much more tasty enfrijoladas. Ideally, the tortillas should be from 5½ to 6 inches (14–15cm) in diameter. If they are not of the best quality or have been frozen, heat them well before using or go one step further and heat them through in very little melted lard or oil before immersing them in the sauce.

For cooking and seasoning the beans, follow the recipe on page 228 for bean tamales, but reduce for about 8 minutes. You will need about 3½ cups (875ml) sauce for the twelve tortillas. I suggest you reduce the beans to a very loose paste and then dilute with bean broth or water to that amount: when the tortilla is immersed it should emerge well coated, neither too thick nor too thin.

In Oaxaca, the black beans for enfrijoladas are flavored with any one of a variety of herbs—poleo, hierba de conejo, hoja santa, epazote—but it is more usual to see them flavored with avocado leaves for this recipe.

Enfrijoladas

Enfrijoladas are served most frequently for almuerzo, *midmorning breakfast—to accompany eggs, or* tasajo *(semi-dried beef), or chicken coated with oregano and garlic topped with sliced white onion and crumbled queso fresco. They should be eaten as soon as they are prepared.*

Of course, the black bean purée can be prepared well ahead and any left over can be frozen and will keep well for about three months.

MAKES 12 ENFRIJOLADAS

3½ to 4 cups (875ml–1L) Oaxacan
  black bean purée (page 228)
12 corn tortillas, 5½ to 6 inches
  (14–15cm) in diameter
1 medium white onion, cut into half-
  moons

¾ cup (188ml) crumbled queso fresco
⅓ cup (83ml) flat-leaf parsley leaves
Rajas de Chile de Agua (page 40;
  optional)

Heat the bean purée and the tortillas. Immerse the tortillas one by one into the bean purée—they should be well coated—and fold them into fours. Sprinkle with the onion, cheese, and parsley leaves. If you care to, pass separately the chile strips.

Papadzules

This is a classic Mayan dish from Yucatán made with the minimum of ingredients. Warmed corn tortillas are dipped into a pumpkin seed sauce from which the green oil has been extracted, and flavored with epazote. The tortillas are filled with chopped hard-cooked egg and topped with a tomato sauce. The final touch is given by little decorative pools of the green oil. Great care has to be taken to ensure that these ingredients are the freshest— slightly rancid or bitter pumpkin seeds can ruin it—and great care also should be taken in the preparation.

MAKES 12 PAPADZULES

2½ cups (657ml) water
2 large leafy stems of epazote
1 scant teaspoon sea salt
8 ounces (225g) hulled raw pumpkin
    seeds, about 1⅔ cups (313ml)
12 freshly made, warm corn tortillas,
    5 to 5½ inches (13–14cm) in diameter
5 large hard-cooked eggs, shelled, roughly
    chopped, and salted

FOR SERVING
1 cup (250ml) Salsa de Jitomate Yucatecan
    (page 203)
2 large hard-cooked eggs, white and yolks
    separated and finely chopped
12 epazote leaves (optional)

Have ready a warmed, not hot, serving dish or warmed individual dishes.

Put the water, epazote, and salt into a small pan and bring to a boil. Lower the heat and simmer for about 5 minutes.

Spread the pumpkin seeds in a thin layer over the bottom of a large skillet and heat through gently over low heat, turning them over from time to time. The seeds will swell, but take care not to let them become even slightly golden or the sauce will lose its fresh green color. You might want to keep a lid handy because often some of the seeds will start jumping out of the pan. Spread the seeds onto a metal tray to cool completely before grinding to avoid the blades seizing up with the volatile oil.

Using an electric coffee/spice grinder, grind a portion of the seeds at a time to a slightly textured consistency, 5 to 6 seconds. If the seeds are ground too fine, then it will be more difficult to extract the oil.

Have a small glass bowl ready for the oil.

Put the ground seeds onto a plate that has a slight ridge around the rim. Measure out ¼ cup (63ml) of the epazote broth and little by little sprinkle it—don't, for

recipe continues on page 262

BELOW: SQUEEZING OIL FROM SEEDS;
DIPPING TORTILLA IN PUMPKIN SEED
SAUCE; FILLING PAPADZULE WITH
COOKED EGG.

FROM TOP: EPAZOTE BROTH; TOASTING
THE PUMPKIN SEEDS; ADDING BROTH
TO GROUND PUMPKIN SEEDS.

MAKING TORTILLAS   261

goodness' sake, pour the whole lot—over the seeds and work it in with your hands, first having put the telephone on automatic answering. Gradually add the liquid until you have a crumbly but cohesive paste.

Tilt the plate a little to one side and put a folded cloth underneath to hold it in that position. Start squeezing the paste and you will see that drops of oil will begin to extrude. Add a little more warm liquid if necessary—you probably won't need the whole amount—and keep squeezing until you have collected almost 4 tablespoons of dark green oil. (This is pure vitamin E, and great for the hands.) Crumble the paste into a blender jar, add the remaining strained epazote broth, if desired, and blend until smooth.

Transfer the sauce to a skillet and warm through over the lowest possible heat, stirring almost constantly because the starch content of the seeds begins to swell and the particles tend to coagulate in the bottom of the pan.

Dip one of the warm tortillas into the sauce: it should be lightly covered. If the sauce is too thick, dilute it with a little extra warm water. Work as quickly as you can, dipping each tortilla into the sauce, holding it with tongs but supporting it with a spatula so you don't get left with a bit of broken tortilla in your tongs. Sprinkle some of the chopped egg across one-third of the tortilla, roll it up, and place it on the warmed dish.

When all the papadzules are assembled, pour the remaining sauce over them. (If the sauce has thickened and become grainy looking, put it back into the blender with a little extra warm water and blend until smooth.) Now pour on the tomato sauce and sprinkle the chopped egg whites and yolks. Decorate with the optional epazote. As a final touch, spoon in little pools of the oil. Serve immediately or the oil will sink back into the sauce and all that work will have been for naught! Of course, it is more colorful and attractive to serve the papadzules together on one serving dish.

Tacos

Tacos are the snack food par excellence, eaten throughout the day at the drop of a hat in the marketplaces or sidewalk stands of Mexican towns. A soft tortilla rolled around, or two small ones doubled over, and practically any type of filling constitutes a taco. They can be soft, fried crisp, or *sudado*—sweated or steamed.

While there are no limits to what goes inside a taco (and I am talking about a snack, not how you eat the main dish of a meal with a tortilla filled with the meat and sauce), you would not normally have a taco of mole or pipián, nor would you have a very soupy filling that would run out at the ends. Use shredded pork or chicken seasoned with tomatoes and chiles, shredded beef in a slightly different guise, nopales, mushrooms, or chorizo and potato, barbacoa. All these recipes and suggestions are in my other books.

TO PREPARE SOFT TACOS: Put some of the filling and sauce—if called for—across one-third of a freshly made or warmed corn tortilla and fold the edge of the tortilla across the filling, making a slight upturn as shown in the photograph. Then roll firmly but not too tightly. Eat immediately, tipping up the end so that the filling does not fall out.

IF YOU ARE GOING TO FRY THE TACO: Heat the lard or oil in a small pan and place the filled and rolled tacos seam side down, pressing to seal more securely. Fry until golden and crisp on the underside, then turn and fry until completely crisp, but not hard, all the way round.

TACOS SUDADOS (LITERALLY "SWEATED"): These are more unusual and delicious if you have a good-quality tortilla and not one that becomes gummy in the steam. For this I use a fan-type steamer in a shallow pan. Heat the water to boiling and lower the heat a little. Fill the tortillas and roll in the usual way, or double them over and secure with a toothpick. Place them in the steamer, cover, and

FROM TOP: FILLING AND ROLLING A TACO TO READY IT FOR FRYING.

heat the tacos through until flabby but not disintegrating. This will take about 3 minutes, depending on the thickness and quality of the tortilla. Eat immediately.

FOR TACOS DE CANASTA: These "basket tacos" are essentially the same as tacos sudados, but not quite. They are typical of the prepared foods sold every morning by women in marketplaces, usually in central Mexico, who arrive with their cloth-lined baskets filled with tacos that have been prepared and stacked while still hot. They are, in fact, steamed and succulent.

Wheat Flour Tortillas

Wheat was one of the first crops introduced into Mexico by the Spanish, both to provide their indispensable basic food, bread, and for communion wafers. In fact, the first mill was licensed in 1525, in the name of Cortes, Rodrigo de Pax and Hernando López de Ávila, only two years after the conquest. Wheat very soon flourished in Tacubaya (now part of Mexico City), and in parts of Tlaxcala and Atlixco it was possible, with irrigation, to have two crops a year. Very much later wheat was introduced into the plains of north and northwest Mexico, where today the wheat tortilla is predominant.

Sizes of wheat tortillas vary as one travels west, and obviously you can always come across exceptions. In Nuevo León, the standard (although I hate to use that word) flour tortillas made in the homes of my friends are 4 to 5 inches (10–13cm) in diameter. They are thin and have small patches of bubbles in the dough or, better still, they inflate totally and are thus very light. Some are now made with a proportion of whole wheat flour. In Chihuahua, the flour tortillas tend to be larger, about 6½ inches (16 cm); they are also thicker and do not bubble or inflate. In fact, I have seen cooks making them in a ranch in Chihuahua and pressing the dough down while cooking with a flat iron to ensure a smooth surface. Another interesting note from that area is that when the ranch-hands go out for days into the prairie to inspect cattle, one of them is always designated as the cook. It is he who will prepare the tortillas from scratch, taking along the smallest board and rolling pin for the process. They always turn out to be larger than those made by the women! But the largest, thinnest flour tortillas of all are those known as *tortillas de agua,* made in Sonora, and are about 18 inches (46cm) in diameter. They are vulgarly known as *tortillas de sobaco,* "armpit," as they are flung dramatically from side to side.

The flavor of these tortillas varies slightly with the type and milling of the wheat. There are local brands in each entity specially produced for these tortillas, and bread. You will obtain the best result by using a hard-wheat bread flour, but if this is not available, add a small proportion of gluten (¼ cup/83ml) to 1 pound/450g all-purpose flour. Without a doubt, pork lard or melted beef fat was originally used for these tortillas, but most cooks today prefer to use vegetable shortening, which seems to make the dough more flexible, apart from dietary factors.

I prefer to make these tortillas by hand, despite the fact that it takes a little longer to work the dough than if you use either an electric mixer or a Cuisinart. Besides, you judge more accurately the amount of water that the flour will absorb. Flour tortillas keep well for a day or two in the refrigerator, but to avoid mold it is best to freeze them. They will keep well for about two weeks. After that time they tend to disintegrate when reheated.

Tortillas de Harina

FLOUR TORTILLAS

MAKES 24 6- OR 7-INCH (15–18-CM) TORTILLAS

1 pound (450g), approximately 4 scant cups, bread flour or all-purpose flour with ¼ cup (63ml) gluten added
4 ounces (115g) solid vegetable shortening, cut up and softened (about 1 cup/250ml)

1 scant teaspoon sea salt
1 cup (250ml) warm water

Have ready a lightly greased tray.

Put the flour in a circle on your work surface and rub in the fat with your fingertips. Dissolve the salt in the water and mix it into the flour, a little at a time to see how much it will absorb. Never pour it all in at once; your mixture may turn out to be too wet.

Scrape up all the peripheral flour with a dough scraper and work the ingredients into a cohesive dough. Continue kneading until you have a very smooth, elastic dough, about 4 minutes. You could also use a food processor, with the metal blade, for mixing, but take care not to add too much liquid. I don't see much point in using a heavy mixer for this; it is not a difficult dough to work.

Divide the dough into, say, 24 pieces—depending on the size of the tortillas you want. Balls of about 1½ inches (4 cm) will make tortillas of 6 to 7 inches (15–18cm)

recipe continues on next page

FROM TOP: MIXING FAT INTO THE FLOUR;
KNEADING THE DOUGH; CUTTING DOUGH
INTO PIECES.

in diameter. Roll each piece into a smooth ball; set them onto a lightly greased tray, cover loosely with greased plastic wrap, and set aside to rest for about 1 hour or more at room temperature.

Heat an ungreased comal or griddle over medium heat.

Take one of the balls and flatten it out on a lightly floured work surface, then roll it out with a narrow rolling pin or, better still, a dowel, turning as you go to keep the circular shape as even as possible. To make it even larger and thinner, lay the tortilla over the back of your cupped hand and gently stretch it out around the edges. When the tortilla is the required size, then lay it (see photograph opposite) onto the hot griddle—there should be a sizzling sound as it touches the comal. After a few seconds the dough will be bubbling up unevenly and the underside will be speckled with brown patches. Flip the tortilla over and cook for a few seconds more or until the surface is blistered but opaque. It should still be flexible. If left too long on the heat it will overcook and become brittle.

Cover immediately with a cloth to keep warm.

To reheat, place the tortilla briefly on a fairly warm comal for a few seconds or until heated through, and serve immediately, or keep covered as before.

ROLLING A TORTILLA WITH A DOWEL.

STRETCHING THE
TORTILLA.

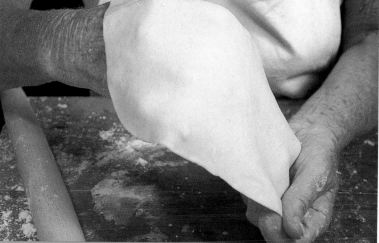

THE BRIEF COOKING OF
THE FIRST SIDE.

MAKING
VINEGAR

The types of vinegar used in traditional Mexican recipes tend to be mild and often on the sweet side. A mild white commercial vinegar is generally used for chorizo, and a more fruity, homemade vinegar is the choice for pickles and escabeches. Many provincial housewives and cooks still make their own, most often using the peel of the pineapple with *piloncillos* (raw sugar cones) to hasten the fermentation. In the Zitacuaro, Michoacán, market one storeowner does a brisk trade with his vinegar made from overripe fruits collected from the neighboring stands. In Tabasco and southern Veracruz, a delicious vinegar is made from fermenting unpeeled bananas. The results may be different with every batch and the methods are totally unscientific, but when they do turn out well, it is a culinary triumph. I have two jars in my kitchen started in 1992. I have no idea how, but they have acquired a rich dark brown color and taste very much like a commercial balsamic.

Pineapple Vinegar

MAKES ABOUT 6 CUPS (1.5L)

The peelings from a medium pineapple   1½ quarts (1.5L) water
4 heaped tablespoons crushed piloncillo
**   or dark brown sugar**

Mix the ingredients in a 3-quart (3L) glass container, cover, and set in a warm place
in the kitchen or on a sunny windowsill. Within a day or so you should see the liquid
beginning to ferment. It will continue to do so; leave it until the liquid becomes a
clear light amber color, which will take about six weeks. It will look messy and foamy
as the mixture ferments, and small flies will crowd around the surface, but the flavor
will change from sweetish to a pleasant acidity. You will need to strain it after about
six weeks. A thin gelatinous "mother" should form after two months (leave the
mother). The vinegar will then be ready
to use.

   If things don't go according to order,
small white maggots will float on the top
(they may anyway). Strain the liquid, and if
it doesn't become acidic within a month,
throw it away and start again. Of course,
the mother and more sugar can be used as
a starter for another batch, but I prefer to
start afresh with pineapple peelings—the
flavor always seems to be superior.

Banana Vinegar

This delicious vinegar can be made from any overripe bananas or plantains. If you don't have them and want to try the recipe, perhaps your local fruiterer will be glad to supply you with some. Of course, the fatter and juicier bananas are best, like the red ones that are sold in Latin American markets. I am afraid the uniformly long, starchy, uninteresting, mass-produced ones will never give the best results. (Mexico can boast many delicious varieties of banana, naturally organic to boot.)

The following is a rough guide, and a very unscientific one, since neither I nor anyone else ever knows the quantity of bananas they use. I keep adding the bananas as they blacken and become soft.

You will need a nonreactive perforated container that sits securely on top of another nonreactive container (I used two unglazed clay pots, one with perforations) to catch the liquid that drips from the fermenting bananas.

MAKES APPROXIMATELY 3½ CUPS (875ML)

4 pounds (1.8kg) overripe bananas	**Approximately 2 ounces (60g) piloncillo for every 1 cup (250ml) liquid**

Slit open but do not peel the bananas and place them in the top, perforated container. Cover with a double layer of cheesecloth and set in a very warm place. Depending on the quality of the bananas and the amount of heat, they will start to disintegrate. Turn the mass over from time to time and gently press down to extract the liquid. Lots of little flies will swarm around because of the fermentation. When the residue of the bananas seem dryish and no more liquid is exuding—in two to three weeks, depending on heat, etc.—measure the cloudy liquid in the bottom container and strain the liquid into glass jars. For every cup (250ml) of liquid, stir in 2 ounces (60g) crushed piloncillo, cover with a loosely fitting lid, and leave to ferment once more. Gradually, the liquid will become quite clear and pleasantly acidic, about two months.

Strain the liquid once more, taking care not to eliminate any gelatinous disks, "mothers," that may have formed. The vinegar will become a brownish-amber color.

MAKING YEAST BREADS

Pan Dulce

Sweet Yeast Rolls

Throughout Mexico, *pan dulce,* the sweet yeast rolls made in countless shapes and often given different regional names, are a joyous part (if they are well made) of everyday meals: for breakfast, tea, or supper with coffee, hot chocolate, or atole. They are usually produced en masse twice a day, early morning and evening. The morning pace is faster as housewives, maids, children (if there is no school), even men, blue- and white-collar workers (not the management-class businessmen, who will be making political or business deals over breakfast at some fancy hot spot) grab their trays and tongs and rapidly select the household's favorites. Then they rush to join the line where shopgirls rapidly count as they pop the breads into a brown paper bag. With the tally in hand they pay the cashier, often—in the towns of Oaxaca and San Cristobal—a formidable-looking woman of uncertain age with markedly Spanish features, and hurry home for breakfast.

I have written in *The Essential Cuisines of Mexico* (and earlier in *Mexican Regional Cooking*) about my experiences working in a bakery in Mexico City in the seventies that produced the following few recipes. They represent a very minor, but popular, selection from the dozens of different types of sweet yeast rolls. (I am afraid their U.S. counterparts, although made by Mexican bakers, fall far short of expectations because everyone hurries the doughs, often with synthetic additives. This is true but to a lesser degree in Mexico itself.)

I do hope you will at least try these trusty recipes because not only are they a culinary challenge but they will give you a benchmark by which to judge what you are buying and eating. As I said before, it is always best to use fresh cake yeast, finely ground sea salt, and unsalted fats. This is the time to buy that great kitchen scale. And do use an electric mixer since the doughs are rather messy to handle.

Equipment for Mexican Yeast Baking

A good heavy scale that indicates the weights in both kilograms and pounds for the United States. (Start the changeover to the metric system, at least in your mind.)

A small diet scale for weighing small quantities if your ordinary scale does not show them clearly enough.

In addition to a normal-size rolling pin, a skinny one 12 to 15 inches (30.5–38cm) long and just under 1 inch (2.5cm) in diameter (or cut off a broom handle or dowel to the required size).

2 plastic dough scrapers—they just work better than anything else.

A portable room thermometer so you can find the right spot for raising dough.

Rubber spatulas of various sizes.

Recycled plastic bags. Let's start thinking much more of using less plastic wrap in the kitchen and instead recycling those thicker plastic bags that inevitably turn up with purchases. They can be opened up, greased, and used to cover rising dough at any stage of making bread, sweet rolls, etc. But as handy as plastic is, it is always preferable to use greased waxed paper.

Some pieces of toweling, which are always useful for keeping the dough cozy.

A heavy-duty electric mixer with a dough-hook attachment—the heavy KitchenAid mixer is my first choice for this heavy work.

A large wooden board for working the dough.

Cutters for decorating *conchas* or *chicharrones*.

4 very heavy baking sheets—I prefer black metal.

Ingredients for Mexican Yeast Baking

FLOUR. Unless otherwise specified, use unbleached, all-purpose flour. Although cup measures are also given, I suggest you weigh your flour for accuracy's sake. I have taken 1 cup (250ml) flour at 4 ounces (115g), knowing that it can vary depending on the flour and how you fill the cup, although generally a high-protein flour will weigh more than a low-protein one.

FATS. Because of the volume of breads made—and eaten by everybody—a special vegetable shortening or margarine is generally used. But in some areas, especially in southern Mexico, where the bakers pride themselves on the quality of their bread, pork lard is used.

Again I prefer to weigh; there is nothing messier to wash up than a measuring cup smeared with fat. However, as a rule of thumb:

1 cup (250ml) vegetable shortening weighs about 6½ ounces (185g).
1 cup (250ml) lard weighs about 7 ounces (200g).
1 cup (250ml) butter weighs about 8 ounces (225g).

Fats should be weighed at room temperature. When weighed cold, straight from the refrigerator, there can be a difference of 21g (roughly ¾ ounce) less per cupful.

YEAST. I personally prefer to use cake yeast over the dry. I think the former develops a better flavor while the latter is easier to buy and store. I buy ½ large brick (200g/7 ounces), cut off what I need right away, then cut the rest into 1-ounce (30-g) cubes—about 2 tablespoons crumbled—to store in the freezer. There is always a difference of opinion as to whether the yeast is as effective after freezing or not. If it is fresh when you buy it, and you don't store it for more than a month, it doesn't seem to lose its strength.

EGGS. It seems that all eggs are large in the United States, and a standard one should weigh about 2 ounces (60g).

Biscuits de Queso

CREAM CHEESE BISCUITS

These are yeasty American-type biscuits, or flaky scones, the dough enriched with cream cheese and folded as for puff pastry.

In "my" Mexican bakery they were made with margarine, but I prefer to use just a small proportion of butter for even better flavor. While the biscuits are best eaten fresh, the high proportion of eggs helps keep the dough tender for a day or two.

It is worth making this quantity while you are going to all the trouble; both the raw dough and the cooked biscuits freeze very well. Don't try and hurry the dough along. If you do you will never get that satisfying deep flavor.

MAKES ABOUT 40 3½-INCH (9-CM) BISCUITS

recipe continues on next page

THE STARTER

6 ounces (180g) all-purpose flour, about
  1½ scant cups (370ml), plus extra for
  dusting
2 ounces (60g) sugar, about ¼ cup (63ml)
¼ teaspoon finely ground sea salt
1 ounce (30g) cake yeast, about
  3 tablespoons finely crumbled
1 tablespoon warm water
⅓ cup (83ml) lightly beaten eggs
2 ounces (60g) unsalted margarine, about
  scant ¼ cup (58ml), softened

THE DOUGH

8 ounces (225g) sugar, about 1 cup
  (250ml)
8 ounces (225g) cream cheese, 1 scant
  cup (230ml)

2 teaspoons finely ground sea salt
1⅓ cups (335ml) lightly beaten eggs
  (about 7 large)
1 cup (250ml) whole milk
2½ pounds (1.125kg) all-purpose flour,
  about 9½ cups (2.375L)
3 rounded tablespoons baking powder
8 ounces (225g) unsalted margarine,
  about 1 cup (250ml), at room
  temperature
5 ounces (140g) unsalted butter, rounded
  ⅔ cup (170ml), at room temperature

THE GLAZE

2 large eggs, well beaten with 1 tablespoon
  water

FOR THE STARTER: Put the flour, sugar, and salt into the bowl of an electric mixer and mix well. Crumble the yeast into a small bowl, add the warm water, and smooth out the lumps with a wooden spoon until it has the consistency of thin cream. Add this together with the eggs and softened margarine to the flour and mix just until the eggs are well incorporated, about 3 minutes. The dough should be soft and sticky.

Scrape the dough out onto a floured surface and let it rest for about 1 minute. Lightly grease and flour a baking sheet. With well-floured hands, shape the starter into an elongated cushion shape and place it on the baking sheet. Make three deep diagonal slashes across the top, cover with buttered waxed paper, and set aside in a warm place, about 70°F (21°C), to rise and double in volume. This will take about 2 hours.

Prepare the baking sheets by greasing them well.

FOR THE DOUGH: Tear the starter up roughly and place it in a mixing bowl. Add the sugar, cream cheese, salt, and eggs and mix until well combined, about 3 minutes. Add the milk and mix for 3 minutes longer and set aside.

Sift the flour and baking powder together into a separate bowl. Cut the fats into the flour and rub lightly with your fingers until the mixture resembles fine bread crumbs. Gradually combine this with the starter mixture until you have a soft, sticky dough. Flour your work surface well. Turn the dough out and let it rest for 1 minute. Flour your hands and form the dough into a round cushion shape. Leave for 1 minute more.

Flour your hands well again and press the dough out to a thick rectangle. Then roll out to a rectangular shape, the long side toward you, about 21 × 13 inches (53.5 × 33cm). The dough should be about ½ inch (1.25cm) thick.

Dust the surface of the dough lightly with flour. Starting from the left side, fold one-third of the dough over onto the middle third, then fold the right-hand side over the top to form a neat package—make sure that the edges meet neatly. Give the dough one more turn to the right clockwise, roll out again to a rectangle, dust the dough with flour, and repeat the folding process. Repeat the whole process once more. Set aside to rest for 1 minute. (If your dough becomes difficult to handle, leave it for a longer period. If the weather is damp and hot you will probably need to let the dough rest in between the turns for about 15 minutes in the refrigerator.)

To form the biscuits: Dust the work surface well with flour and roll the dough out until it is about ¾ inch (2cm) thick. Dip a plain, round cookie cutter about 2½ inches (6.25cm) in diameter into flour and cut out the biscuits. Place them about 1½ inches (4cm) apart. Flatten each one slightly and stamp the center with a small cutter about ½ inch (1.25cm) in diameter.

Set the biscuits aside to rise, uncovered, in a warm place, about 70°F (26°C), until they almost double in size, about 2 hours.

Arrange two racks in the top half of the oven. Preheat the oven to 375°F (190°C).

Brush the surface of the biscuits with the egg glaze and bake for about 10 minutes. Reverse the position of the trays and bake until they are spongy to the touch and golden brown on top, about another 10 minutes. Allow the biscuits to cool off for about 10 minutes without attempting to transfer them from the trays to the cooling racks.

Conchas or Chicharrones

These most Mexican of sweet yeast rolls are called conchas *(shells) or* chicharrones *(pork rind) depending on the shell-like or cross-hatched patterns of the sugar toppings. The dough itself is spongy and as rich as the bakery owner will allow—and can sell for a higher price. When they first come out of the oven, the aroma and their soft texture are so enticing that naturally you have to eat one, but actually the flavor improves hours later, or even the next day if the atmosphere is not too dry. You can always reheat briefly to revive in a preheated 300°F (150°C) oven. Unfortunately these buns do not freeze well. When defrosted their topping disintegrates, and you need it not only for appearance but as a contrast of flavor and texture.*

You will see that the starter given here is for two batches. It is hardly worth making less; besides, you can always freeze the part you don't use for a future batch of dough. However, I don't recommend keeping it for more than two months.

You really need to weigh your ingredients for this sort of baking; cup measures, as I have said repeatedly, do not give accurate measurements.

MAKES 16 TO 18 BUNS ABOUT 5 INCHES (12.5CM) IN DIAMETER

THE STARTER (FOR TWO BATCHES)
8 ounces (225g) unbleached all-purpose
   flour, about 2 scant cups (425ml), plus
   extra for working
¾ ounce (22.5g) cake yeast, 2 to
   3 tablespoons when finely crumbled
About 3 tablespoons warm water
2 large eggs, lightly beaten

THE DOUGH
1 pound (450g) unbleached, all-purpose
   flour, about 4 scant cups (950ml), plus
   extra for working
6 ounces (170g) sugar, about ¾ cup
   (189ml)
½ teaspoon sea salt
1 ounce (30g) unsalted butter,
   2 tablespoons, softened

1 cup (250ml) eggs (4 to 5 large ones),
   lightly beaten
About ¼ cup (63ml) water

THE SUGAR TOPPING
4 ounces (113g) unbleached, all-purpose
   flour, about 1 scant cup (225ml)
4 ounces (113g) confectioners' sugar,
   about ⅔ cup (166ml)
2 ounces (57g) unsalted butter, about
   ¼ cup (63ml), at room temperature
2 ounces (57g) vegetable shortening
   (about a rounded ⅓ cup/85ml), at
   room temperature, plus 1 tablespoon
   more for the cocoa topping
1 tablespoon ground cinnamon
1 tablespoon unsweetened cocoa powder

Begin the day before.

FOR THE STARTER: Sift the flour into the bowl of a standing mixer. Crumble the yeast into a small bowl, add the warm water, and press out the lumps with a wooden spoon until it has the consistency of thin, smooth cream. Add to the flour with the eggs and beat with the dough hook for about 2 minutes. The dough should be fairly stiff and sticky. Throw a little more flour around the bowl and beat for a few seconds longer or until the dough comes cleanly away from the side of the bowl.

   Flour the work surface well. Scrape the dough out and let it rest for 1 minute. Flour your hands and shape the dough into an oval cushion. Place on a well-greased and floured baking sheet and make three deep diagonal slashes across the surface. Cover with a piece of buttered waxed paper and a thick towel and set aside to rise in a warm place, about 70°F (21°C), until doubled in size, about 1 hour.

FROM TOP: ADDING STARTER TO THE BOWL; THE TEXTURE OF THE DOUGH.

At the end of the rising period, cut the dough into two equal parts—weigh them to make sure they are equal. Put one part in the refrigerator for a later batch of conchas (it will last about two days, or in the freezer for a maximum of two months) and the other into the bowl of an electric mixer.

FOR THE DOUGH: Add the flour, 4 ounces (113g) of the sugar, the salt, butter, eggs, and water to the starter and beat with the dough hook at high speed for 4 minutes. Add the rest of the sugar and beat for 4 minutes longer; the dough should now be soft, sticky, and shiny and form a cohesive mass. Throw a little more flour around the inside of the bowl and beat for 2 seconds more until the dough pulls cleanly away from the bowl.

   Flour your hands and work surface well. Scrape the dough out onto the board and quickly form it into a round cushion shape. Let it rest for 1 minute while you butter and flour a large bowl.

   Put the dough into the bowl, cover with

recipe continues on page 281

BELOW: ROLLING THE DOUGH INTO
EVEN BALLS AND PUTTING ON THE
CINNAMON TOPPING.

FROM TOP: USING CUTTER TO MAKE A
PATTERN IN THE TOPPING; THE BAKED
CONCHAS.

buttered waxed paper and a thick towel, and set aside in a warm place, about 75°F (24°C), for 2 hours. Then place in the refrigerator for the dough to rise very slowly and season well for about 12 hours.

FOR THE SUGAR TOPPING: Just before the end of the long rising period, butter some cookie sheets, and prepare the sugar topping for the buns. Sift the flour and confectioners' sugar together. Cut the fats into the flour and mix thoroughly with your hands until you have a soft, pliable dough. (You could use the smallest food processor, but it is hardly worth having another thing to wash up.) Divide the mixture into two equal parts. Add the cinnamon to one and mix well—it should be soft and malleable. Add the cocoa powder to the other with 1 tablespoon more of the shortening and mix thoroughly. Set aside at room temperature.

After the long rising period, turn the dough out onto a floured surface and let it rest for 1 minute. Flour your hands and quickly work the dough into a round cushion shape. With a plastic dough scraper or very sharp knife, cut the dough into four equal portions. Divide each into four again to make sixteen portions. I like to weigh pieces of about 2 ounces (60g), and then end up with about 18 pieces (they could be made smaller if desired; if smaller, you will need to make more topping).

Lightly flour your hands and roll each piece into a smooth ball by rotating your cupped hands and pressing the dough down firmly. (I learned this trick during my apprenticeship at the bakery.) If the working surface has too much flour, then you can't get any traction. If the dough sticks to the surface you will need a little more flour.

Place the balls on the baking sheets about 3 inches (7.5cm) apart, then grease your hands and flatten each ball a little. Take a small piece of the sugar topping and roll into a ball about 1 inch (2.5cm) in diameter. Again dust your hands with flour, and with your fingers, flatten out a ball of the topping into a disk of about 3 inches (7.5cm) in diameter in the palm of your hand. Press the disk very firmly onto one of the balls of dough so that they adhere well. Repeat until all the balls are covered with either the cinnamon or the chocolate topping. Then decorate with a traditional cutter, or improvise, cutting the topping in a shell, or cross-hatched pattern.

Set the buns aside to rise, uncovered, at a temperature of about 75°F (24°C) until almost doubled in size, about 2 hours. Preheat the oven to 375°F (190°C) and place one or two of the racks in the top half of the oven. Bake the conchas until the dough is light and spongy to the touch and the exposed surface around the topping is a rich brown color, about 12 minutes. Carefully transfer the conchas to a rack to cool in a place free from drafts.

Pan de Muertos

This type of pan de muertos is made for the celebration of the Days of the Dead, November 1 and 2, when families honor their dead by setting up a colorful altar in the house and preparing special foods to put on it and take to the graveside. While this custom has its roots in pre-Columbian central Mexico, it has become popular even in the north (though a friend from Sonora says that her mother considered it very bizarre).

This semisweet yeast bread enriched with egg yolks and other similar breads are circular in form, transversed with "bones," and topped with a "skull." The same dough is used for the rosca de reyes, made for the celebrations for Twelfth Night, January 6. Don't try to hurry the dough along; the flavor will develop better with slow rising. I certainly advise an electric mixer with dough hook for this type of dough, which is rather messy to handle.

MAKES 1 LARGE BREAD ABOUT 11 INCHES (28CM) IN DIAMETER, OR TWO SMALL ONES (AS IN STEPS BELOW).

THE STARTER

1 pound (450g) all-purpose flour (about 4 scant cups/950ml), plus extra for bowl and working surface
1¼ teaspoons sea salt, finely ground
2 ounces (60g) sugar, about ⅓ cup (83ml)
⅔ ounce (20g) crumbled cake yeast, about 2 tablespoons, or 1 scant tablespoon active dry yeast
½ cup (125ml) plus 2 tablespoons water
3 large eggs, lightly beaten
Unsalted butter, for greasing bowl

THE DOUGH

8 ounces (225g) sugar, about 1 cup (250 ml)
7 ounces (200g) unsalted butter, softened, plus extra for greasing baking sheets
1 pound (450g) all-purpose flour, about 4 scant cups (950 ml), plus extra for board and bowl
8 egg yolks, lightly beaten with 2 tablespoons water
About ¼ cup (65ml) water
1 teaspoon orange flower water and/or grated rind of 1 orange

THE GLAZE

4 egg yolks, well beaten
About ¼ cup (65ml) melted, unsalted butter
⅓ cup (83ml) granulated sugar

FOR THE STARTER: Put the flour, salt, sugar, and yeast into a mixing bowl and gradually beat in the water and eggs. Continue beating until the dough forms a cohesive mass around the dough hook. It should be sticky, elastic, and shiny, about 5 minutes. Turn the dough out onto a floured board and form into a round cushion. Butter a

clean bowl and sprinkle well with flour. Place the dough into it, cover with greased waxed paper and a towel, and set aside in a warm place—ideally about 70°F (21°C) —until the dough has doubled in volume, 1½ to 2 hours.

FOR THE DOUGH: Tear the starter into pieces and put it, the sugar, and the butter into the bowl of a mixer and mix well with the dough hook, gradually beating in the flour alternately with the yolks. Beat in the water and flavoring—you should have a slightly sticky, smooth, shiny dough that just holds its shape (since eggs, flours, and climates differ you may need to reduce or increase the liquid). Turn the dough out onto a lightly floured board and form into a round cushion shape.

Butter a clean bowl and dust well with flour and place the dough in it. Cover with greased waxed paper and a towel, and set aside in a warm place, about 70°F (21°C), until it is almost doubled in size, about 1½ hours. *Or,* if you have the time, set it aside gently weighted down in the refrigerator overnight. (If you choose the latter, allow the dough to come up to room temperature before shaping it.)

Liberally grease four baking sheets—two for main "bodies" and two for the "heads and bones." Turn the dough out onto a floured board and divide into two equal pieces. Set one piece aside under plastic wrap while you work with the first.

recipe continues on page 285

FROM TOP: THE RISEN STARTER; FORMING THE FINISHED DOUGH; CUTTING A PIECE OF DOUGH FOR THE SKULL AND BONES DECORATION; FORMING THE BASE OF THE BREAD.

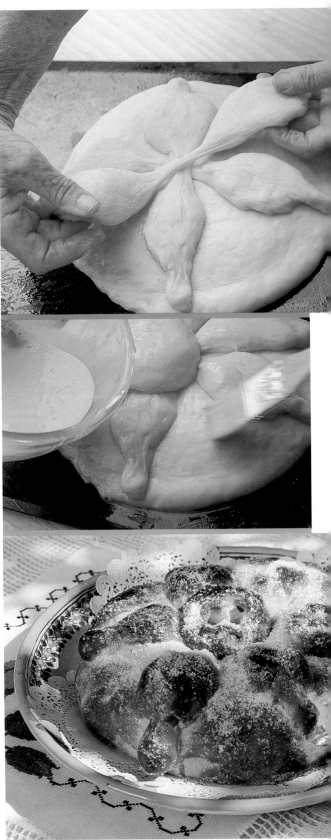

FROM TOP RIGHT: PLACING THE
"BONES"; GLAZING WITH BEATEN EGG;
THE FINISHED PAN DE MUERTOS.

Take three-fourths of the dough and roll it into a smooth ball. Press it out to a circle about 8 inches (20cm) in diameter—it should be about 1 inch (2.5cm) thick. Press around the edge of the dough to form a narrow ridge of about 1 inch (2.5cm)—like the brim of a hat—and transfer to one of the baking sheets. Cover loosely with greased waxed paper and set aside in a warm place, about 70°F (21°C), to rise about half its size again, about 1 hour.

Divide the remaining one-quarter of dough into four equal parts. Roll one piece into a smooth ball—that will be the head. Roll out the other three pieces into strips about 8 inches (20cm) long, forming knobs as you do it. Place these onto a second tray, cover as before, and set aside to rise for about 1 hour. Repeat the steps to form the second bread.

Preheat the oven to 375°F (190°C). At the end of the rising period, place the three "bones" at regular intervals across the dough with the round ball in the middle and make two indentations for "eyes." Brush the surface of the dough with the beaten eggs and bake until well browned and springy to the touch, 15 to 20 minutes. Turn the heat off, open the oven door, and let the breads sit for about 5 minutes.

Transfer the breads to racks, brush with the melted butter, and sprinkle well with the sugar. It is best to let the breads cool off for about 2 hours before eating. If well stored, they will keep soft for several days and, in fact, improve in flavor.

Rosca de Reyes

TWELFTH NIGHT RING BREAD

January 6—Reyes, as it is known in Mexico—is the time for giving presents to children and to have a merienda, *with a rosca de reyes, a sweet yeast bread made in the form of a ring. Hidden in the dough is a tiny plastic doll. Times have changed; it used to be made of fine china. The person who gets it then has to give a party on Candelaría, February 2.*

This rosca is made with the same dough and method as the previous recipe for pan de muertos and also brushed with butter and sugar. The only difference is the shaping and decorating with crystallized fruits. Here in Michoacán the fruits or just the peel have been cooked, really preserved to a dark brown color, frutas en tacha. *From the photograph on the next page you can see that I have used candied figs and slices of peel, but use whatever good crystallized or dried fruits you can find.*

MAKES 2 LARGE ROSCAS ABOUT 12 INCHES (30CM) IN DIAMETER

recipe continues on next page

Dough for Pan de Muertos (page 282)

Follow the directions for making Pan de Muertos. After the final rising, divide the dough into two equal pieces and coax each one into a round cushion shape. Don't forget the dolly, or even a dried fava bean (an old French custom) in each one. Set one aside while you work with the first.

There are two methods:

Roll the dough out to a compact sausage shape about 3 inches (7.5cm) thick. Dampen the ends with a little water and join them together, molding the dough so that you can hardly see the join. Place on a well-greased tray, decorate with the fruits, cover with well-greased waxed paper, and set aside in a warm place, about 70°F (21°C), until it has risen about half its size again. Glaze, bake, and finish following the instructions for Pan de Muertos.

Or punch a hole with your fist in the center of the dough cushion and stretch until you have an opening about 6 inches (15cm) across. Then follow the above instructions.

FROM TOP: FORMING METHOD ONE; FORMING METHOD TWO; GLAZING THE UNBAKED ROSCA. RIGHT: THE BAKED ROSCA.

Pan de Sal

Nonsweet Yeast Rolls

Pan de sal, or salt bread, generally refers to bread rolls, or *bolillos,* of white flour that accompany a meal, or *teleras,* flattish rolls, used for tortas—a Mexican sandwich. There are, too, regional variations of round breads, like the *pambazos* and *pambacitos* of Veracruz.

While the dough for these rolls is raised with commercial yeast, in many country villages the local bakers, like my neighbors, still prepare their doughs for the panes de sal with pulque.

These breads are usually formed into round, flat shapes of different sizes and are about 1 inch (2.5cm) thick. The crumb is soft and rather compact, not porous, and the flat tops acquire a natural, almost glossy, dark brown surface from the baking in wood ovens. It is always rather frustrating to try to duplicate these types of breads. Every ingredient—flour, yeast, and even water—differs, and as much experience as I have had in baking Mexican (salt) breads—pambacitos excepted—I can never quite achieve a complete look-alike.

Bolillos

Mexican Bread Rolls

The elongated, crusty little bread rolls called bolillos *are an indispensable part of any (urban) Mexican meal. I have always likened them to fat bobbins, but with little knobs at either end. They have naturally changed during the years I have been in Mexico: in texture—because a soft-wheat flour is now used and machines for kneading—and in appearance—because of modern diesel ovens instead of the wood-fired ones (although the latter still exist in many small towns and villages). Fast-rising additives, too, including sugar, have become the order of the day.*

Trying to duplicate breads, especially, from one country to another is always a challenge—one that has been met very successfully by a growing number of enormously talented and dedicated bakers in the United States. But somehow turning out bolillos to look like those of a provincial bread-baking village has escaped that challenge, especially when you see what is turned out by the majority (perhaps all) of the Mexican bakeries in the United States.

I am including this recipe because I know there is always a group of aficionados who want to make their own, even if they aren't perfect. It is based on the first ones I learned to make in a bakery in Mexico City over twenty-five years ago, with minor changes that have become necessary with different materials, ovens, and the like.

Of course, in a home kitchen the climatic conditions will never be the same as the steady heat of a commercial bakery, where the ovens are in action for the greater part of the day—unless you have a cozy kitchen with an Aga cooker. How depressing it is to see a cloudy, damp day just when you want to start! But there is the culinary challenge: how to coax that dough into behaving! It seems as though breads made with a starter and then three stages of slow rising take forever, but all this can be worked in between other chores, or the rising delayed by putting the dough into the refrigerator overnight. The resulting flavor, especially when the bread is a day old, is incomparable.

Once the bolillos are formed, if you want to cook them on a baking sheet, put them seam side up onto the baking sheets so that they open attractively. If, on the other hand, you will be cooking them on the floor of a wood-fired oven, put them on well-floured canvas for the final rising and then turn them over onto the peel.

For this sort of bread it is ideal if you have special bricks in your oven and spray them with water to form steam, as advocated in many bread-baking articles and specialized books.

MAKES ABOUT 24 5-INCH (12.5-CM) ROLLS

¼ teaspoon crumbled cake yeast,
  or ⅛ teaspoon dried
1 teaspoon sugar (optional)
½ cup (125ml) warm water
½ teaspoon sea salt
8 ounces (225g) all-purpose flour, plus
  extra for working

THE DOUGH

2 pounds (900g) all-purpose flour, plus
  extra for working
The starter
½ ounce (15g) cake yeast (about
  1½ tablespoons crumbled), or
  2 teaspoons active dry yeast
About 2 cups (500ml) warm water
1 tablespoon sea salt
Softened shortening, for your hands when
  forming the dough

Cream the yeast and sugar together in a small bowl with 2 tablespoons of the water. Dissolve the salt in the remaining water.

USING AN ELECTRIC MIXER: Put the flour into the bowl of an electric mixer and work the yeast mixture in thoroughly before adding the salted water—always reserve a little to see how much the flour will absorb. Beat with the dough hook until you have a smooth, rather firm but sticky dough, about 2 minutes.

Throw in a little more flour around the edge of the bowl and beat briefly until the dough pulls cleanly away from the surface of the bowl. Scrape the dough onto a lightly floured surface and form into a round cushion shape. Place the dough into a lightly greased bowl, cover with greased waxed paper and a towel, and set aside in a cool place, about 55°F (14°C), for a minimum of 8 hours or overnight.

MIXING BY HAND: Place the flour in a circle on your work surface, forming a well in the center. Add the creamed yeast and mix well into the flour. Gradually add most of the salted water, always reserving a little until you see what the flour will absorb, and work all the ingredients together, scraping any stray flour—with a plastic dough scraper—into the middle. Work the dough, adding the rest of the water if necessary, to form it into a cohesive mass. Knead, adding a little more flour if necessary, to make a springy, fairly firm and slightly sticky dough, about 3 minutes. Transfer to a greased and floured baking sheet or bowl, cover with greased waxed paper and a towel, and set aside in a cool place, about 55°F (14°C), for a minimum of 8 hours or overnight.

recipe continues on next page

USING AN ELECTRIC MIXER: Put the flour into the mixer bowl and add the starter torn into small pieces. Cream the yeast with 2 tablespoons of the water and mix into the flour. Dissolve the salt into the remaining water and gradually beat it into the flour, reserving, as always, a little to see how much the flour will absorb. Beat with the dough hook until you have a smooth, flexible, slightly sticky dough, 2 to 3 minutes. Throw a little more flour around the bowl and beat briefly until the dough cleans itself from the surface of the bowl.

MIXING BY HAND: Put the flour in a circle on your work surface and make a well in the middle. Break up the starter into small pieces and put into the well. Cream the yeast with 2 tablespoons of the water and add to the starter. Work all this together thoroughly. Dissolve the salt in the rest of the water and add gradually to the flour, reserving a little, as always, to see how much the flour will absorb. Keep scraping the dough and peripheral flour together with a plastic dough scraper until it becomes a cohesive mass. Then knead, adding a little more water or flour as necessary to have a smooth, flexible but very slightly sticky dough, about 5 minutes.

FROM TOP: ROLLING A PIECE OF DOUGH WITH A DOWEL; STEP ONE IN FORMING A BOLILLO; FORMING STEP TWO; THE FORMED BOLILLO READY FOR THE LAST RISING.

FIRST RISE: Scrape the dough out onto a floured work surface and coax it into a round cushion shape. Put the dough either into a large greased bowl or on a floured board, cover, and set aside in a warm place—ideally 65° to 70°F (18–21°C)—until tripled in volume, about 5 hours.

SECOND RISE: Scrape the dough out onto a floured work surface and cut with a plastic dough scraper into 24 equal pieces. Scrape flour off your work surface to get traction. Lightly greasing your hands, roll each piece of dough under the palm of your hands as shown to form smooth balls. Leave them on the work board about 2 inches (5cm) apart. Cover with greased waxed paper and leave until they have grown to half their size again and are spongy but tender, about 1½ hours.

At this stage prepare the baking sheets: you will need four large ones liberally greased and floured (see the headnote).

FORMING THE BOLILLOS: Grease your hands well with shortening. Take one of the balls of dough and flatten it, either with your hand or a dowel, and then pull out to a fat oval shape. Double the dough over, pound on each side with the heels of your hands, then begin folding about one-fourth of the dough and press down very hard before continuing with the second and third folds. By this time the dough will be formed into a small roll slightly raised in the center. Roll smoothly under your palms, letting a little of the dough escape at each end to form the ears. Grease the top lightly and place seam side up on a baking sheet; again cover with greased waxed paper. Set aside to rise until spongy and inflated to about half again the original size.

In the meantime, preheat the oven to 450°F (230°C).

Bake the bolillos until they are golden and have a crisp crust and sound hollow when tapped, 15 minutes. The temptation is to eat hot bread right away, but more flavor will develop if left for an hour or so, or even until the next day and then reheated.

This type of bread keeps well for a few days, but if it dries out a little, sprinkle with water and put into an oven preheated to 400°F (205°C) until very hot and crusty, about 15 minutes.

It can also be frozen for a month or two, and revived with or without defrosting in a very hot oven. Please—no microwaving unless you are having trouble with your teeth!

Teleras

FLAT BREAD ROLLS

In Mexico, the flat bread rolls with two parallel grooves in the surface are called teleras. *The name came from Andalusia in Spain, where it referred to whole wheat—considered second-class—bread made for laborers. Now they are made of the same bread dough as bolillos and used principally for that greatest of sandwiches, the Mexican torta stuffed with layers of meat, cheese, beans, avocados, and so on (see* The Art, *page 373).*

Follow the bolillos recipe (see page 288) up to forming the dough into 24 balls. Taking one ball—the Mexican bakers do two at a time—and using a dowel, roll into an oval shape. With the long side toward you, make two horizontal grooves, pressing hard until you think you are going to go right through the dough. Reverse the telera onto a prepared baking sheet and set aside to rise, uncovered, at 70°F (21°C) until it has expanded to half its size again, about 1 hour.

Meanwhile, preheat the oven to 400°F (205°C).

Reverse again onto another baking sheet and bake until crusty and a deep golden color, 15 to 20 minutes. See the information on page 291 for storing and reheating.

FROM TOP: MAKING THE TWO MARKS IN A TELERA; THE TELERA READY FOR ITS FINAL RISE.

Pambacitos de Jalapa, Veracruz

I have eaten these attractive and delicious little bread rolls, very lightly baked and coated with flour, many times in Coatepec, Veracruz, and always wondered how they were made. At last I came across a recipe in La Cocina Veracruzana, *attributed to Dulce Maria Dauzón. At first, they didn't turn out exactly as I remembered them; they had rather a tough crust. I have therefore adjusted the recipe slightly to give them their characteristic spongy crumb and brittle, shell-thin crust. Do not expect these rolls to rise spectacularly; they are close-textured and, as you can see, baked at a lower than usual oven temperature for other types of bread. And please don't make the mistake, as I did on the first try, of using strong bread flour.*

Traditionally these pambacitos are filled with a paste of black beans, chorizo, or sardines, tomatoes, cheese, and lettuce. I warn you they go down very easily and are somewhat addictive! I prefer to follow the recipe and use pork lard because the flavor is incomparable, but you could use vegetable shortening, or at least half and half. If they dry out, sprinkle them with water and put them into a 350°F (180°C) oven for 15 to 20 minutes, but they can be frozen successfully for about one month.

MAKES 15 ROLLS ABOUT 3 INCHES (7.5CM) IN DIAMETER

½ ounce (15g) fresh yeast, about 1½ tablespoons when finely crumbled
½ cup (125ml) warm water
17 ounces (380g) all-purpose flour (about 4 rounded cups/1.05L), plus more for rolling

1½ teaspoons sea salt
1 teaspoon sugar
2½ ounces (about 75g) pork lard, about a rounded ⅓ cup (90ml)
⅓ cup (83ml) water
⅓ cup (83ml) whole milk

Mix the yeast to a cream with the ½ cup (125ml) warm water. Add 1¼ cups (313ml) of the flour and mix to a dough. Form into a ball, score a cross in the top, cover with greased waxed paper, and set aside to double in volume at a temperature of about 65°F (17°C).

Meanwhile, put the rest of the flour in a mound on a work surface (ideally it should be wood) and form a well in the center. Mix in the salt, sugar, and lard. Add the water and milk and mix well, working in the fermented dough torn into small pieces. Knead the mixture until you have a smooth dough that comes cleanly away from your hands and the board. Form into a round cushion shape; put into a well-greased bowl. Lightly grease the surface, cover the bowl with greased waxed paper and a towel, and set in a warm place to double its volume for a minimum of 6 hours at a temperature of about 65°F (17°C), or in the refrigerator for 12 hours. (I recommend the latter because the dough develops a wonderful flavor.)

Grease two large cookie sheets and preheat the oven to 325°F (about 165°C).

Divide the dough into 15 pieces and roll each into a round, smooth ball. Set out at least 2 inches (5cm) apart on greased cookie sheets. Cover and set in a warm place, about 70°F (26°C), until risen half its volume again. Bake either one or two trays at a time—if the latter change them around—until they are very slightly colored on top and have a shell-like crust, about 30 minutes. While still hot, roll the pambacitos in lots of flour and replace on the baking sheet until completely cool.

UTENSILS

raditional cookware is perhaps better described as cookware for traditional Mexican food, because some of the utensils described here, like the metal corn grinder, tamale steamer, and tortilla press, are certainly newcomers and probably never heard of until the early part of the twentieth century.

The oldest pre-Columbian grinding utensils for preparing food were the basalt metate and mano—grinding stone and muller—and the molcajete and tejolote—mortar and pestle. And what is so fascinating about them is that their modern replicas have almost the same form, and are certainly as efficient, as their forebears.

The comal, an earthenware griddle, probably appeared on the scene later, according to archaeological finds in most areas of Mexico (of course, they were much more fragile and their remains more difficult to identify). The methods for glazing cazuelas—clay cooking casseroles without lids—was introduced by the Spaniards, but cazuelas, too, are still used today mostly in the rural parts of central Mexico. They are at once both functional and decorative.

Cazuela

There is no accurate translation for the word *cazuelas*. They are traditional earthenware cooking "bowls" flared out toward the top and with a handle on either side of the rim. They do not have a lid. Cazuelas are used in traditional kitchens in Mexico for cooking rice, and dishes like moles and pipianes.

Because the clay is relatively thin with the glaze on the inside and the pots have not been fired in a high-temperature kiln, cazuelas can be used for cooking directly on a bare flame, or over a wood or charcoal fire. However, it is not advisable to use them on the hot plates, or elements, of an electric stove since the intense heat will crack them.

Cazuelas are made in all sizes, some much deeper than others. Their form, with the type of glaze and decoration, denotes the village or area in which they were made.

Like almost every other type of craft, the quality of decoration has deteriorated in the last decade or so. There is now much more homogenization of design, especially in central Mexico, while the more isolated villages tend to adhere more to their traditional shapes and patterns.

When choosing a cazuela, tap the bottom firmly: a dull sound warns of an elusive, unnoticed crack, while a more hollow, dry sound means that it is unblemished. Before using a cazuela it should be "cured" to seal the pores and ensure that the first foods cooked in it do not taste of raw clay. There are many ways of doing this, and traditional cooks, who still prefer to use them for cooking (they say food cooked in them has a very special flavor), have their preferences. Some cover the outside with a paste of diluted cal, or lime; others smother them with grease and bake them. The variations are countless. I still adhere to the way I was first taught: fill the cazuela to the top with water, add a whole head of garlic, and put over low heat until the water has evaporated. I do this a second time, then rinse and dry the cazuela. It is now ready to use. After use, they are washed in the usual way by hand.

A note of warning: The Food and Drug Administration has warned about the leaching of lead from the glaze of Mexican and other types of rustic cazuelas when acidy sauces are cooked or left in them for any length of time. This is because they have not been fired at a high enough temperature to render the lead in the glaze inactive. More information can be obtained from the FDA.

Chilmolera

The *chilmolera* (the name indicates that it is used for grinding chiles) is a small, round clay bowl, usually with the sides flaring outward. It is deep and the surface inside is ridged from cross-hatched scoring while the clay was still wet; this abrasive surface helps in the grinding process.

I have seen chilmoleras used more, but not exclusively, in remote places in Guerrero and Oaxaca.

Comal

In Mexico, the griddle on which tortillas (an indispensable part of a Mexican meal) are cooked, or ingredients for sauces, etc., are toasted is called a *comal*, from the

Nahuatl word *comalli.* It is a thin disk of either unglazed earthenware or a light metal, the latter often recycled from the scrap heap. Comals are made in all sizes and for all purposes. The most traditional ones are of unglazed clay, which are used mostly in the villages over a wood fire. Traditional cooks insist that if tortillas, and for that matter tamales, are not cooked over wood they are not very good.

Comals are mostly flat with a low, rounded ridge around the edge, but in some rural areas—Tabasco, for instance—they are concave, although not very deep. In a few areas in the south the surface is burnished with a stone to give them a shiny, impervious look. Depending on the area where they are made, they are either light beige in color, or reddish brown with patches of black fire clouding. I have even seen ones that are made of black clay with a matte, dull surface in a highland market of Oaxaca.

The surface of a clay comal has to be sealed before using for the first time so that the dough of tortillas or *antojitos* will not stick to the surface. To do this, dilute some powdered lime with a little water to make a thin paste. Spread this paste in a thin, but opaque, layer over the surface and set the comal over medium heat—over a gas or wood or charcoal fire (but *not* on an electric hot plate). As the surface heats up the paste will turn from whitish to brown. Remove the comal from the heat and brush off the dry lime. I sometimes do this a second time to make sure. It is now ready to use.

Always have a backup comal, because when you least expect it, it could crack. No one is ever to blame, but occasionally someone puts a heavy pot on it inadvertently.

To clean the comal, brush with a soapy, stiff brush, or scour lightly with pumice and rinse it well, but I don't advise immersing it completely in water.

A heavy tin or light metal comal, which I have mentioned before, is most likely to be used in kitchens in urban areas or restaurants. Again, before using the comal it is necessary to temper it by wiping the hot surface with a thin vegetable oil (not a thick viscous type). Then reheat and wipe any residual oil off with a piece of absorbent paper. I usually do this twice before making tortillas. This sort of comal can be used over any type of heat, but avoid a very hot element on an electric stove as the metal tends to warp.

The comal can be washed with soap and water, or scoured lightly with pumice to dislodge bits of food adhering to it. Make sure it is stored only when completely dry to avoid rusting.

Of course, if you have neither of these you can use a heavy, iron griddle (see the manufacturer's instructions for curing before using), although I don't particularly like it for tortilla making because of the thickness of the metal and the time it takes to transmit the heat. You could even use a heavy skillet, but take care not to burn your hand on the high sides when turning a tortilla.

Surfaces to avoid: Teflon and similar nonstick surfaces, aluminum, or stainless steel, which reflect the heat and do not cook the tortilla dough fast enough. The tortillas will remain pale and underdone, or stiff as a board.

Clay comals are not so easy to come by outside Mexico except in the markets of some of the border towns. In the first place, the demand would not be that great and second, they are fragile and the breakage rate in transporting them is very high. Metal ones are much easier to find in Mexican stores and large supermarkets.

Metate and Mano

The *metate* is a thick rectangular grinding stone supported on three legs, and cut in one piece from volcanic rock. Its accompanying grinding stone, the *mano,* or in Nahuatl, *metlapil,* is either fat and blunt-ended or long and tapering. It is "cured" by grinding with either rice or dried corn, but it may not be for the uninitiated.

The metate is used now only by the older traditional cooks who live in the country and have been using the metate since childhood for grinding nixtamal (corn cooked and soaked in a solution of lime), cacao, pumpkin seeds, chiles, and other ingredients for moles. It is back- and knee-breaking work.

Use the same guidelines for choosing a metate as for a molcajete, although good-quality ones are not easily available outside of Mexico.

Molcajete and Tejolote

In my opinion this volcanic rock mortar and pestle is an indispensable piece of kitchen equipment for any cook, but primarily, of course, for aficionados—or professionals, for that matter—who pride themselves on their Mexican sauces (table sauces as opposed to cooked sauces). The qualities of a sauce prepared in the molcajete are incomparable: the flavors extracted from the ingredients crushed against the abrasive surface of the rock are more intense compared to those cut, however finely,

with the blades of a blender. There is the added aesthetic pleasure of presenting a sauce in its most natural historical setting, for molcajetes, albeit in a slightly more rustic form, have been used from pre-Hispanic times.

Molcajetes are available in many sizes, from very large ones for restaurant use—about 15 inches (38cm) in diameter—down to the smallest (either for children or for simply crushing spices)—about 4 inches (10cm). The most useful sizes I have found are 5½ inches (14cm) in diameter for everyday sauces and 6½ inches (16.5cm), which, believe it or not, will hold enough guacamole for about eight servings.

The molcajete is in effect a bowl set on three sturdy legs hewn out of the same piece of black or gray volcanic rock. The quality varies considerably from closely, medium, or coarsely grained rock. The latter should be avoided simply because it is more difficult to clean. Neither should it be too porous, and you can test this before buying by adding water to see if it seeps out through the legs. Another test of the quality of the rock is to grind the surface with the tejolote: some dust should be loosened, but if there is too much then the molcajete will never be any good.

The tejolotes, or pestles, made of the same rock come in several shapes: stocky and blunt at both ends or like a blunt cone. When choosing one to go with the molcajete, make sure it is big enough for you to grasp firmly and grind efficiently.

Before using the molcajete, the inside of the bowl should be ground several times with the tejolote to smooth the surface. My very first teachers used raw rice for this, and I have continued to use it. Put a small handful of rice into the bowl of the molcajete and grind until you have reduced it to a grayish powder. Brush it out, rinse, and dry the surface before the second grinding. After three or four grindings the rice powder will not look so gray and that should do it. Of course, it is always preferable to get somebody else with a strong wrist to do this! (If your sauce or guacamole does at first seem a bit gritty you will only be ingesting some natural minerals!)

After use, I wash the molcajete using a brush and natural, unscented soap and let it dry well. With proper care it should last a lifetime!

Molcajetes of varying quality can be found in the United States in Mexican markets and large supermarket chains catering to a Latin American population. If you can't find one to your liking, given my norms, then tote one back next time you go to Mexico! You will never regret it. But don't lend it out and make sure the tejolote doesn't get thrown out with the avocado pits; I have lost several that way.

Molino de Maíz

While it is not an essential piece of equipment, I use this metal corn grinder when I want to grind *nixtamal* (dried corn cooked with lime) to a textured, dryish masa for certain types of tamales. It is also useful for grinding toasted (but not soaked) ingredients for moles. I have even seen it used for fresh corn for making tamales.

The round, ridged grinding plates can be adjusted to the required texture. But this grinder is for aficionados who are not grinding enormous amounts. I warn you, it is hard work!

These corn grinders are sold in Mexican groceries and supermarkets catering to a large Hispanic population.

Olla

It is difficult to translate the word for the earthenware *olla*, which is made in many sizes for multiple uses. They are bulbous-bottomed cooking vessels with a high collar around the top and handles on each side. Like cazuelas they are glazed inside and used for cooking on gas or wood or charcoal fires. Milk, atoles, hot chocolate, soups, brothy stews, pozoles, and so on, are traditionally cooked in ollas.

Use the same instructions for choosing and curing ollas as those for cazuelas.

Tamale Steamer

Mexican cooks are very inventive when it comes to improvising ways of steaming tamales: recycled capacious square cans, earthenware ollas, even old galvanized buckets with some thick twigs or bits of wire in the bottom, holding a bed of corn husk or banana leaves above the water level and on which to support the tamales. And they all work! However, the commercial tamale steamers shown in the

photograph are cheap enough and now widely available. (See Sources, page 308.)

The steamers consist of four parts: the main container and its lid, a rack to hold the tamales just above the waterline, and a divider for holding the tamales upright. These steamers are very practical and you can buy them in varying sizes, but unless you are going into the tamale business in a big way, I have found the steamer that measures about 12 inches (30cm) high and 11 inches (28cm) across to be the most practical—it will hold about fifty tamales.

To prepare the steamer for use:

1. Fill the lower section with water to come just below the level of the rack. Place three light coins in the water—these will let you know, when they stop jingling, that the water is getting dangerously low and should be topped up with boiling water.

2. Place a double layer of corn husks, banana or avocado leaves, or whatever the tamale wrapping to cover the rack and set over medium heat. When the water comes to a boil, it is time for the tamales to be put in the top section.

Try never to let the water in the steamer go off the boil once you have started cooking.

Tortilla Press

Even if you think you will never make a tortilla for the rest of your life, you can never be really sure, so buy a tortilla press to have on hand anyway. Somebody else may want to use it for making any one of the delicious *antojitos* or for the addictive Tostones de Plátano (*My Mexico,* page 335).

Tortilla presses are readily available in Mexican groceries or big supermarkets catering to a Latin American population. I have even seen them in Chinese markets! But beware of the lightweight alloy ones that look more elegant than the heavier, rougher-looking cast-iron tortilla presses made in Mexico. You will never be able to flatten a ball of masa into a thin tortilla without using a lot of pressure, and the alloy press is liable to snap in two—evidence, of course, that the person who designed it has never made a decent tortilla in his life.

The large wooden presses look very impressive and folkloric, but I find them more difficult to handle. These are also harder to come by. You would most likely have to bring one back from Mexico, since I have never seen one north of the border.

Through the years I have found that the heavy Mexican press with plates measuring from 6 to 7 inches (15–18cm) is the most practical for most cooks.

Try to keep the metal press as dry as possible because it does tend to rust, especially if the metal plates are not properly dried after cleaning. Just to make sure, when the press is not in use I keep paper towels between the plates.

OTHER USEFUL COOKWARE

The greater part of Mexican cooking—apart from pit barbecues and grilling—is done on top of the stove, so with that in mind I recommend the type of utensils you might need:

CASSEROLES: For cooking Mexican rice, moles, pipianes, and stews, you will need thick-bottomed pans so that particularly the rice dishes and thicker sauces will not stick and scorch in the long cooking time or when reducing a thick sauce over high heat. They will also need to be deep, so I recommend the LeCreuset ware that I have used for many years: for normal use, the round casseroles 10 and 11½ inches (25 and 29cm) in diameter, and the larger 14 inches (35cm) if you are cooking a much larger quantity. Heavy stainless rondeaus of various sizes are good as well.

SKILLETS: The preparation of ingredients for many dishes involves a good deal of frying and toasting, so I suggest you have a series of heavy skillets. I favor cast iron and do not like nonstick. I use pans 6, 8, and 10 inches (15, 20, and 25cm) in diameter. I also find heavy sauté pans with lids, 10 and 12 inches (25 and 30 cm) in diameter, very useful.

OVENWARE: Oval or rectangular oven dishes, at least 2 inches (5cm) deep, of china, ovenproof glass, or earthenware are essential for dishes like vegetable budines, casseroles of layered tortillas or pasta, baked fish in sauces like Red Snapper a la Veracruzana (see *Essentials*, page 368).

GRIDDLE: As I have mentioned on page 298, if you can't lay hands on a comal, a cast-iron griddle is necessary for making tortillas or *antojitos*, for charring ingredients for sauces, and so on. A useful size is 8 or 10 inches (20 or 25cm) in diameter. But do not be tempted into buying one that is a light-colored or shiny, or it will reflect the heat and not cook the ingredients properly.

SLOW-COOKER: The old-fashioned hot pot is great for beans or grains that take a long cooking time (but not if you live at a high altitude or they will take days to cook); they never burn and you can sleep soundly and have that delicious aroma in your kitchen the next morning.

PRESSURE COOKER: This is essential if you are cooking beans or hard grains at a high altitude, especially if fuel is in short supply or very expensive. I know it is not the best way of cooking beans, but I finish them off for the last 30 minutes in a Mexican bean pot, or olla. The pressure cooker is also essential in Mexico, where much of the meat tends to be tougher than that in the United States. I have found a 4- and 6-quart (4- and 6-L) capacity to be the most useful.

KITCHEN SCALE: It should be a good, reliable one—not one that bounces around or one with a container that slides around and falls off easily. It saves all that bother of cramming things into cups and less washing up to boot.

USEFUL ELECTRICAL EQUIPMENT

BLENDER: It is absolutely necessary to have a really good, heavy blender (not the built-in countertop model with plastic jars). It is best to have two jars and ideally they should be of glass, with straight sides and detachable blades. That is the optimum for really efficient blending of sauces, and there is a lot of it in this type of food preparation. Why the blender? It will do a far more efficient job for these textures than the food processor.

FOOD PROCESSOR: This is invaluable for grinding cooked fruits—for example, for making ates, or fruit pastes. I even use mine for mashing the milk curds for queso fresco or grinding fresh corn for tamales.

COFFEE/SPICE GRINDER: I mention the word *coffee* here because that is how this excellent little grinder is identified. It is useful for grinding not only spices but also nuts and seeds, and even the hard annatto seeds for the Yucatecan achiote seasoning, although not in large quantities because the blades are worn out in the process.

MIXER: The KitchenAid mixer, with most important attachments—the paddle, whisk, meat grinder, and dough hook—is indispensable. (I specify this brand because over the years I have found it to be superior to other brands.) It is indispensable because, while I am willing to knead yeast breads by hand, I flinch at the idea of the long beating required for the pan dulce doughs.

ACITRONAR: to sauté until translucent.

AGUJAS: literally means "needle," but beef ribs are called *agujas* in the north of Mexico.

AHUMAR: to smoke. *Ahumado,* smoked.

AJO: garlic. *En ajillo,* fried usually in olive oil with a lot of garlic.

ALBÓNDIGA: a meat- or fishball.

ALMÍBAR: a syrup.

ALMUERZO: a large breakfast, or brunch; in a very few areas it means a lightish lunch.

AL PASTOR: meat cooked over an open fire or on a revolving spit.

ANTOJITO: a snack made of corn masa.

ASAR: this is a difficult word to translate because there is no concise equivalent in English. When ingredients like tomatoes, onions, garlic, or fresh chiles are put onto a comal or griddle, slightly charred and partially cooked, they are *asados;* while *carne asada* refers usually to meat cooked directly on a very hot surface or on a grill. But there are some local dishes like the Asado Placero Sinaloense (*Essentials,* page 289) that belie these explanations since the meat is actually cooked in water. *Asado de puerco* can also mean roasted pork.

ASIENTO: particles that have settled in the fat remaining in the base of a *cazo* (after the cooking of chicharrón; see page 143).

ATE: a fruit paste.

ATOLE: a gruel, usually made of corn masa.

BACALAO: dried salted cod. *Bacalao fresco* is fresh cod.

BAÑAR: to cover with. *Bañado* means "covered with sauce," for instance.

BARBACOA: pit-barbecued meat, generally mutton or goat. In a few areas it is beef—wrapped in large maguey leaves (*pencas*). However, there are some recipes for barbacoa de pollo or rabbit, for instance, where the meats are wrapped in banana leaves or mixiotes and steamed. In the eastern part of Michoacán the whole head (*rostro*) of a cow is wrapped in maguey leaves and cooked in an oven usually used to bake bread. In the southeastern Mayan areas, the pit-barbecue is called *pib.*

BARNIZAR: to glaze.

BATIR: to beat. *Batida,* beaten.

BIFSTEK: literally translated as "beefsteak," it is one, if not the most, popular way of eating beef, particularly in the provinces. It is prepared from various cuts of beef, depending on taste, and pounded until flattened. This way of preparing meat has two advantages: it appears larger than it is and it cooks very quickly.

BOLITA: a little ball.

BOTANA: a snack, usually with drinks.

BUDÍN: plural *budines,* translates literally as "pudding." The word is often used for a casserole of tortillas or solid vegetable custard rather like an Italian *sformato.*

BUÑUELO: a thin pancake or flour tortilla fried crisp and served either with a syrup or powdered sugar and cinnamon. One exception is the buñuelo de viento prepared in Veracruz; it resembles a fried cruller served in a syrup perfumed with aniseeds.

CALDO: a broth, although a clear chicken broth is usually called *consome* [*sic*] *de pollo,* which is often fortified with a piece of poached chicken or a little rice and topped with cilantro, chile serrano, and white onion, all finely chopped. A very popular family dish is caldo de res, a hearty and delicious stew of beef ribs or brisket and lots of vegetables: onion, carrot, cabbage, corn, etc., often served with the traditional toppings of cilantro and chile. One particularly delicious version is the Chile Caldo of Cuicatlán, Oaxaca (see *My Mexico,* page 449), made when the local chiles are ripe and pumpkins and wild broad beans are ripe. In Oaxaca the caldo de cuatro oreganos is a very fragrant broth of beef seasoned with fresh local oregano, marjoram, etc. There are the *caldos largos,* fish broths of Veracruz.

CALENTADO: heated, from the word *caliente,* or hot.

CAPA: a layer.

CAPEAR: to cover with eggs beaten to a froth—not a batter, which would imply that flour was included. The ingredients to be *capeado* or *rebozado* are just dusted with flour, as for chiles rellenos.

CEBOLLA: onion. *Encebollada* means cooked smothered in sliced onions.

CEDAZO: sieve.

CENA: supper. *Cenaduría* is usually a modest supper place.

CHICHARRÓN: pork rind double-fried until crisp.

CHULETA: a cutlet or a chop.

COCINA: kitchen. *Cocinar* means to cook.

COLADERA: colander or strainer.

COMPOTA: stewed fruit.

CUAJAR: to set or to clabber. The word is usually applied to milk clabbered for cheese making. The word could also be applied to an egg custard, or even to a gelatin dessert.

CUCHARA: spoon. *Cuchara sopera* is a soup spoon; *cucharita,* a teaspoon.

CUCHILLO: knife.

DERRETIR: to melt. *Derretida,* melted.

DOBLAR: to double over. *Doblado,* doubled.

DORAR: to fry until golden. *Dorado,* golden.

EMPANADA: a half-moon-shaped filled pastry.

EMPANIZADA: bread-crumbed.

ENCHILADA: a corn tortilla dipped into a chile sauce, stuffed, and rolled.

ENFRIJOLADA: a corn tortilla dipped into puréed beans.

ENTERRAR: the word used in the Yucatán Peninsula for pit-barbecuing meats in what is locally called a *pib.*

ENTRADA: the first course. See *platillo fuerte.*

ENVOLVER: to wrap.

ESCABECHE: a light pickle or sause, often just called *en vinagre.*

ESCALFAR: to poach.

FIDEO: a popular Mexican-type Italian pasta like fine vermicelli. It is usually fried before adding to a dish—to the horror of the Italians and aficionados of real Italian food—but this is done probably because the pasta is made of a much softer flour than the traditional Italian pasta, which tends to quickly soften and lose its texture when cooked.

FREIR: to fry. *Frito,* fried.

FRUTA: fruit, but the word is also used as in *fruta del horno* applied to cookie-type baked goods.

GORDA: literally, fat. *Gorditas* is usually applied not only to different types of *antojitos* but also to rather thick flour tortillas, sweet or savory, made in northern Mexico.

GUISO: a cooked dish.

HOJALDRE: puff pastry.

JOCOQUE: "soured milk" like yogurt prepared by families of Lebanese descent; it also refers to soured cream like crème fraîche (see especially *My Mexico,* page 80).

JUGO: means juice, whether of meat or fruit. *Jugoso* means juicy.

LONGANIZA: a sausage of ground meats, like chorizo, but not tied into links. It is usually made of inferior cuts of meat—often pork and beef—to that of the more prestigious chorizo. It is cheaper to buy than chorizo but used in the same way.

MANJAR: a delicacy.

MANTECA: pork lard.

MANTECA VEGETAL: shortening.

MANTEQUILLA: butter.

MARINAR: to marinate.

MARISCO: shellfish.

MASA: an uncooked dough of either bread or ground corn for tortillas, etc.

MERIENDA: afternoon tea or coffee, usually with a pastry.

MILANESA: meat cut thin or butterflied, breaded, and fried.

MIXIOTE: the membranous tough skin that is stripped from the immature leaves or pencas of maguey. It is used for wrapping meats to keep in all the juices. Its use is now illegal because the plant cannot survive and the demand is so great.

MOLER: to grind. *Molido,* ground.

NATAS: in the singular *nata* means "skin that forms on top of a liquid"; in culinary terms the plural refers to the thick skins that form after scalding several lots of raw milk.

PAMBAZO: a roll specially made for filling as a sandwich.

PAN: bread.

PASTEL: a cake.

PESCADO: fish.

PIB: the Mayan word for a rather shallow, often rectangular, pit used for cooking seasoned meats wrapped in banana leaves in the Yucatán Peninsula.

PICAR: to chop or to pierce. *Picada,* chopped or pierced.

A LA PLANCHA: cooked pressed flat onto a hot surface, usually of metal.

PLATILLO FUERTE: the main course of a meal.

POZOLE: a hearty soup-stew, generally made of pork (sometimes of chicken or dried shrimp) that is fortified with hominy cooked until it opens up like a flower. It is usually served with accompaniments that may differ regionally, but generally with chopped onion, sliced radishes, shredded cabbage, and oregano with a hot sauce, lime slices, and fried tortillas, or tostadas. In Guerrero, pozole is usually topped with chicharrón as well. There are three main types of pozole, the most prevalent comprising a "white," or natural, broth. In parts of Michoacán it is seasoned and colored with guajillo or ancho chiles with an addition of chickpeas. But the most fragrant and interesting is a green pozole prepared best in Chilapa, Guerrero, seasoned with wild sorrel and epazote, and enriched with toasted ground pumpkin seeds (see *The Art,* page 108). In parts of southern Mexico, a cold corn drink is named *posol,* and even *pozole.*

PUERCO, CARNE DE, or **CERDO:** both mean pork.

RALLAR: to grate. *Rallador,* grater.

REBANAR: to slice. *Rabanada,* a slice.

RECETARIO: cookbook.

RELLENAR: to stuff or fill. *Relleno,* stuffing or filling. In central Mexico, blood sausage is also referred to as *relleno.*

RES: beef.

SABOR: flavor. *Sabroso,* tasty.

SALTEAR: to toss lightly in oil or fat.

SANCOCHAR: partially cooked in water.

SOPA: a fairly substantial soup; see also *Caldo.*

SOPA AGUADA: literally "watery soup," refers to any liquid soups, or broths.

SOPA SECA: literally "dry soup." It is served like a pasta course in Italy, just before the main dish. In fact, it often consists of Mexican-style pasta, but more frequently a dish of rice, either cooked with blended tomato and seasonings or plain white rice often dotted with carrots and peas. In southern and coastal areas it is often served plain with strips of fried plantain. It is with rare exceptions *picante* (hotly seasoned), but sometimes served with a hot sauce on the side.

TACHA: as applied to *frutas en tacha,* means fruits cooked for a long time in sugar, usually with piloncillo (raw sugar cones) until dark brown.

TENEDOR: fork.

TIERNO: tender.

TORTA: a fritter, or a filled bread roll, or a type of baked cake or layered casserole.

TOSTAR: to toast. *Tostado,* toasted.

The exodus of Mexicans from Mexico continues unabated despite the dangers of illegal entry, and as a result in the most unexpected places I continue to discover or hear about small restaurants or groceries catering to their compatriots or bringing in ingredients for the dishes that are their "soul food." There is nothing like traditional food and shared meals to soothe the soul and make one feel at home, however fleetingly.

It would be an impossible task to list all the sources for ingredients in all your particular areas; apart from the fact that many are continually changing, it is so frustrating when addresses and telephone numbers become obsolete so rapidly. In the last five to ten years the main supermarket chains almost everywhere seem to have begun carrying a constant stock of fresh chiles—serranos, jalapeños, and even poblanos (often mislabeled fresh *pasillas,* an oxymoron if there ever was one!)—jicama, cilantro, packages of the most popularly used dried chiles, real cinnamon, pepitas, Mexican "oregano," and dried shrimp, to name just a few items distributed by this phenomenal and still-growing industry. I was surprised by the latest newcomer: packaged dried hoja santa leaves, albeit rather shattered and at a ridiculously high price.

After skimming the Yellow Pages for tortilla factories, Mexican bakeries, restaurants, and groceries, take the time to seek them out and see what additional or extensive stock they carry. But much of what is available, especially the more specialized items, will depend on which region of Mexico the majority of the local customers come from. For instance, it was a great surprise to find in Brooklyn small food stores and even a large market owned by a Middle Easterner carrying guajes, papaloquelite, sour tunas, chilacas, "Arabic" squash (called *calabacitas italianas* in Mexico). The owner obviously was catering to people from central Mexico. A good source of information for ethnic foods is the weekly food section of your local newspaper or magazine—it might even list websites!

I must warn you that there is always a certain amount of mislabeling—this especially applies to the packaged ingredients—and although it is a nuisance, it is advisable to take this book with you until you become familiar enough with the ingredients. Before resorting to substitutes, make the effort to reproduce as faithfully as possible—at least on a first attempt—the true flavors of an unfamiliar dish. If you don't, you will never know the pleasure that a combination of new (to you) ingredients can give—besides, cooking is always a learning experience.

The Fiesta Market in downtown Austin, Texas, is always a pleasure to shop in with a vast range of Mexican produce and ingredients, while the Fiesta in suburban Dallas has gone blandly and disappointingly upscale. The Central Market of downtown Los Angeles can always be relied on to provide the staples for good Mexican food, except now, alas, for the poor quality of the tortillas (made from one of those innocuous tortilla flours), and there may be produce items that are very fresh and appealing in Asian markets. Surprisingly, I have never fared well in the Phoenix area!

Here is a list of just a few of the sources that I have come across when giving classes in different cities of the United States and Canada:

Alpha Beta and **Safeway**
markets, located throughout
Arizona, carry several types of
Mexican produce.

Flores Bakery
8402 South Avenida del Yaqui
Guadalupe, AZ 85283
(480) 831-9709

Mercado Mexico
8212 South Avenida del Yaqui
Tempe, AZ 85283
(480) 831-5925

**Mi Ranchito Mexican Food
Products**
601 North 43rd Avenue
Phoenix, AZ 85009
(602) 272-3949
www.mi-ranchito.com

La Tolteca
1205 East Van Buren
Phoenix, AZ 85009
(602) 253-1511

CALIFORNIA
Northern

Cal Foods
195 South 28th Street
San Jose, CA 95116
(408) 293-0550

Casa Grande Products, Inc.
1730 Broadway
Sacramento, CA 95818
(916) 443-5039
www.casagrande.com

Casa Lucas Market
2934 24th Street
San Francisco, CA 94110
(415) 282-2400

Casa Sanchez
2778 24th Street
San Francisco, CA 94110
(415) 282-2400
www.casasanchez.com

Don Juan Foods
1737 Crows Landing Road
Modesto, CA 95351
(209) 538-0817

La Esperanza (bakery)
5028 Franklin Boulevard
Sacramento, CA 95820
(916) 455-0215

La Estrellita
2387 University Avenue
Palo Alto, CA 94303
(650) 328-0799

La Estrellita
2205 Middlefield Road
Redwood City, CA 94063
(650) 369-3877

Latin American Imports
3403 Mission Avenue
San Francisco, CA 94110
(415) 648-0844

Mi Rancho Market
3365 20th Street
San Francisco, CA 94110
(415) 643-5959

La Palma
2884 24th Street
San Francisco, CA 94110
(415) 647-1500

La Tapatia Tortilleria
411 Grand Avenue South
San Francisco, CA 94080
(650) 589-5881

Southern

Claremont area
Many of the large supermarkets
in the area carry a variety of

Mexican ingredients. Seville
orange trees along the streets
are abundant for those inter-
ested in Yucatecan cooking.

Casa Magui, S.A.
Avenida Constitucion 932
Tijuana, B.C., Mexico 5-7086

Los Cinco Puntos
3300 East Cesar E. Chavez
   Avenue
Los Angeles, CA 90063
(323) 261-4084

Fruteria Jacaranda
Stand 90
Interior Mercado
Tijuana, B.C., Mexico

El Indio Tortilla Shop
3695 India Street
San Diego, CA 92103
(619) 299-0333

Liborio Market
864 South Vermont Avenue
Los Angeles, CA 90006
(213) 389-4444

Main Market
(Revolucion)
Tijuana, B.C., Mexico

El Nopalito Mexican Food
560 Santa Fe Drive
Encinitas, CA 92024
(760) 436-5775

Peter Pan Market
2791 Pica Boulevard
Los Angeles, CA 90006
(323) 731-9596

El Toro
1340 West First Street
Santa Ana, CA 92703
(714) 836-1393

Borges Supermarket
223 Washington Avenue
Homestead, FL 33030
(305) 245-4655

El Charrito Mexican Market
1621 NE 8th Street
Homestead, FL 33030
(305) 247-9772

Diaz Supermarket
1215 NE 8th Street
Homestead, FL 33030
(305) 246-2262

La Guadalupana Groceries
4690 US Highway 1
Vero Beach, FL 32967
(561) 770-9222

La Reina Supermarket
1200 North State Road 7
Hollywood, FL 33024
(954) 989-9682

MASSACHUSETTS
Stop and Shop markets, located
throughout Massachusetts,
offer a range of Mexican foods.

Harbar Corporation
25 Broad Street
Quincy, MA 02169
(617) 769-0023
www.harbar.com

India Tea & Spice Inc.
445 Common Street
Belmont, MA 02478
(617) 484-3737

MICHIGAN

Algo Especial
2628 Bagley
Detroit, MI 48216
(313) 963-9013

Honey Bee La Colmena
Bagley at 17th Street
Detroit, MI 48216
(313) 237-0295

La Jalisciense
2650 Bagley
Detroit, MI 48216
(313) 237-0008

MINNESOTA

El Burrito Mexican Foods
196 Concord Avenue
St. Paul, MN 48216
(651) 227-2192

MISSOURI

Inserra Produce Soulard Market
730 Carroll Street
St. Louis, MO 63104
(314) 231-2520

La Tropicana Market Inc.
7304 South Broadway
St. Louis, MO 63111
(314) 352-5118

NEW MEXICO

The Chile Guy (wholesale only)
168 Calle Don Francisco
Bernalillo, NM 87004
(505) 867-4251
www.chileguy.com

NEW YORK
The **Union Square
Greenmarket** in New York City
on Wednesdays and Saturdays
offers a large range of fresh
chiles, epazote, and other herbs
as well as squash flowers and
other very fresh produce.

Carniceria Mexicana
4805 5th Avenue
Brooklyn, NY 11220
(718) 437-4520

Empire Meat Co.
4603 5th Avenue
Brooklyn, NY 11220
(718) 437-4520

International Grocery & Meat
543 9th Avenue
New York, NY 10018
(212) 279-5514

Kitchen
218 Eighth Avenue
New York, NY 10011
(212) 243-4433

Laraia's Cheese Co.
5 Seegar Drive
Nanuet, NY 10954
(845) 627-2070

Trinacria Importing Co.
275 East Main Street
Mount Kisco, NY 10549
(914) 242-5499

OHIO

La Borincana Foods Inc.
2127 Fulton Road
Cleveland, OH 44113
(216) 651-2351

Danny Boy Farm Market
24579 Lorain Road
North Olmsted, OH 44070
(440) 777-2338

Super Mercado Rico
4506 Lorain Avenue
Cleveland, OH 44102
(216) 631-1156

OREGON

La Milpa Tortilleria
16560 SE 362nd Drive
Sandy, OR 97055
(503) 668-5391

Su Casa Imports
11755 NE Marx Street
Portland, OR 97220
(503) 262-7030

1050 SE Walnut Street
Hillsboro, OR 97123
(503) 648-5779

PENNSYLVANIA

La Cantina Provisions
2700 East Lehigh Avenue
Philadelphia, PA 19125
(215) 425-8280

J & J Foods Inc.
1301 North Second Street
Philadelphia, PA 19122
(215) 425-3300

TENNESSEE

Emilio's Grocery
2757 Getwell Street
Memphis, TN 38118
(901) 365-3015

Mega Market
5150 American Way
Memphis, TN 38115
(901) 795-0128

Mercado Latino
3210 South Perkins Road
Memphis, TN 38118
(901) 365-7948

TEXAS

Fiesta Stores and **H-E-B Food Stores,** two food chains with locations throughout Texas, offer a range of Mexican groceries and produce.
www.heb.com

Danal's Stockyard Stores and **Super Mercado Mexico,** two chains in Dallas, offer Mexican produce and groceries.

Alamo Masa
1603 North Laredo Street
San Antonio, TX 78207
(210) 732-9651

Antone's Import Co.
2424 Dunstan Road
Houston, TX 77005
(713) 521-2883
(many stores in the Houston area)

Generation Farms (herbs)
1109 North Mckinney Street
Rice, TX 75155
(903) 326-4263

It's About Thyme (herbs)
11726 Manchaca Road
Austin, TX 78748
(512) 280-1192

Mexicatessen
302 West Crosstimbers
Houston, TX 77018
(713) 691-2010

Mozzarella Co.
2944 Elm Street
Dallas, TX 75226
(214) 741-4072
www.mozzco.com

Pendery's Inc. (spices)
1221 Manufacturing Street
Dallas, TX 75207
(214) 357-1870
www.pendery.com

WASHINGTON

Krueger Pepper Gardens
462 Knights Lane
Wapato, WA 98951
(509) 877-3677
(seasonal)

El Mercado Latino
1514 Pike Place #6
Seattle, WA 98101
(206) 623-3240

El Ranchito
352 Griffin Avenue
Enumclaw, WA 98022
(360) 825-8511

WASHINGTON, D.C.
Safeway has locations throughout the Washington, D.C., area.

Arlington Bodega
6170 Arlington Boulevard
Falls Church, VA 22044
(703) 532-6849

Casa Lebrato
1733 Columbia Road NW
Washington, DC 20009
(202) 234-0099

Casa Pena Mexican Grocery
1636 17th Street NW
Washington, DC 20009
(202) 462-2222

CANADA

Dinah's Cupboard
50 Cumberland Street
Toronto, ON M4W 1J5
(416) 921-8112

Portuguese Fish Market
821 Dundas Street West
Toronto, ON M6J 1V4
(416) 603-6168

Que Pasa Mexican Foods
1637 5th Avenue West
Vancouver, BC V6J 1N5
(604) 737-7659
www.quepasafoods.com

Sanci Tropical Foods
66 Kensington Avenue
Toronto, ON M5T 2K1
(416) 593-9265